Traveling With Bears:

In Search of

MarkTwain

JACK DOLD

authorHOUSE®

AuthorHouse™
1663 Liberty Drive
Bloomington, IN 47403
www.authorhouse.com
Phone: 1 (800) 839-8640

Published by AuthorHouse 01/24/2020

ISBN: 978-1-7283-4414-0 (sc)
ISBN: 978-1-7283-4412-6 (hc)
ISBN: 978-1-7283-4413-3 (e)

Library of Congress Control Number: 2020901092

Print information available on the last page.

This book is dedicated to

Watson (Mac) Laetsch

My friend, mentor, and fellow traveler
Who inspired and shared twenty-eight
Wonderful adventures with
U.C. Berkeley Alumni

INTRODUCTION

> "...nothing so liberalizes a man and expands the kindly instincts that nature put in him as travel and contact with many kinds of people."
>
> Letter to San Francisco *Alta California*, dated May 18th, 1867; published June 23, 1867

I have often theorized that there is no author in American literature, or even the world's for that matter, who could inspire by their life an almost endless series of tours. Over the years Mark Twain has inspired five tours with the Golden Bears, the alumni of the University of California Berkeley, six if we count our time in India a few years ago. Jack London and Robert Lewis Stevenson traveled a great deal, but they are far surpassed by Twain. The fact is, Sam Clemens/Mark Twain was a world traveler, and his experiences are all documented beautifully, as we found out a couple of years ago in Hawaii. He was a natural-born travel writer.

For more than twenty-five years, I have traveled with a notebook in hand, keeping a journal that would later remind me of travel details, restaurants, contact names, etc. Being a tour operator made such a journal seem normal, not to mention important. I think I first had an inkling that in Samuel Clemens I had found a travel soul mate when I read *Roughing It*. I was amazed when he dredged from his notes the names of most of Nevada's rivers and reported that many of them ended in "sinks." He even included the Reese River, one of the great geographic trivia names available.

> "At the border of the desert lies Carson Lake, or the "Sink" of the Carson, a shallow, melancholy sheet of water some eighty or a hundred miles in circumference. Carson river empties into it and is lost—sinks mysteriously into the earth and never appears in the light of the sun again—for the lake has no outlet whatever.
>
> There are several rivers in Nevada, and they all have this mysterious fate. They end in various lakes or "sinks," and that is the last of them. Carson Lake, Humboldt Lake, Walker Lake, Mono Lake, are all great sheets of water without any visible outlet. Water is always flowing into them, none is ever seen to flow out of them, and yet they remain always level full, neither receding nor overflowing. What they do with their surplus is only know to the Creator."
>
> *Roughing It*, p. 131-132

Over the years, I have written and escorted scores of tours for the University of California Alumni, in programs that were part of Bear Treks and later Cal Discoveries. Primarily with Professor Watson (Mac) Laetsch, we have wandered throughout America on historic trails such as Lewis and Clark, the Oregon Trail, Santa Fe Trail, Route of the Klondike, Route 66 and the Lincoln Highway. With Mac, I also traveled to India twice and with Cal through much of Europe and Asia. But perhaps the most unusual of those trips were designed to follow Mark Twain around the world.

One of the treasures to be found at U.C. Berkeley are the Mark Twain Papers. The massive inventory of writings from this prolific author, passed after his death through the hands of a series of editor/executors: Albert Bigelow Paine, from 1910 to 1937; Bernard DeVoto at Harvard (1938-1946); Dixon Wecter (1947-1950) at the Huntington and Bancroft Libraries. It was he who brought the papers to the Bancroft Library in Berkeley in 1949. Henry Nash Smith edited the collection from 1953 to 1964 and Frederick Anderson, also at the Bancroft, from 1971 to 1979. Most of the original collection of documents was bequeathed to the University of California Regents in 1962 by Samuel Clemens' middle daughter, Clara Clemens Samoussoud.

It is a massive collection, of an estimated 11,000 letters by Clemens and his family and over 17,000 letters received by them, about 50 notebooks kept by the author and 600 manuscripts unpublished or unfinished, and photocopies of the manuscripts of all his major works known to be extant. In addition there are books from his personal library, many annotated in the margins, and innumerable business documents, photographs, scrapbooks, clippings and other ephemera from the author's life.

In 1980, Robert Hirst was named as editor of the papers, creating the Mark Twain Papers Project, with the stated aim of publishing every word that Mark Twain ever wrote. It is a daunting task. To date, the letters alone have been edited and published in six volumes, comprising only those up to 1875!

Bob Hirst, now in his 39th year as General Editor, remains as energetic and enthusiastic as ever. And as accessible. He is always willing to share his expertise with anyone interested in Mark Twain, and he shares that knowledge in the most congenial way. It took only a suggestion from Mac to begin a series of tours on the life of Samuel Clemens to get Bob to agree to accompany the tours as a lecturer. To date, that includes five tours, four of which are included in this book ("Mark Twain in the West" was repeated once.) Also included, although Bob did not accompany us, are notes from a Cal Alumni tour to Calcutta and Darjeeling, which formed a major part of the author's lecture tour to India, chronicled in *Following the Equator*.

The world was Mark Twain's home. By the end of his life his travels had taken him to at least thirty-seven countries, using today's political borders. He lectured in twenty-three states and four Canadian provinces and visited many more. And throughout his travels, he catalogued the people, the cultures, the landscapes and the governments he encountered, always with an eye for detail, and humor. He is unquestionably one of the world's great travel writers. He filled his wonderful "travel books," *Roughing It, Innocents Abroad, A Tramp Abroad, Life on the Mississippi,* and *Following the Equator,* with insightful and detailed descriptions of the land and people he encountered. Among countless numbers of such descriptions, many stand out for me. I admire his description of South Pass in Wyoming which the wagon trains crossed on the Oregon Trail. Most of the travelers didn't even realize that they were actually cresting the Rockies. Sam Clemen's description is as poetic as it is accurate.

"As a general thing the Pass was more suggestive of a valley than a suspension bridge in the clouds—but it strongly suggested the latter at one spot. At that place the upper third of one or two majestic purple domes projected above our level on either hand and gave us a sense of a hidden great deep of mountains and plains and valleys down about their bases which we fancied we might see if we could step to the edge and look over. These Sultans of the fastnesses were turbaned with tumbled volumes of cloud, which shredded away from time to time and drifted off fringed and torn, trailing their continents of shadow after them, and catching presently on an intercepting peak, wrapped it about and brooded there—then shredded away again and left the purple peak, as they had left the purple domes, downy and white with new-laid snow... In the one place I speak of, one could look below him upon a world of diminishing crags and canons leading down, down, and away in a vague plain with a thread in it which was a road, and bunches of feathers in it which were trees."

Roughing It, p. 80

Through his eyes, the reader can travel confidently to New York, Philadelphia, Washington D.C., London, Calcutta, San Francisco, Hawaii, South Africa, Paris, Rome, and hundreds of other places, and be confident that he is seeing those places as they looked in the author's day.

BOOK ONE

Mark Twain & The Mississsippi

I

> "For a few months I enjoyed what to me was an entirely new phase of existence—a butterfly idleness, nothing to do, nobody to be responsible to, and untroubled with financial uneasiness. I fell in love with the most cordial and sociable city in the Union. After the sage-brush and alkali deserts of Washoe, San Francisco was Paradise to me. I lived at the best hotel, exhibited my clothes in the most conspicuous places, infested the opera, and learned to seem enraptured with music which oftener afflicted my ignorant ear than enchanted it, if I had had the vulgar honesty to confess it.... I attended private parties in sumptuous evening dress, simpered and aired my graces like a born beau, and polked and schottisched with a step peculiar to myself—and the kangaroo."
>
> *Roughing It*, p 396

In true Twain fashion, at least during his initial few weeks in San Francisco, we gather tonight at the elegant Sheraton Palace Hotel. It is the kick-off of our first Bear Treks' tour on Mark Twain, which combines a two-day California segment, a six-day bus tour along the Mississippi and a seven-day cruise on the *Mississippi Queen* riverboat from Memphis to New Orleans. It will feature Bob Hirst, Director of the Mark Twain Papers & Project at UC's Bancroft Library, as well as Watson (Mac) Laetsch, professor emeritus of botany and former vice chancellor at U.C. Berkeley. I am in charge of logistics and paying bills. Pretty top-heavy in administration!

Dinner at the Palace is scheduled in the French Parlor overlooking the famous Garden Court, and tonight will be serenaded by one of the six or seven weddings that paraded through the Palace lobby this afternoon. One of them has taken over the entire Garden Court on a Saturday night, no little assault on the wallet of the father of the bride, and my fears are aroused by six-foot speakers I see down there that are certain to bombard our senses and rattle our tonsils up on the mezzanine. By the time our salads arrived, I knew my fears were well placed. We shouted our way through dinner, and I started looking around for a lecture site for Bob, whose voice won't have a chance against those woofers.

I found a large rather elegant room nearby with an impressive barrel vault ceiling and we adjourned after coffee to hear Bob introduce Mark Twain. The subject for Bob, tonight and tomorrow morning is Mark Twain in San Francisco, a logical place to start, since he lived only a few blocks from where we are staying and describes in his letters and sketches much of the region from south of Market to the financial district to the Cliff House.

જ્જ ✖

Born in 1835 "in the almost invisible village of Florida, Missouri," Sam Clemens was twenty-five years old when he arrived in Nevada in 1861, joining his brother Orion to escape the Civil War, and unsuccessfully attempting to avoid catching the silver bug. He began writing as a local reporter for Virginia City's *Territorial Enterprise,* generally poking fun at most everything. He came for a short visit to San Francisco in May and June, 1863, before returning once again to Virginia City.

In May, 1864, he returned to San Francisco with his friend, Steve Gillis. Sam scoured the city, scraping up material for a column in the *Morning Call.* Financially he was often in dire straits but he and Gillis generally terrorized the city. On December 4, 1864 he was "encouraged" to leave town, having put up bail for Gillis who had come into problems with the law. Gillis jumped bail, escaping back to Virginia City, leaving his friend with a bill he couldn't pay. Sam also left, joining Steve's brothers, Jim and Billy, in a cabin on Jackass Hill, outside of Angels Camp in the heart of the gold country. He stayed for three months, (eighty-four days), during which time he tried to write his now famous story of the Jumping Frog of Calavaras County.

By now having adopted his famous pen name, Twain returned to San Francisco where he stayed from late February, 1865 to March 7, 1866. From that period of his life only four letters have survived. But one of those was of utmost importance in Sam Clemens' life.

"I never had but two powerful ambitions in my life. One was to be a pilot, & the other a preacher of the gospel. I accomplished the one & failed in the other, because I could not supply myself with the necessary stock in trade—*i.e.* religion. I have given it up forever. I never had a "call" in that direction, anyhow, & my aspirations were the very ecstasy of presumption. But I *have* had a "call" to literature, of a low order—*i.e.* humorous. It is nothing to be proud of, but it is my strongest suit, & if I were to listen to that maxim of stern *duty* which says that to do right you must multiply the one or the two or the three talents which the Almighty entrusts to your keeping, I would long ago have ceased to meddle with things for which I was by nature unfitted & turned my attention to seriously scribbling to excite the laughter of God's creatures."

Mark Twain's Letters, Vol. 1, Letter to Orion and Mary Clemens, October 19-20, 1865

In March, 1866, securing a commission for the *Sacramento Union* to report on the sugar industry, he moved to Hawaii. Returning to San Francisco from Hawaii in November, 1866, he launched his career as a humorous lecturer.

"I was home again, in San Francisco, without means and without employment. I tortured my brain for a saving scheme of some kind, and at last a public lecture occurred to me! I sat down and wrote one, in a fever of hopeful anticipation. I showed it to several friends, but they all shook their heads. They said nobody would come to hear me, and I would make a humiliating failure of it. They said that as I had never spoken in public, I would break down in the delivery anyhow. I was disconsolate now. But at last an editor slapped me on the back and told me to "go ahead." He said, "Take the largest house in town, and charge a dollar a ticket." The audacity of the proposition was charming; it seemed fraught with practical worldly wisdom, however. The proprietor of several theatres endorsed the advice, and said I might have his handsome new opera-house at half price— fifty dollars. In sheer desperation I took it—on credit, for sufficient reasons. In three days I did a hundred and fifty dollars' worth of printing and advertising, and was the most distressed and frightened creature on the Pacific coast. I could not sleep—who could, under such circumstances! For other people there was facetiousness in the last line of my posters, but to me it was plaintive with a pang when I wrote it: 'Doors open at 7 ½. The trouble will begin at 8.'"

Roughing It, p. 533

It was the beginning of Mark Twain's remarkable career as a lecturer and an orator. The "Sandwich Island Lecture" was the first in a long string of subjects he would unleash on the world, beginning with a series of lectures from San Francisco to Virginia City, and then moving to the Midwest, Canada and the Eastern seaboard. In all he would lecture in twenty-three states and four Canadian provinces.

II

This is my wife Mary's day, September 9, California Admission Day, commemorating that day in 1850 when we officially became a state, some years before, the wags would say, it degenerated into a state of mind. Mary appeared this morning clad in a white sweatshirt, the Bear Flag emblazoned across her chest. Bear flags decorated her ears. A faux leather purse, made in India, also bore the flag on one side, and a California license plate on the other. I wondered aimlessly if the factory worker in Delhi had the slightest idea of what she was making, but Mary is an irrepressible collector of flags and the origin of the item doesn't matter in the least, as long as there is a bear, a star and a white field. Having been wed to her for thirty-eight years, I know that her undies were probably bearing bears as well and socks would be completing the ursine theme. I used to get embear-assed by all this patriotic fervor, but long ago decided that if she could appear in public decked out like that, the least I could do is record her for the great grandkids.

Bear flags were already common by the time Sam Clemens arrived in California, ushering in, at least for us out West, the most famous period of his life. It usually comes as a surprise to his fans that he was only here for five years because most of us associate him with jumping frogs and tall tales of gold rush and Wild West. We mentally claim his river days as "western" and certainly lump the Sandwich Islands into the same geography. Most Californians probably couldn't begin to place him in New York, much less Connecticut.

Today we are determined to find Sam Clemens in San Francisco, a neat trick since the city has completely scrubbed his 1860s world from its face, filling in the coves, asphalting the lanes, demolishing the houses and hotels in favor of high rises. Buildings today have the effrontery to stand defiant even to major earthquakes, a fact that would cause the writer to tremble visibly with disappointment. No, Sam would not enjoy the modern San Francisco, at least not the part he frequented. His stays in the city were varied in style, from elegant to "slinking." He left one of the great descriptions of the former and followed it up a month later with something less grand.

> "To a Christian who has toiled months and months in Washoe; whose hair bristles from a bed of sand, and whose soul is caked with a cement of alkali dust; whose nostrils know no perfume but the rank odor of sage-brush — and whose eyes know no landscape but barren mountains and desolate plains; where the winds blow, and the sun blisters, and the broken spirit of the contrite heart finds joy and peace only in Limburger cheese and lager beer — unto such a Christian, verily the Occidental Hotel is Heaven on the half shell. He may even secretly consider it to be Heaven on the entire shell, but his religion teaches a sound Washoe Christian that it would be sacrilege to say it.
> Letter to the *Territorial Enterprise*, June 1864

Bob Hirst immediately began to stir life into the lost San Francisco world of Sam Clemens/Mark Twain with a series of readings and observations, beginning with a description of two young hooligans rampaging through the city.

"Steve & I have moved our lodgings. Steve did not tell his folks he had moved, & the other day his father went to our room, & finding it locked, he hunted up the old landlady (Frenchwoman,) and asked her where those young men were. She didn't know who he was, & she got her gun off without mincing matters. Said she—"They are gone, Thank God—& I hope I may never see them again. I did not know anything about them, or they never should have entered this house. Do you know, Sir, (dropping her voice to a ghastly confidential tone,) they were a couple of desperate characters from Washoe—gamblers & murderers of the very worst description! ... One night when they were carrying on in their room with some more roughs, my husband went up to remonstrate with them, & that small man told him to take his head out of the door (pointing a revolver,) because he wanted to shoot in that direction. O, I never saw such creatures. Their room was never vacant long enough to be cleaned up—one of them always went to bed at dark & got up at sunrise, & the other went to bed at sunrise & got up at dark—& if the chamber-man disturbed them they would just set up in bed & level a pistol at him & tell him to get out. They used to bring loads of beer bottles up at midnight, & get drunk & shout & fire off their pistols in the room, & throw their empty bottles out of the window at the Chinamen below.... They always had women running to their room—sometimes in broad daylight—bless you, *they* didn't care. They had no respect for God, man or the devil. Yes, Sir, they are gone, & the good God was kind to me when He sent them away."

Mark Twain's Letters Vol 1, Letter to William Wright (Dan DeQuille), July 15, 1864

It was not a prosperous time for the young writer as he "slunk" from meal to meal and scoured the city for material for his daily local squibs for the *Call*. He lived on Minna Street, south of Market in a place owned by Gillis' mother, a house now long gone. If anyone had been stirring on Minna this morning they must have wondered what on earth a tour bus was doing stopped in the vicinity of 44 Minna Street in the center of blank, bare concrete walls and completely nondescript surroundings, a district Twain described as "full of gardens and shrubbery." Today a single dead weed provided the color to this alley.

Twain wandered this world in search of stories, often falling back on the frequent earth tremors which will always be associated with San Francisco. His first he called the "great earthquake," which stirred the reporter to considerable eloquence.

"As I turned the corner, around a frame house, there was a great rattle and jar, and it occurred to me that here was an item—no doubt a fight in that house. Before I could turn and seek the door, there came a really terrific shock, the ground seemed to roll under me in waves, interrupted by a violent joggling up and down, and there was a heavy grinding noise as of brick houses rubbing together. I fell up against the frame house and hurt my elbow. I knew what it was, now, and from mere reportorial instinct, nothing else, took out my watch and noted the time of day; at that moment a third and still severer shock came, and as I reeled about on the pavement trying to keep my footing, I saw a sight! The entire front of a tall, four-story building in Third street sprung outward like a door and fell sprawling across the street, raising a dust like a great volume of smoke! And here came the buggy—overboard went the man, and in less time than I can tell it the vehicle was distributed in small fragments along three hundred yards of street…. The street car had stopped, the horses were rearing and plunging, the passengers were pouring out at both ends, and one fat man had crashed half way through a glass window on one side of the car, got wedged fast and was squirming and screaming like an impaled madman. Every door of every house, as far as the eye could reach, was vomiting a stream of human beings, and almost before one could execute a wink and begin another, there was a massed multitude of people stretching in endless procession down every street my position commanded."
Roughing It, pp. 398-399

I have always been surprised that everyone outside of California thinks that we endure a continuous string of devastating earthquakes out here, a myth that may go back directly to Mark Twain whose reports seem to make that claim.

I will set it down here as a maxim that the operations of the human intellect are much accelerated by an earthquake. Usually I do not think rapidly—but I did upon this occasion. I thought rapidly, vividly, and distinctly. With the first shock of the five, I thought— "I recognize that motion—this is an earthquake." With the second, I thought, "What a luxury this will be for the morning papers." With the third shock, I thought, "Well my boy, you had better be getting out of this." Each of these thoughts was only the hundredth part of a second in passing through my mind. There is no incentive to rapid reasoning like an earthquake. I then sidled out toward the middle of the street- and I may say that I sidled out with some degree of activity, too. There is nothing like an earthquake to hurry a man when he starts to go anywhere.

"The Great Earthquake in San Francisco," *New York Weekly Review*, November 25, 1865. Reprinted in *Early Tales & Sketches*, vol. 2, p. 310.

෴ ෴

Bob had written up a marvelous tour of the city, but we were forced to make radical cuts in it, because this morning the city is hosting its first ever Grand Prix bike race and the whole waterfront is barricaded off. We were fearful that even the financial district, the area of the city that was frequented by Mark Twain and his friends, would be impacted, but traffic was surprisingly Sunday-light.

We were able to double-park to get off the bus and gawk at a new archaeological project—the unearthing of the *General Harrison*, a 126-foot vessel that had been abandoned in 1849 and buried in the land fill of Yerba Buena Cove. It has rested all these years beneath the Jang Sing Dim Sun Restaurant. The old ship is only one of several that support the skyscrapers of the commercial district.

The only indication that Mark Twain ever resided in San Francisco is old Merchant Street, which has been renamed for the author recently. Only a few facades remain from his day, among them that of the old mint on Commercial Street. The offices of the Hudson Bay Company, the *Call*, and the *Alta Californian*, the old Olympic Club, the restaurants and hotels are all long gone, even the Occidental Hotel, "heaven on the half shell", which saw the young reporter whenever he had money or presumed credit. Or his favorite Lick House where he "put on the most disgusting airs."

> "I suppose I know at least a thousand people here—a great many of them citizens of San Francisco, but the majority belonging in Washoe—& when I go down Montgomery Street, shaking hands with Tom, Dick & Harry, it is just like being in Main Street in Hannibal & meeting the old familiar faces. I do hate to go back to Washoe. We fag ourselves completely out every day, and go to sleep without rocking every night. We dine out, & we lunch out, and we eat, drink and are happy—as it were. After breakfast, I don't often see the hotel again until midnight—or after. I am going to the Dickens mighty fast. I know a regular village of families here in the house, but I never have time to call on them. Thunder! we'll know a little more about this town, before we leave, than some of the people who live in it. We take trips across the Bay to Oakland, and down to San Leandro, and Alameda, and those places, and we go out to the Willows, and Hayes Park, and Fort Point, and up to Benicia, and yesterday we were invited out on a yachting excursion, & had a sail in the fastest yacht on the Pacific Coast. Rice says: "Oh, no—we are not having any fun, Mark"…When I invite Rice to the Lick House to dinner, the proprietors send us champagne and claret, and then we do put on the most disgusting airs."
> *Mark Twain's Letters, Vol. 1,* Letter to Jane Lampton Clemens & Pamela Moffett, June 1, 1863

Twain's world around Montgomery, Sacramento, Clay and Bush is difficult to recognize. Even the Monkey Block was demolished to put up the Transamerica Pyramid. I suppose that during this trip the least we can to is to offer up a toast to this lost world of Mark Twain, fittingly tipping a glass filled with one of his own concoctions:

"A tall ale-glass is nearly filled with California brandy and Angelica wine—one part of the former to two of the latter: fill to the brim with champagne; charge the drink with electricity from a powerful galvanic battery, and swallow it before the lightning cools. Then march forth—and before you have gone a hundred yards you will think you are occupying the entire street; a parlor clock will look as big as a church; to blow your nose will astonish you like the explosion of a mine, and the most trivial abstract matter will seem as important as the Day of Judgment. When you want this extraordinary drink, disburse your twenty-five cents and call for an 'EARTHQUAKE.'"

"The Great Earthquake in San Francisco", New York *Weekly Review*, 25 November, 1865, Reprinted *Early Tales & Sketches*, V. 2, 310.

Mac is totally in favor of having an "Earthquake party" this evening, since he publicly moaned "I have been very concerned about people lately because they have not been drinking enough to stay healthy." A good earthquake jolt should remedy that.

Following Twain's advice we finished our San Francisco tour with an excursion to the Cliff House, returning to the hotel via Golden Gate Park.

> If one tires of the drudgeries and scenes of the city, and would breathe the fresh air of the sea, let him take the cars and omnibuses, or, better still, a buggy and pleasant steed, and, ere the sea breeze sets in, glide out to the Cliff House. We tried it a day or two since.....
> Then there's the Cliff House, perched on the very brink of the ocean, like a castle by the Rhine, with countless sea-lions rolling their unwieldy bulks on the rocks within rifle-shot, or plunging into and sculling about in the foaming waters. Steamers and sailing craft are passing, wild fowl scream, and sea-lions growl and bark, the waves roll into breakers, foam and spray, for five miles along the beach, beautiful and grand, and one feels as if at sea with no rolling motion nor sea-sickness, and the appetite is whetted by the drive and the breeze, the ocean's presence wins you into a happy frame, and you can eat one of the best dinners with the hungry relish of an ostrich. Go to the Cliff House. Go ere the winds get too fresh, and if you like, you may come back by Mountain Lake and the Presidio, overlook the Fort, and bow to the Stars and Stripes as you pass.
> "A Trip to the Cliff House," *The San Francisco Daily Morning Call,* June 25, 1864

After lunch, we crossed the Bay en route to a genuine "back to school" experience, with Mac providing the commentary:

"There's Coit Tower, built by Lily Hitchcock Coit. The lady liked firemen very much."

"That ugly gray building blocking the campus vista is the math building, 'the box the Campanile came in.'"

"Soda Hall looks like a tiled toilet."

But the campus still stands and we landed finally on the sidewalk in front of the Bancroft Library where Bob is introducing us to the Mark Twain Papers, one of the university's true treasures. There his colleagues have laid out a special display for our group, demonstrating the enormous scope and breadth of the collection of Mark Twain papers that reside in the library, a collection Bob has been formally collating, editing, annotating and organizing for over twenty years.

Bob positively came alive among his treasures. It was wonderful to observe and appreciate true expertise, as he regaled us with story after story around the captivating career of Mark Twain, and perhaps even more intriguing, the tangled life of his written works.

From the Bancroft we wandered at leisure back to Alumni House where Mac organized cocktails and dinner (no Earthquakes), an informal welcome to the tour. Carolyn and Jackie from BearTreks joined us, as did Professor Robert Middlekauf, one of the country's eminent historians, and a strong supporter of the Mark Twain Papers Project, which Bob Hirst leads. With Mac as MC, each member of our tour group was asked to introduce him/herself. It is no easy task to keep the banter flowing through sixty people, but Mac is an expert in these situations and really succeeded in "breaking the ice." Finally he got around to Bob Middlekauf, who protested, "Maybe I should introduce myself, Mac!" But he emerged unscathed with high praise and laurels, highlighting the evening with a lecture entitled "The Myths and Realities of the Antebellum South."

III

In my experience, this has been the strangest start to a tour, commencing two days ago, but we haven't left yet. It reminds me of our adventure a few years ago in gold rush country when we were two hours away from home for eight days. But on that tour we at least left for somewhere, if only to Sacramento. Here we are, still in the Bay Area and only now beginning to consider leaving. It is strange to get a hotel wakeup call to leave home, but then again you don't have doormen and bellhops at home so we must be "gone" somewhere. But no, there is the Bay Bridge right outside the window. We're still here!

In my mind, the tour begins this morning, a fact confirmed by the powerful feeling of dread that always hits me at these times. There is one main worry: will the bus arrive to transfer us to the airport? For thirty-one years, I have maintained this fear although it has never materialized. The bus has always appeared, late once or twice, but not critically, and we have never missed a flight. On reflecting I think that my real phobia is not to be afraid—if I don't worry, something bad is bound to happen.

My heart beat easier as I peered out on New Montgomery at 5:30 A.M. and spotted the Thunderstar coach rounding the corner onto Jesse St. End of worries! It hasn't occurred to me to be concerned that we might not have collected all the luggage at the hotel, or that the plane might not show up, or that someone might miss the flight, or that the flight be cancelled—no, the bus showed up and all is right in my tour world. Let the tour begin!

"We would like to welcome our large group on board," the TWA stewardess announced, "the University of California, called BearTreks. Is that b-a-r-e?" In the twelve years I have done these Cal trips I have never encountered that cliché, and am a bit chagrined I never used it myself. Mac offered to disrobe for the sake of the flight attendant, but that created a mental vision none of us was willing to endure.

We were met in St. Louis by our drivers, Richard and Phil, two men from Arrow Coach Lines who have driven many of our trips over the years. Richard was driving a bright red and blue coach, which we promptly labeled the Gold Bus, while Phil's green and gold bus was christened Blue. Carolyn, Travel Director at Bear Treks, doesn't like numbers and letters to designate multiple coaches, so colors work fine, and may even correspond to the actual paint of the buses, sometimes.

We are kicking off our St Louis visit with dinner at Bevo Mill on Gravois Street. Bevo, the fox mascot of August Busch, gave his name to this fine German establishment, built in 1916 by Busch, who positioned it halfway between his home at Grant's Farm and the brewery. It served as his rendezvous and clubhouse for cronies around the area and in business. Tonight we supped on German food in Busch's private dining room. Norman was there to greet us, gamely extricating six-packs of Bud and Bud Lite for our consumption, not having thought to bring along a bartender, or even a bar, for our party.

Bob, framed with white lights from the main dining hall, gave us a background lecture on the Clemens family. Sam was born in 1835 in Florida, Missouri, moving four years later to nearby Hannibal. He had an older brother Orion, a sister Pamela (neither of whom ever learned how to pronounce their name properly) and a younger brother Henry (who did). The family owned two slaves at one point, but sold them in hard times and rented others. On his father's death, Sam's mother extracted his pledge not to drink or swear, "but mother, don't make me go to school." In 1847, Sam became a printer's apprentice with Joseph Ament at the Hannibal *Missouri Courier.* By 1850 he was working as a typesetter for his brother Orion at the Hannibal *Journal,* writing three essays in what Orion called, "Our Assistant's Column."

In 1853, Sam left Hannibal for St. Louis, then off to New York, Philadelphia and Washington D.C. Orion worked for Lincoln in his campaign and subsequently moved west to Nevada. Sam first proposed to journey to South America to work in coca production, but decided to pursue his dream of becoming a riverboat pilot instead, a profession that he prized for the rest of his life. He remained a pilot until 1861 and the start of the Civil War. He quickly found out that riverboat pilots were a prime target for sharpshooters along the Mississippi. After the commencement of hostilities, he "hid out in St. Louis" before moving west to Nevada with his brother. His notes from that adventure would materialize in *Roughing It,* a brilliant description of much of his time in California and Nevada. That Western period would last initially from 1861 to December, 1866, with a brief lecture return in 1868.

Bob described Sam's meeting with his bride-to-be, Olivia Langdon, going to hear a Dicken's recital "with a highly respectable, young white woman." (Letter to the *Alta California*, February 5, 1868)

He quickly sought her hand in marriage, but her father, Jervis Langdon, asked for references. Clemens submitted six from his San Francisco days, three of which were from ministers, a disastrous choice, but perhaps his only one. "I would rather bury my daughter than have her marry him," was one of these dubious "recommendations." His suit was somehow successful, and he and Livy were wed in February, 1870, moving into a home in Buffalo, gifted to them by the Langdons. They had four children. After their first child, Langdon, died in his second year, three daughters followed—Susie, Clara and Jean. At twelve, Susie wrote her father's biography, "much the best biography I have read thus far."

In 1871, the Clemenses moved from Buffalo to Hartford, where They built an elaborate Victorian home. From there Mark embarked on a world lecture tour. Susie died of meningitis in 1896, followed by Olivia in 1904 and Jean in 1909. Sam died on April 21, 1910, leaving only Clara. Clara lived until 1962.

IV

September 11, 2001

"TODAY OUR NATION SAW EVIL..."

The headline of the *Quincy Herald-Whig,* in Quincy, Illinois screamed out above a picture of a fireball possible only in doomsday movies or spy novels, bewailing an event that has shaken the world and altered our lives. At 8:45 A.M., American Airlines Flight 11, hi-jacked enroute from Boston to L.A., crashed full-speed into the North Tower of the World Trade Center. Eighteen minutes later United Flight 175 nearly decapitated the South Tower, slicing almost completely through the gigantic building. At 9:40 a third commercial flight, American #70 with 64 people on board, exploded into the Pentagon in Arlington, VA. A fourth hijacked plane, presumably also targeted for the capital, crashed in the countryside near Pittsburg. 266 Americans died on those four flights. Thousands, possibly tens of thousands perished in New York and Washington, far eclipsing Pearl Harbor's terrible "Day of Infamy." The concept of this crime, using fully-fueled 767s as instruments of mass murder, of innocent, completely unsuspecting, unprepared civilians, challenges human reason. Such an act cannot be conceived much less actually carried to completion. No soul can be that empty, so totally devoid of feeling, so utterly consumed by hatred, to forsake every vestige of humanity. Today, as President Bush whispered, we saw evil, we witnessed insanity on the public stage carried out in full video view of the world, and we will never again be quite the same. These fanatic lunatics have destroyed our trust, shaken our psyche as surely as an 8.0 earthquake. No, more. We can accept or at least understand such a loss inflicted by the haphazard hand of unfeeling nature, following the dictates of tectonic physics—such a thing is beyond our control. But it is impossible to comprehend an atrocity inflicted by a fellow human creature. Surely this can't be true.

And yet we must mourn, saddened profoundly at the sight of fellow suffering, appalled at the apparition of inexplicable evil. What are we supposed to do now?

Mark Twain faded into the irrelevant this morning.

Most of us were gathered for breakfast at the Embassy Suites when the word first came on TV of the assault on the World Trade Center, and we had moved off on our St. Louis tour before the full extent of the disaster was known. Our guides met us at the hotel, leading us straight to the Arch and the National Museum of Westward Expansion.

The Gateway Arch is a magnificent work of art, an inverted catenary arch 630' high and the same distance between the legs. Designed by Eero Saarinen, work was begun in 1963, completed two years later with no fatalities. Each leg was built independently with the keystone placed at the end, constructed of concrete and steel and covered with a 1/4" veneer of stainless steel. The tram ride over the arch was installed in 1967, taking cars up in four minutes to a small observation deck, returning in three minutes.

The full impact of our national crisis hit us when we approached the Arch, which was barricaded by Park Service and police who asked us to vacate the entire park. A news crew was already there, approaching me for an interview:

`"What is your feeling about the attack on New York?"

"Are you frightened that other places could be attacked?"

"Do you think the government is right to close places like this?"

So soon it begins—idiot questions that contain their own answers, inane queries demanding an emotional response, preferably in a single syllable.

"America needs to know."

I hope I confused that insipid bottom feeder, because I am deeply offended by her sort, who parade their ignorance by waving a microphone.

Armed with cuttings and cones, Mac, in his real life a professor of botany, gathered the group around a well-shaped, frilly tree that is one of his favorites, the Dawn redwood or *metasequoia*, a tree discovered in coastal China in 1941 with Berkeley roots, so to speak, and related to the Bald cypress we will encounter in the swamps of the south. He announced that it is more palatable than a redwood and is eminently chewable.

"We need to consume more tannins for longevity", and this, augmented by red wine could lead to a life as long as a sequoia. This naturally led him to discuss the age of such a tree. "Age in trees is nonsense since most of the tree is dead." Only six cell layers and the needles are actually alive, he reported. "I don't know about that," one of our travelers whispered to me. "If you want to know the age of a tree, just give it a ring."

Expelled from the park, we settled into the Old St. Louis Cathedral, officially the Basilica of St. Louis, King of France. Guide Joan, declaring that she "knew all about the church," hobbled in on her gimpy knee to enlighten us. First, she mis-defined a basilica and mishandled a cathedral, neither of which, in my view, demanded an immediate refutation or firing squad.

"This is the oldest church west of the Mississippi."

Mac and I gagged in unison, a thing we have gotten very good at when local guides are pontificating. Joan caught her balance but moved a mountain or two— "Except the missions in the Rockies in California."

"New Orleans is west of the Mississippi."

"Have you heard of the Jesuit missions in Texas?"

"And Arizona?"

"California is not in the Rockies."

Totally undismayed, Joan went on, seeking bigger game, jumping off to a preview of Bellefontaine Cemetery, where we would find the grave of Captain Isaiah Sellers, "the first Mark Twain, who wrote *Life on the Mississippi*."

Bob's head snapped up so fast his clavicle jumped over his chin. Mac let out a laughing guffaw, while I just quietly sighed, realizing that I was paying for this, trying to crawl into hiding beneath the pew. We escaped to the bus.

Cathy, the guide on our bus had not been in the basilica, or cathedral, or whatever that place is, and she immediately started to tell us about Cap. Sellers, "the first Mark Twain."

"No, stop!" I commanded. "That's not true. Don't even try to say that."

Totally flustered, she retreated. "I just heard that this morning. It's not true? Okay, I never said it. You never heard it." End of discussion!

From then on Cathy was fine, but Joan, totally unstoppable, spewed information at Mac's bus in a random deluge that left everyone drowning as they swam off the coach at Bellefontaine Cemetery and staggered toward the marker at Captain Seller's grave. Bob gave the talk at the monument while Mac kept Joan at bay by blocking her away from the crowd. Bob explained that Sam Clemens wrote several times that he never adopted his pen name until after Sellers died, because the famous captain used to sign his letters "Mark Twain." However there is no indication of this. Clemens had served as clerk and steersman under Captain Sellers aboard the *William M. Morrison* for three months in 1857-58. In 1859, Clemens wrote a biting, sarcastic piece that was published in the *New Orleans True Delta* in May, 1859, in which he unmercifully parodied the letters which Sellers routinely sent in to the "River Intelligence" column.

Clemens wrote a long, sarcastic appraisal of Sellers' river reports, signed "Sergeant Fathom."

> "I burlesqued it broadly, very broadly, stringing my fantastics out to the extent of eight hundred or a thousand words. ... There was no malice in my rubbish; but it laughed at the captain. It laughed at a man to whom such a thing was new and strange and dreadful. I did not know then, though I do now, that there is no suffering comparable with that which a private person feels when he is for the first time pilloried in print.
> *Life on the Mississippi*, p. 497

"When me and De Soto discovered the Mississippi River..." (New Orleans *Crescent*, May 17, 1859), said Captain Fathom of the steamer *Trombone*. Twain was forever ashamed of this work.

The cemetery director, Mike Tiemann, a good amateur historian, took over from here, walking us across to the grave of Susan Blow, who founded the first American kindergarten in St. Louis, and the tomb of August Busch, whose wife kicked all the relatives out of the plot to erect his ostentatious mausoleum. It presides over its cushy neighborhood, sitting there with Caesar's *"Veni, vidi, vici"* inscribed above statues of a knight (August Busch?) and the Virgin Mary. This beer baron, who ultimately created the world's largest brewery, hated beer, which he called *"der Schlapp"* and drank only wine. However hops, not grapes, decorate his crypt. "No tap, though," one of our wags complained.

Mike walked us around the whole Busch family who had been pushed to the rear—Anna, Carl, Buffy, Eddie, Walter, Peter and some odd brothers and sisters, causing another comment, "You can't take this cemetery for granite!"

There is most certainly a high rent district in Bellefontaine, surrounding the Busch monument, a place of postmortem elegance where marble is the coin of the day. Joanie was in her element,

"There's MacMillan Furniture, and over there is Brown Shoes, you know, Buster Browns? And that's Stubbs Iron next to Moon Autos. Nickolson Whiskey is under that big tree and there lies Shinkle Shoes. Oh, and that one is Bixby Brick." She would have gone on, but someone wanted to know just who decided how big a brick should be anyway.

Our last stop was at the grave of William Clark, that intrepid explorer who has become a household word in America because he had the good fortune to have known Sacagawea. For four years he and Meriwether Lewis led their Company of Adventurers around the Far West, immortalized just recently for their *"Undaunted Courage."* Clark has continued to wander long after his death, moved to his present home from his nephew's estate in time for his own centennial celebration in 1904. His slumber is again disturbed by jackhammers as we near the bicentennial festivities of 2004, at which time they will probably try to reconvene the whole company, or at least the important leaders, Sacagawea, York and Seaman, whose figures grace nearly every modern monument striving for political correctness.

We left Bellefontaine, returning to the city, past the monumental courthouse, which Cathy reported was at first much opposed by the citizenry when it was built in 1861. "The only thing of value is the caretaker's turtle," ran the complaint. Today, of course it forms a magnificent artistic subject with the Arch as its frame, certainly the signature of St. Louis.

Historically it has its place as well, witnessing the Dred Scott case and later the first trial for women's suffrage.

A marker outside the courthouse announces the start of the Oregon and Santa Fe Trails, causing both Mac and I to object on our respective buses, since Becknell most certainly started his trek to Santa Fe from Old Gardner well west of St. Louis and Independence is certainly more important for the Oregon Trail. But we have found that any city worth its salt claims all the firsts and bests, starts and ends it can, defying argument once they are chiseled into stone.

We headed for beer country south of the city center, driving through a restored area called the Soulard District, a place that reminded me strongly of Philadelphia's Society Hill, with rows of restored red brick townhouses along tree-lined streets. It is the old German neighborhood that once boasted twenty-six other breweries besides that of Anheuser and Busch. Budweiser's biggest rival was Lemp Brewery, whose eccentric owner finally spent himself into oblivion. "If you don't spend your $1000 today," he reportedly told his wife, "you won't get another tomorrow." Lillian Lemp did spend her daily $1000 allotment, always dressing in purple, the color of royalty, becoming known as the Lavender Lady. The Lemp mansion still stands in Soulard, but the brewery was sold to the International Shoe Co.

"First in shoes; first in booze; last in the American League," Joanie had told us, probably unaware that the Cardinals are actually in the National League.

St. Louis is made up of neighborhoods, and we bounced from the Soulard to the Benton Park to the Lafayette Park neighborhood (filled with elegant mansarded Victorians), finally stopping for lunch at the imposing Union Station, whose spectacular grand hall and eleven-acre train shed were designed by Theodore Link in 1891.

We gave folks the option of returning to the hotel, since many wanted to find out the extent of the damage back east, and only one bus continued on through the Downtown Neighborhood, and the Mid-Town Hood (which is not actually in mid-town) to the Central West End Neighborhood, to visit the "New Cathedral" of St. Louis. It is a massive structure with green tiled domes visible for miles, housing "the largest mosaic collection in the world, 83,000 acres of mosaics," boasted Cathy. It was the fastest question/ exclamation mark I have ever written into my notes, and just about every head in the audience snapped to disbelieving attention. Of course she meant 83,000 *square feet*, and even that number is mind-boggling. There is hardly a tiny spot in this church that is not filled with saints and angels, apostles and beasts, executed in bits of colored tile. It is a breathtaking collection, put together between 1907-1914.

I harvested some neat words in the New Cathedral. We met in the *narthex,* the entrance hall where you are supposed to gather. Inside, the cathedral is a mosaic of mosaics—in the two massive domes, filling the half domes of the transept. Triangular areas between round dome and square bays, called *pententives,* are filled with angels. Mosaics in the under-arches (*soffits*) tell the story of Catholicism in St. Louis. *Lunettes* or half-round walls tell of the works of Cardinal Ritter and early clerics who labored on the Mississippi. Twenty artists, working over seventy-five years installed 41 million pieces in over 8,000 colors, using a variety of mosaic styles. This church can hold its own among the artistic marvels of Christianity, going several degrees farther in mosaic sophistication than Ste.-Anne-du-Beaupre, another historic Romanesque basilica in Quebec province. I have been to St. Louis a dozen times and never visited its New Cathedral, surprisingly never having heard it existed.

All of us returned to the grim reality of the crime inflicted on America by these Arab terrorists. It is unthinkable. Both World Trade towers have collapsed. Once the tallest in the world, they are no more, having imploded to gigantic heaps of twisted rubble, a grisly bier which will house thousands of ill-fated office workers, who left home this morning never conceiving the nightmare they would experience. We must all pray for them.

V

With heavy hearts we depart for Hannibal, about 100 miles north on the river, entering the world of Sam Clemens, of Huck, and Becky Thatcher, Indian Joe, Pudd'nhead Wilson and, of course, Tom Sawyer. Perhaps, in this mad post-9/11 world, it is a proper time for a dose of fiction.

You know immediately when you are nearing Hannibal because whitewashed fences start proliferating and businesses get named things like Huck and Becky Thatcher, Sawyer and, of course, Mark Twain. I quickly noted the Hotel Clemens, Mark Twain Dinette, Huck's Home Stand, Becky's Old-Fashioned Ice Cream Emporium, Mrs. Clemens Shop, Pudd'nhead Antiques, Clemen's Landing, Tom Sawyer's Dioramas and the Mark Twain Card Shop. There seems to be a homogeneous theme about this place. The town's first citizen certainly didn't see it the way we do today.

> "Hannibal has had a hard time of it ever since I can recollect, and I was "raised" there. First, it had me for a citizen, but I was too young then to really hurt the place."
> Letter to the *Alta California*, dated April 16, 1867; published May 26, 1867. Quoted in www.twainquotes.com

We were met at the new Mark Twain Museum in Hannibal by director Henry Sweets, who introduced us to the society of Mark Twain's day, expanding on the social structure, the economy, religion, school system that could produce this largely self-taught, but world-wise genius. "Hannibal 1819-1860" was a welcome background introduction to the author. From there we wandered off to explore the white-washed world of Tom, Becky and Huck, a world that Henry Sweets would expand on when we reconvened in the afternoon. Henry is an earnest speaker, with pleasant manner and style, probably better extemporaneously, fielding questions, where his depth of knowledge shines through. Having tied all of Twain's characters to their real-life Hannibal personalities, he regaled us with letters and inquiries routinely received at the museum, drawing continuous smiles of understanding and nods of approval from Bob who encounters such things daily at his Mark Twain Project. It was a pleasant hour.

We checked in to the Hannibal Inn before driving back to town to dine at the Riverview Cafe. Given a wide choice of entrée items, I settled on a combination I had never seen in real life—turkey and prime rib, barnyard and pasture. The restaurant proved to be rather deliberate in their service techniques, starting slowly and then gradually grinding to a halt, sometime just before coffee. I went to inquire about coffee and dessert and was heading back upstairs when the first of our gang wandered down, inspiring me to pay the bill and head back to the Hannibal Inn. "Where's dessert?" would start as a gentle heckle and escalate to a rather sarcastic battle cry in the days to come. That night I checked my contracts and found that I had indeed ordered and paid for some sort of apple crisp, too late to do any good. But anyway, why would anyone miss dessert in a restaurant that offers magnum bottles of Delicato merlot and chardonnay for $12? The Bears are going to have to get their priorities in order. Mac is probably right—they need more tannins, not sugar.

VI

It took all morning to drive south of Saint Louis to the lovely old town of Sainte Genevieve, with a rest break at the McDonald's in Troy, Missouri. Bob moved to the Blue Bus to repeat a lecture he had done for the Gold Bus people yesterday.

As we departed the Hannibal Inn, he announced "I'm going to wait a bit until the bus is a little more awake."

"It'll never happen, Bob. Hit 'em now!" I advised.

9 A.M. is the golden moment for bus lectures on a travel day. An hour of warm drone has a narcotic effect on the most interested traveler and you never want to waste these precious first moments. So Bob carried forth, and I patrolled with my tithing stick to urge the audience to active participation. This is not at all necessary with the Golden Bears. This is my twenty-third trip with them, and I have never met a batch of folks with such an active curiosity and love of learning. Oh, you have to offer their material in attractive, fun packages, but a more questioning audience is not to be found. A speaker is only as good as his audience, and I have seen the Bears turn a bunch of stutterers into orators. I remember a poor guide on Campobello Island who was petrified to find herself in front of a whole busload of college graduates and she was totally tongue-tied. Graduates— and from Berkeley! She was tongue-tied and petrified.

"They won't hurt you," I had counseled. "Just tell us about your neighbors, the weather, anything you know about the island." She was wonderful!

"They're such lovely people!" she oozed at the end of her tour.

So Bob carried forth from that inexhaustible reservoir of expertise, based on the material that comprises the Mark Twain papers, thousands of letters, a fraction of those actually written, augmented by articles, notebooks and of course the novels, short stories and essays, many in multiple versions. More than anyone, Bob has access to the whole incredible body of materials.

"If Mark Twain says something and you can't confirm it, he's right!"

Bob expanded this morning a bit on the author's general view of life and his place in it. He was very anxious to be successful, to be regarded well by the world. Part of his attraction to river piloting was that the job carried respect and prestige. Looking at his life he regarded himself as being very fortunate.

"You will decry this egotism, but I tell you there is a stern joy in it."

I like it best when Bob chooses passages where Twain ventures into the realm of pure imagination, like his letter to Annie Taylor on the subject of "Bugs!" described as a religious mass meeting attracted by the candles in the pilot house.

> "Night before last I stood at the little press until nearly 2 o'clock, and the flaring gas light over my head attracted all the varieties of bugs which are to be found in natural history, and they all had the same praiseworthy recklessness about flying into the fire. They at first came in little social crowds of a dozen or so, but soon increased in numbers, until a religious mass meeting of several millions was assembled on the board before me, presided over by a venerable beetle, who occupied the most prominent lock of my hair as his chair of state, while innumerable lesser dignitaries of the same tribe were clustered around him, keeping order, and at the same time endeavoring to attract the attention of the vast assemblage in their own importance by industriously grating their teeth...."

> "It would take a ream of paper to give all the ceremonies of this great mass meeting. Suffice to say that the little press "chawed up" half a bushel of their devotees, and I combed 976 beetles out of my hair the next morning, every one of whose throats was stretched wide open, for their gentle spirits had passed away while yet they sung and who shall say they will not receive their reward? I buried their motionless forms with musical honors in John's hat."
> *Mark Twain's Letters*, Vol. 1, Letter to Ann E. Taylor, May 21 and 25, 1856

Twain's "letters" seldom just present news or gossip. ("Pamela has got a baby!") Rather they are discussions, essays on anything, nothing apparently outside the scope of his interest, be it real or imaginary, serious or comical. Mark Twain could reduce a calamity to comedy. I wonder how his friends and family responded to such letters, if they tried to respond in kind, or just rolled their eyes, had a good laugh, and relayed his words on to friends. Bob mentioned how subtly he used letters, especially to his mother, trapping her with the content, assuming that she would be reading it to neighbors, probably without proofing it beforehand, trapping his audience without ever seeing it. It would be interesting to find out how many of his letters were written for publication.

Eyes were still open when we arrived in Troy and Bob had used up his golden hour.

By noon we reached Sainte Genevieve, self-proclaimed "the oldest town west of the Mississippi." I have given up on anyone in Missouri recognizing New Orleans, but I am willing to accept Sainte Genevieve as the oldest town west of the Mississippi and north of New Orleans. Then there is always Santa Fe!

When Sam Clemens was first on the river as a cub pilot, Sainte Genevieve was as well. But like many towns along the Mississippi, the town was literally moved inland by the meanderings of the great river.

> "...for these people were evidently bound for a large town which lay shut in by a tow-head (i.e., new island a couple of miles below this landing. I couldn't remember that town; I couldn't place its name. So I lost part of my temper. I suspected it might be St. Genevieve—and so it proved to be. Observe what this eccentric river had been about: it had built up this huge useless tow-head directly in front of the town, cut off its river communications, fenced it away completely, and made a "country" town of it. It is a fine old place, too, and deserved a better fate. It was settled by the French and is a relic of a time when one could travel from the mouths of the Mississippi to Quebec and be on French territory and under French rule all the way."
> *Life on the Mississippi*, pp. 262-263

Today Sainte Genevieve is perfectly charming, having been spared the ravages of war and flood, and maintaining an atmosphere of Creole French that almost feels like something that belongs north of the border in Quebec, and south of the border in Barbados. Sainte Genevieve has concentrated its history in about four square blocks around the Visitor Center, where Judy put on a video for us describing the town and its history, condensed as we are wont to do, into seventeen minutes—a *USA Today* capsule, perfect for American travelers. Then, armed with maps that conveniently marked all restaurants with an "F" for "Food", everyone dispersed for lunch and exploration.

Three houses in town are open for tours: the Bolduc House, built in 1770; the neighboring, and younger Bolduc-LeMeilleur House (1820); and the Felix Valle House from 1818. All are examples of early French Creole architecture, unique to this area. Sainte Genevieve's official seal says it was founded in 1735. Gregory Franzwa, an old Santa Fe and Oregon Trail friend who has written a history of the town, scoffs at that date and puts the settlement in the late 1840s. What is certain is that the area was visited in the seventeenth century by LaMothe Cadillac who was looking for silver and struck lead. The region has been producing valuable lead right up to modern times, only recently closing the last mine. Generally the French settled the opposite, east shore of the river, with Kaskaskia being the leading village. With the Treaty of Paris in 1763 and the English takeover of the Ohio Valley, some 300 settlers moved across to Saint

Mary's and Sainte Genevieve, building their homes on the river, their farms stretching in long, *arpent*-wide strips (192') back to the hills. Later because of recurring floods, they moved the town away from the river, next to *le Grande Champs*, a huge, fertile meadow that had attracted them in the first place.

The town remains distinctly French to this day, provincial in the extreme and sometimes most curious in their customs. Franzwa, in *The Story of Old Ste. Genevieve*:

> Nicknames are especially popular with the settlers...The custom persists in Ste. Genevieve today. There is Punkin' Basler, Fuclos La Rose, Horse Maurice, Flakes Bahr, Toothpick Bollinger, Possum Grass, Bigfoot Basler, ... and an entire family bearing the names of Izzy, Dizzy, Nuts, Boats and Nooney... One man has his nickname, "Boob" painted on his mailbox.

The old French had a New Year's custom called *La Guignolée*, where on New Year's Eve, people dressed as Indians or in black face, going from door to door begging food, which is stored for a banquet on Twelfth Night. Sainte Genevieve remains one of those curious national enclaves that are to be found in every part of the U.S.

We took the river road south from Sainte Genevieve to Cape Girardeau, only jogging off on Road KK to give the folks a little, county-road experience. Phil mentioned that single-letter roads run north-south and double-lettered ones east-west, a Harry Truman idea.

These roads are great to drive in the South. Usually narrow and winding, they wander through dense woods and over undulating hills. They offer the visitor views of kudzu and dead armadillos, and cute little red-necked box turtles ambling across the road. You are sure to find a supply of plastic pink flamingos, looking absolutely natural in their Southern setting. They will be in front of a house whose driveway is lined with old tractor tires, sitting up, half sunk in the dirt, and painted white for decorative purposes. A few plastic deer and half a dozen Canada geese add to the décor, the scene completed by one or more of the Purple martin condo complexes, some with hanging gourd appendages. Businesses are a bit different in the South. I spotted a house that advertised Sandra's Cut

& Curl and Joe's Taxidermy, a curious combination that seemed more natural the longer I thought about it. In another town I found Big Buck's Barbecue Smokehouse, which probably could merge with Sandra and Joe without an eyebrow being raised.

The landscape is a painter's canvas. Dense forests of pine and big leaf oak, with hardwoods interspersed, completely wall off the road. Wherever there is an opening, that voracious vine, kudzu, imported from the Far East as a ground cover, suffocates everything. It oozes completely over large trees, strangling the life out of them, climbs telephone poles and creeps along the wires. I was told once that it can grow a foot a day.

A bus driver told me once, "If y'all have a neighbor y'all don't like, wait for him to go away for the weekend. Plant some kudzu in his back yard. He won't be able to find his home when he comes back."

I am always saddened by the sight of kudzu running wild. It symbolizes, I think, life gone completely berserk, running over everything without distinction, ultimately choking everything it encounters. It is like green chaos—an unstoppable riot of growth—sad.

Here in the country, besides the armadillos, which always seem to turn on to their backs after they get run over, there are the hound dogs. In every dirt driveway there is a hound, sitting there watching the world go by. They don't bark at you or chase you down the road; they are just sitting there watching. Stop and a bunch of them will descend on you, this time barking, and keep you at bay until someone comes to call them off.

Just north of Cape Girardeau is the Trail of Tears State Park, part of the national historic trail tracing the route of the Cherokee expulsion from North Carolina to Oklahoma in 1838, one of the most dastardly deeds in our history. The route crossed the Mississippi in this region on its way across Missouri and Arkansas.

As a cub pilot, Sam Clemens stopped at most of the river towns between St. Louis and New Orleans. Twenty-one years after he left the piloting profession, he made a return trip down the river, describing many of those places, often remarking on the change effected by more than two decades.

> "Cape Girardeau is situated on a hillside, and makes a handsome appearance. There is a great Jesuit school for boys at the foot of the town by the river… There is another college higher up on the airy summit,—a bright new edifice, picturesquely and peculiarly towered and pinnicaled—a sort of gigantic casters, with the cruets all complete. Uncle Mumford said that Cape Girardeau was the Athens of Missouri, and contained several colleges besides those already mentioned…He directed my attention to what he called the "strong and pervasive religious look of the town." But I could not see that it looked more religious than the other hill towns with the same slope and built of the same kind of bricks. Partialities often make people see more than really exists."
> *Life on the Mississippi*, pp. 274-75

We checked in to the Victorian Inn in Cape Girardeau, nestled comfortably in the midst of the typical neon desert that has driven most small American towns to near extinction. There is a particularly good fast food wasteland, here in Cape Girardeau, probably inspired by I-55 and Southeast Missouri State College. Modern American students minor, perhaps even major, in Fast Food Consumption. Here they have quite a selection, able to choose from:

> McDonalds, Burger King, KFC, Wendy's, Taco Bell, Hardees, Denny's, Applebees, Red Lobster, El Torito, Baskin Robbins, Dairy Queen, Long John Silvers, Fasoli's, Ruby Tuesday's, Lion's Choice, Bob Evan's, Great Wall of China, Outback Steakhouse, Pizza Inn, Cedar Street, Ryans, Steak n Shake, Cracker Barrel, Sonic, Blimpies

It was the best such dining pollution I have seen since the one surrounding Notre Dame in South Bend, Indiana. There were more in that famous college town, but my pen ran out of ink. I think that a Cape Girardean could "dine" in a different quick-thawed cuisine every night of the year, and still be able to get a sausage McMuffin with egg in the morning. I believe that this proliferation of fast food emporiums completely supports Sam Clemens' observations in the preceding quote.

Our choice for dinner was worlds above this, at the Old New Orleans Restaurant on Broadway in town, a fine establishment fashioned out of the old Firehouse. There we were met by Dr. Frank Nicholl from the State University, whose subject is the Mississippi River.

"It is a pleasure to be here tonight. We haven't had this much brain power in Cape Girardeau since Rush Limbaugh left town." Of course this was Rush's hometown, and evidence of his association is all over town, in books, pictures, posters, and of course on their Wall of Fame.

The Mississippi drains 40 percent of the U.S., with its mighty tributaries, the Missouri, Ohio, Arkansas and all the streams which feed them. 60 percent of North America's water flows past Cairo at the confluence with the Ohio. The Missouri's contribution is soil, the "Big Muddy" spewing 60 percent of the sediment carried down to the Gulf, enough every day to raise 100 acres six feet. The Ohio doubles the volume of the water itself.

Scientists tracked the river waters after the flood of 1993. A huge stream of sediment flowed into the gulf, turned east past the Florida Keys, then ambled all the way into the North Atlantic. The great 1927 flood created a lake near Greenville 100 miles wide, leaving 600,000 homeless. 620 cities get their drinking water from the Mississippi, including Cape Girardeau.

"We have had seven floods in the last twenty years," Dr. Nicholl reported. "I've lived here twenty years and in that time, we have had three so-called "500-year floods."

Mark Twain has many descriptions of the Mississippi, but he is deeply interested in its constant state of flux.

"An article in the New Orleans "Times Democrat," based upon reports of able engineers, states that the river annually empties four hundred and six million tons of mud into the Gulf of Mexico—which brings to mind Captain Marryat's rude name for the Mississippi— "the Great Sewer." This mud, solidified, would make a mass a mile square and two hundred and forty-one feet high....

The belief of the scientific people is, that the mouth used to be at Baton Rouge, where the hills cease, and that the two hundred miles of land between there and the Gulf was built by the river.

The Mississippi is remarkable in still another way—its disposition to make prodigious jumps by cutting through narrow necks of land, and thus straightening and shortening itself. More than once it has shortened itself thirty miles at a single jump! These cut-offs have had curious effects: they have thrown several river towns out into the rural districts, and built up bars and forest in front of them...

A cut-off plays havoc with boundary lines and jurisdictions: for instance, a man is living in the State of Mississippi today, a cut-off occurs tonight, and to-morrow the man finds himself and his land over on the other side of the river, within the boundaries and subject to the laws of the State of Louisiana. Such a thing, happening in the upper river in the old times, could have transferred a slave from Missouri to Illinois and made a free man of him."

Life on the Mississippi, pp. 23-24

"Since my own day on the Mississippi, cut-offs have been made at Hurricane Island; at Island 100; at Napoleon, Arkansas; at Walnut Bend; and at Council Bend. These shortened the river, in the aggregate, sixty-seven miles. In my own time a cut-off was made at American Bend, which shortened the river ten miles or more.

Therefore, the Mississippi between Cairo and New Orleans was twelve hundred and fifteen miles long one hundred and seventy-six years ago. It was eleven hundred and eighty after the cut-off of 1722. It was one thousand and forty after the American Bend cut-off. It has lost sixty-seven miles since. Consequently its length is only nine hundred and seventy-three miles at present."

Life on the Mississippi, p. 207

VII

Marge Thompson was glued to her TV set when we arrived at the River Museum this morning, the events in New York having expunged everything else from her interest, and she completely forgot she was supposed to meet us. She arrived fifteen minutes late, out of breath and embarrassed, to admit us to a hot, airless collection of small-town memorabilia, the kind of country ephemera that always seems to survive. This museum, centering on a Missouri river town, had some unique gems:

***The biggest barge tow in history was 72 barges.

***Marie Watkins Oliver designed the Missouri flag.

***It was Willard Vandiver who said: "I come from a state that raises corn, cotton, cockleburs and Democrats. Frothy eloquence neither convinces me nor satisfies me. I am from Missouri. You've got to show me." I'll bet everyone thinks Harry T. said that.

***The best trivia is about Missouri's famous mules. There are different sorts:

Jack, jackass—males of ass family

Jenny, Jaunet—female

Mule—offspring of male ass and a mare

Hinny—offspring of stallion and a jenny

Burro—small Mexican or Spanish ass

Donkey—name for all of them when you don't know any better.

That is some fine cocktail party trivia!

Linda Hill, a guide from the Cape Girardeau Visitor Center guided Mac's bus around the town while ours was at the museum and now switched to our group for her tour.

Cape Girardeau is a town of 50,000 including university students, "the largest town on the west bank of the Mississippi between St. Louis and Memphis." The superlatives are a bit more constrained here. We drove down Morgan Oak Rd. to the Mississippi River Bridge, then turned on Spanish St., the old El Camino Real that once stretched from St. Louis to Memphis. Near the river is the Wall of Fame, pictures of famous Missourians painted on the flood wall, of course including Rush, Harry T., Sam Clemens, obvious inclusions, but other less well known such as Vincent Price, Calamity Jane, Frank & Jesse James, Pulitzer, J.C. Penny, Jack Buck, Marlin Perkins, Generals Pershing and Omar Bradley, T.S. Eliot, George Washington Carver, Scott Joplin, Burt Bacharack, Eugene Field, Dale Carnegie, Walter Cronkite and Tennessee Williams.

From the wall we drove past the court house and a somewhat nondescript downtown area to the Cape Rock which gave the town its name after Jean Baptiste Girardot moved over from Illinois to set up a trading post. The actual town was founded by Don Louis Lorimer, whose statue graces the downtown area, notable only because his braided hair was so long he could use it as a horse crop.

Morgan Oak Avenue leads across a rickety old bridge to Illinois, into one of the most depressed areas of the nation. Even the bridge is for sale, someday soon to be superseded by a modern new span. There are no buyers. Across the way, in the flat sandy Illinois tongue that sticks out at the junction of two great rivers is a place that was once prosperous, the vital heart of the valley that supported Grant's Union Army, and housed 30,000 people in the last decades of the nineteenth century. Today it is a land of scraggily cotton, goose-reserve marshes, time-forsaken towns, burned out, boarded-up buildings, few hopes. Once this was "Little Egypt" flowing with grain, bursting with promise, a place that fed the cities, manufactured ironclads, supplied armies, hosted presidents, supported industrial millionaires. No longer. Today this land of Cairo and Thebes, Olive Branch and Mound City is reduced to sad emptiness, epitomized by the weed-infested vacant, double highway entering Future City just outside Cairo (pronounced "kay-row"). Race riots in the 1960s were the final nail in Southern Illinois' coffin, as the place succumbed to vice, drugs, and despair. That was not the case in Sam Clemens' day.

> "Cairo is a brisk town now; and is substantially built, and has a
> city look about it which is in noticeable contrast to its former estate,
> as per Mr. Dickens's portrait of it. However, it was already building
> with bricks when I had seen it last—which was when Colonel (now
> General) Grant was drilling his first command there. Uncle Mumford
> says the libraries and Sunday-schools have done a good work in Cairo,
> as well as the brick masons. Cairo has a heavy railroad and river
> trade, and her situation at the junction of the two great rivers is so
> advantageous that she cannot well help prospering."
> *Life on the Mississippi*, p. 280

Ten years ago I came to Cairo aboard the *Mississippi Queen*. At that
time, most of the town was boarded up, with eroded levies, cracked up
sidewalks, dilapidated, ugly buildings. Only a few sad stores offered a
Vincent de Paul inventory to the eager cruise shoppers. There was nothing
to buy! I have always told people how sad Cairo, Illinois was.

Surely, I thought, in ten years they would have fixed up this place,
given the increasing tourism and the escalating value of waterfront
property everywhere in America. How wrong I was! Even St. Vincent has
now deserted Cairo. There is not a single business left open in the river
area. A lonely clock tower, a spin-off of the one in Cape Girardeau, newly
constructed of bricks with donors' names incised on them, is the only
indication that life exists in this forlorn place. But there is nothing left alive
around it. A few blocks away sits a monumental Customs House, and the
impressive brick Cairo Baptist church. But the town is gone, moved away
from the river leaving only the shell of former grandeur.

Last month I revisited Cairo, hoping to find a book or two on the
town's history. That Customs House spoke of a very important place, and
I knew that Cairo had once had 30,000 or more inhabitants. There must
be more to it, and at least a good, if sad story to be read. I stopped at two
bookstores in Cape Girardeau but they knew of no history of the river
towns. Maybe in Cairo I would find something. On the way into town,
there is a sign advertising Magnolia Manor, a historic home that is open
to the public. I turned on 27th Street and found Washington Avenue, lined
with a row of magnificent mansions suitable for Natchez or Savannah. I

stopped at Riverlore, a stately French Second Empire Mansion built in 1865, to see if they had any books.

"Oh yes, I have a copy of a history of Cairo," reported the volunteer lady proudly handing me her copy, called "The History of Cairo."

"Is it well written," I asked not knowing what else to say to her enthusiasm.

"Oh I've never read it. But there are lots of pictures, of the sewing machine plants, and the Coca Cola plants. There was a lot of history here."

"Can I buy a copy?"

"Oh no, this is my personal copy. Your best bet would be the library."

I didn't really want to apply for a library card in Cairo, Illinois, so I bade her adieu and drove off down "Millionaire's Row" which she had called this elegant magnolia-lined avenue. Across the street from Riverlore sits Magnolia Manor, built in 1869, four stories of Italianate elegance in brick and wrought iron. At the end of Washington Avenue sits the Safford Memorial Library, this one done in 1883 Queen Anne style, an imposing edifice in its own right. On an impulse, I stopped for a visit, warmly greeted by the librarian, a middle-aged woman who might be the prototype of the profession—hair-bunned, bespectacled, matronly.

"Do you by any chance sell any books on the history of Cairo?"

"Well, yes," she responded, quickly producing the very book I had just seen.

"Is it well written?" I asked, having now perfected the question.

"Well, I haven't actually read it."

"How much is it?"

"$12.50," she replied, obviously thinking that was way too dear for something that had apparently never been read.

"Could I have two copies?"

I wish I could describe her look of astonishment. Her bun positively sat up on top of her head, as the matter beneath it tried to puzzle out why someone would want two books on Cairo's history. I started to explain how I needed a copy for Mac but decided it would be more fun to leave her perplexed, with a great story to relate to the illiterati of the town. I fully intend to find out what happened to this once thriving place. Just from the few buildings I discovered, it is obvious that Cairo owed its wealth to the Civil War. Charles Gallagher, who built Magnolia Manor, supplied the

Union Army with flour, and became a close friend of General Grant. Cairo supplied Grant's army during his Mississippi campaign. For a half century after the war, this must have been the economic center of the region.

At the confluence of the two great rivers is Fort Defiance State Park, called in the Cairo brochure (which I had also found in the library) "probably the ugliest park in America. The park that no one wants." That was way too much to pass up, so with heightened expectations, I drove out the peninsula, having no idea what I would find. For a place like Cairo, which has taken ugly to an art form, to call her park "ugly", this must be some cesspool. What I found was a pleasant grassy place with good views of both bridges, one running east to Kentucky, the other south to Missouri.

Today, Frank Williams, the mayor of Cairo was at Fort Defiance Park, talking of reviving the town beginning with paving the riverside streets and cleaning up the park. The work has surely started because the park is on the rise, with new picnic tables, a bandstand under construction, and a litter-free RV park to attract visitors. Tomorrow they are hosting a Harley bike rally. It's a start!

Our lunch today is at a Southern institution, Lambert's Restaurant in Sikeston, Missouri, the home of "throwed rolls." A sign on the highway bragged "We've thrown 13,578,485 rolls." I am anxious to see how our college-cultured Bears react to Southern mountain heehaw. The place takes no reservations because they are always full, and I called from Cairo to see how busy they were.

"Oh, we're a might bit slow. Y'all ain't gonna have no problem."

There wasn't an empty booth in the place when we arrived a half-hour later and I spit and moaned at the manager, vowing verbally never to come again.

"Won't take but a minute to git y'all seated," he assured me and he was right, placing all fifty-six of us in less than fifteen minutes. Scrunched into heavy wooden booths, grabbing paper towels from rolls to hold fried okra and piping hot rolls, "throwed" from the aisles with precision accuracy, where they were ladled with molasses. Many of the Bears got their first good look at the cliché of mountain culture. Fried chicken, hog jowls, onion-fried potatoes, hot wings, polish sausage—such delicacies poured out of Lambert's kitchen, served by loud, happy young waiters. A few of our crowd made the mistake of ordering chef salads and were served with massive constructions resembling a vegetable garden atop one of the Cahokia Mounds. This is a place to *EAT*!

It was 2 P.M. by the time we exited Lambert's and a decision had to be made about ducks and New Madrid. I had planned a stop at New Madrid (pronounced Mád-rid), site of America's worst-ever earthquakes in 1811-12 and one of the most famous spots on the river—the legendary New Madrid Loop, where the Mississippi does a sideways "S" turn requiring twenty miles to proceed a single one. Nearby is strategic Island #10, the scene of a pivotal battle in Grant's 1863 drive toward Vicksburg. Except for its strategic position on the river, New Madrid has never been a big tourist attraction.

> "The town of New Madrid was looking very unwell; but otherwise unchanged from its former condition and aspect. Its blocks of frame-houses were still grouped in the same old flat plain, and environed by the same old forests. It was as tranquil as formerly, and apparently had neither grown nor diminished in size. It was said that the recent high water had invaded it and damaged its banks. This was surprising news; for in low-water the river bank is very high there (fifty feet), and in my day an overflow had always been considered an impossibility."
> *Life on the Mississippi*, p. 290

For us today, with our bellies full of "throwed rolls," New Madrid was one touring choice. Opposed to this endemically plain town are five mallards in Memphis, the incomparable Peabody Hotel ducks, who walk every afternoon precisely at 5:00 from the fountain in the lobby to the elevator for a ride to their penthouse palace. We can't do both. Which will it be—New Madrid where an 8.9 earthquake lowered 300 square miles twenty feet, threw the Mississippi out of its bed, caused it to run uphill before bringing it back in the form of giant lakes and a violent river; New Madrid, whose revitalized river front features a fine new museum, a wonderful observation deck running out over the levee affording a view of the unique 'loop'; New Madrid, which at the same time is north, south, east and west of Kentucky?

Or five ducks waddling to an elevator?

Have you ever watched a full-grown woman deliberately place herself supine on a hotel rug, supported by chin, boobs and belly in front of a couple hundred people for the sole purpose of photographing a waddling bird heading for the roof? Today academic curiosity took a huge beating in favor of touristic banality, as the Bears turned their backs on New Madrid and opted for the most ridiculous tourist scam "west of the Mississippi." Oh, wait! Memphis is east of the Mississippi, but it is west of Dollywood. The path from the pond to the elevator was lined three-deep with intellects by the time our buses disgorged our folks at 4:30, a full half-hour before the spectacle. Additional gawkers lined both sides of the mezzanine, mostly breathless with anticipation. I heard a more subdued buzz at one of the Wednesday Papal Audiences at the Vatican.

A red carpet ran the gauntlet between the two lines of spectators who were already on hands, knees and stomachs, Minoltas straining to spring into action. Finally a red-coated top-hatted Caylen Housdan, the Duckmaster, approached the fountain, duck wand in hand, carrying himself proud and erect as only a leader of ducks can manage. He stood stiff and straight in martial splendor, now and then consulting his chronometer for the precise moment where he would spring into action and command his charges to attack. Suddenly a stentorian voice boomed out, "Ladies and Gentlemen..." A John Phillips Souza march filled the room. All eyes focused on the fountain chiseled out of the finest Italian travertine marble, topped by a sensational floral arrangement of lilies, massive proteas, magnolia blossoms, and ginger. All the ladies and their gentlemen hushed themselves in reverent awe as the Duckmaster positioned a red-bedecked stairway outside the pond, turned and tapped the marble with his duck wand. The tired drake and his harem of four swam on cue to the ramp, proposing to exit stage left. They botched it! Two orderly canards calmly walked over the pond wall. One jumped, missed and crashed back into the water. Another went the wrong way. One completely lost composure and *flew out of the pond!* The crowd watched stunned. The Duckmaster shrank with shame. Such an exit had not been seen since Randy Duck had gone AWOL and ended up in Berkeley playing basketball.

In thirty-seven seconds, the waddlers, finally organized and composed by the Duckmaster, disappeared into the elevator, at least that is my assumption, because the crowd crush enveloped them the second they left the pond. The lady whose chin was on the floor was left with a wet duck print on the top of her bun and two tiny pellets in one ear.

"It was worth ten New Madrids," enthused Bob Hirst, his cheeks trembling with emotion.

"The best thing about the ducks is the people kneeling there watching," opined Leo, our resident observer, who had apparently missed the whole point.

"I hope nobody saw me there," moaned Alice, clasping her camera to her bosom and removing a feather from her sleeve.

"Do we have time to see New Madrid?"

They probably wouldn't be much impressed by Yosemite either.

VIII

"We were approaching Memphis, in front of which city, and witnessed by its people, was fought the most famous of the river battles of the Civil War. Two men whom I had served under, in my river days, took part in that fight: Mr. Bixby, head pilot of the Union fleet, and Montgomery, Commander of the Confederate fleet....

The boat was to tarry at Memphis till ten the next morning. It is a beautiful city, nobly situated on a commanding bluff overlooking the river. The streets are straight and spacious, though not paved in a way to incite distempered admiration. No, the admiration must be reserved for the town's sewerage system, which is called perfect; a recent reform however, for it was just the other way, up to a few years ago—a reform resulting from the lesson taught by a desolating visitation of the yellow-fever....

But there is life enough there now. The population exceeds forty thousand and is augmenting, and trade is in a flourishing condition. We drove about the city visited the park and the sociable horde of squirrels there saw the fine residences, rose-clad and in other ways enticing to the eye; and got a good breakfast at the hotel."
Life on the Mississippi, p.323

Mary Elizabeth and Lex are our Memphis guides, the former a fast-talking, enthusiastic Southern lady, the latter a droll slow-mumbling expatriate from a Tennessee Williams play. I wanted to go with both, but since I had inflicted St. Louis Joanie on Mac, I should take Memphis Mary Elizabeth. "That's two names, Mary - Elizabeth. Ah neva' sho'tins it."

What a wonderful surprise is Memphis! I remember the city as depressed, dirty and dangerous, boasting Graceland, the Peabody, Mud Island and a couple of Victorian houses that gave tours. You couldn't walk anywhere after dark, and there wasn't anywhere to go if you did go for a nervous stroll. The last ten years have been very kind to Memphis, which has drawn in new business and industry as have many of the Southern cities and has reclaimed its downtown as a result of the new revenue. Last month I visited the new Museum of Rock and Soul, a collaboration with the Smithsonian, and I was very impressed, both with the concept as well as with the execution. I also toured the new Mississippi River Museum on Mud Island, which is equally impressive. Today we drove by the Museum of Civil Rights, based in the old Lorraine Motel where Martin Luther King was murdered on April 4, 1968. $12 million has been expended to create the modern complex, which extends behind the restored façade of the motel. Later we visited the Danny Thomas Memorial at his St. Jude Hospital for Children. While it struck me as a bit garish, too much Robert Shuler Crystal Cathedral-ish, it is nevertheless a spectacular venue. We need not necessarily raise Danny Thomas to canonization status, but his work is certainly worth remembering and praising, both of which have been accomplished.

All these sites emphasize the renaissance that Memphis is experiencing, a rebirth that is epitomized by the Pyramid that dominates the cityscape. It houses the basketball facility of Memphis University, seating 20,000 for games and other events. Since it was built, it has welcomed a world-class procession of exhibitions, the Wonder Series, which has included King Tut, Catherine the Great, Napoleon and the Titanic, a new program scheduled every two years. It is a most impressive structure, thirty-two stories high above the West Memphis Bridge. Visitors enter past a stone replica of Rameses II, a fitting symbol of a city called Memphis. Of course, this is made understandable because Memphis is the southern terminus of that nineteenth century region known as "Little Egypt," also featuring Thebes and Cairo.

The city was founded in 1819 by John Overton, James Winchester and Andrew Jackson, who purchased the land from the Chickasaw Indians. Winchester, who admired the career of Napoleon, named the city after its river-based counterpart in Egypt. Today Memphis is the eighteenth largest city in the U.S., five times named the cleanest city in the nation. Once half of the cotton in the U.S. came across its docks and warehouses, though now only "spot cotton" remains and the warehouses have been turned into what Mary Elizabeth called "precious apartments."

There is more that is new in the city. Near the Peabody we passed the brand new 14,000-seat stadium of the Memphis Red Birds, attracting sellouts most nights and bringing thousands back into town. Beale Street has been cleaned up and is now heavily patrolled by the local gendarmes, making it a considerably more attractive destination for tourists. We drove out on Mud Island to find a gorgeous line of upscale condos and "doctors' houses" lining the river. Mary Elizabeth called these "zero lot line houses", mostly three stories with elevators, many costing up to $1 million.

I can't recall being more surprised by a city, pleasantly surprised. Memphis has come bounding like a frisky colt into the twenty-first century, memorializing its heritage but packaging it for the modern person. I am going to have to reconsider our time allotment here, because half a day for Mud Island and Elvis is no longer sufficient.

I am most eager to get our people's reaction to the Rock 'n Soul Museum. Most of our groups hated Elvis and if they ever got into Blues, they probably think it is too loud. We were having a hamburger in the Hard Rock Cafe, one of the more subdued in the chain, when a couple from our group walked in. They heard the music, eyes bugged out and they called the waitress over.

"Can you recommend a place to eat that is not so noisy?"

On Beale Street?!

"If you can't find your youth here, you never will," marveled Russ as he left the museum. One after another our folks came down the stairs at Rock 'n Soul with positive, sometimes effusive things to say. Mary Elizabeth came over with a big grin, saying that there were people dancing in there. It was Ernie. "I danced the whole time," she affirmed. I think this place is a must for future groups regardless of age. Besides, we "youngsters" were raised with Elvis and Otis Redding.

Across from the museum is an old church surrounded by urban renewal empty parking lots. It is the Black African Methodist Episcopal Church, the starting point for the Martin Luther King garbage strike protests of the late 1960s. From there he led the protesters down Beale St., the traditional Black shopping street of Memphis, along Front to the Courthouse and back to the church. Of course he was staying in the nearby Lorraine Motel the night he was killed by James Earl Ray. The Young & Morrow Building on South Main, from which Ray shot, is currently under restoration and will become part of the complex of the Museum of Civil Rights.

Danny Thomas, born Amos Jacobs in 1914 in Michigan, will forever be associated with St. Jude and Memphis. His hospital, built in 1962, now largely financed by ALSAC, his American-Lebanese-Syrian Associated Charities, serves young cancer victims. Thomas died in 1991.

Our last stop before boarding the *Mississippi Queen Riverboat* was at the Mud Island Museum of the Mississippi River, which Mary Elizabeth said, "runs from 10,000 B.C. to Elvis," a conceptual sequence possible in few other places in this world. In fact, she was right. The museum traces a timeline from pre-history through the Mound Builders, to European exploration and settlement, continuing through ante-bellum slavery days, Civil War, Reconstruction, to Black music and ending with Elvis. Wonderful!

Also on Mud Island is a neat model of the Mississippi from Cairo to the Gulf, showing all the twists and turns, tributaries, towns and special features. Mileposts are listed at each town, all accompanied by the letters AHP. This stands for "Above Head of Passage," that spot on the delta where the five "passes" or fingers of the river meet, i.e.. the last point in the delta where "they is only one river passage." All mileage is measured from that spot.

We had dropped our luggage at the *Mississippi Queen* this morning, so it was an easy process for us to board. Mr. Bob, the Hotel Manager, was surprised and very pleased to see us.

"We figured that with a name like Golden Gate, no way you were going to get here for the cruise." In fact they had booked 406 people this week, and we would sail with only 186, fallout from the World Trade Center attack in New York. Airplanes just began flying again yesterday and the fears of being stuck in New Orleans are beginning to lessen. We tend to underestimate American resiliency, a quality that has stood us well in time of crisis, and which always amazes our European friends. The fact is, we can't keep still for very long, in good times or bad. We don't mourn for long, and the great joy we express today is dissipated by noon tomorrow. We can't handle one of those three-hour French dinners, or a two-hour lunch in Spain. A few years ago Italy celebrated its World Cup victory for a month. We cheer our World Series champs in October for a day, move on the NFL that night. We are likely to push aside tragedy just as fast, filling our grief with activities of a dozen natures. We are a nation of fast foods and McDonald service, assembly line activities and one-column bylines. We guzzle our beers and gulp our food, because there are other things to do. A news story, no matter how compelling has a shelf life of a few days, and then we begin to think elsewhere. Politicians count on this, knowing that their most heinous transgression will disappear in the environmental waste container before the newsprint is dry. Manufacturers love us because the latest fad lasts only until next Tuesday, when Beanie Babies are replaced by Diaper Dolls or some such and there is something new for them to sell and us to buy. Longevity in America is measured in Barbie clothes changes—keep the body, but for God sake change the dress!

As horrific as the World Trade Center destruction was, we started healing almost immediately, as we box up our terror and grief and place it with other experiences, moving on with our lives, because to stay there too long is to invite personal disaster. It is the media that tries to create the conceptual bridges that keep the event before our eyes, and in our concerns; to write an event in a thousand variations to keep it fresh and important, to manage our emotions. I have no doubt that the terrorist attack will be with us for months, perhaps years, as events ebb and flow and crises come and go, but now that the horror of first strike is over we will put it in place and resume our lives, but in this case, maybe taking a glance or two over our shoulder just to be sure. We are a resilient, resourceful people, the result of almost four centuries of ancestors who were not afraid to try something new. But we are not stupid.

A week floating down the lazy river looks awfully good right now.

IX

Not much to do today, what with an entire day of what they call "Steamboatin'." Bob Hirst is scheduled for a talk in the theater this morning, and that is an event. He protests a bit that he is not prepared, but I have never seen anybody better able to convey his knowledge, at almost any time, even for an audience of one. The best condition a speaker can find himself in is to be thoroughly conversant with his subject matter. There is nothing quite as satisfying as to be confident that you can field whatever questions might arise, solve any problem that appears. That is where Bob finds himself, after years of poring over Mark Twain's letters, books, notebooks, newspaper articles, and scraps, he is an expert, enjoying the prize perquisite of that condition—confidence.

Today his subject is "Sam Clemens as a River Pilot." Sam was twenty when he apprenticed himself to Horace Bixby in 1851. A few letters exist from this period, in addition to some notes he made, which he "found in an old box of rubbish" in 1880. It is certain that he loved the life of the river pilot and was most proud that he had mastered the craft, receiving verification from two licensed pilots to get his own papers.

> "A pilot, in those days, was the only unfettered and entirely independent human being that lived in the earth."
> *Life on the Mississippi,* p. 166

> "...*all* men—kings & serfs alike—are *slaves* to other men & to circumstance—save alone, the pilot—who comes at no man's beck and call, obeys no man's orders & scorns all men's suggestions... It is a strange study,—a singular phenomenon, if you please, that the only real, independent & genuine gentlemen in the world go quietly up & down the Mississippi river, asking no homage of any one, seeking no popularity, no notoriety, & not caring a damn whether school keeps or not."
>
> *Mark Twain's Letters*, Vol. 1, Letter to Will Bowen, August 24, 1866

"I was a good, average St. Louis to New Orleans pilot."

Sam quit piloting because of the Civil War. Most Mississippi pilots were Southern sympathizers, forced to turn to the Union, which largely controlled the river, if they wanted to keep their jobs. It was a dangerous job because the pilot was a sitting target in the wheel house and Sam didn't have much of a stomach for that sort of risk, or perhaps for war in general. He hid out in St. Louis before leaving for Nevada. He says he learned lots about one aspect of military life—retreating.

> "I could have become a soldier myself, if I had waited. I had got part of it learned: I knew more about retreating than the man that invented retreating."
>
> *Private History of a Campaign that Failed*, Rise of Douai Publishing, p. 35

Bob easily filled our hour, an hour that flew by. He stood before us, armed with half a dozen books, all marked with various sorts of blue and white scraps and more substantial papers, hanging out on three sides. He would grab a tome, turn it virtually upside-down searching for a certain letter or passage. Nothing ever fell out! I found myself like the jurors in a Clarence Darrow trial, watching his cigar ash grow longer and longer, fearing, hoping, that it wouldn't fall off and completely missing the whole argument. Bob's papers all stick, even the ones that aren't post-ems, largely because of moral necessity, I think.

He talks rather deliberately, a tiny version of Mark Twain lecturing. He will be moving along on a subject, when he will stop for a moment, considering. "Let's see if I can find a letter for that!" He picks up a book, the blue one, with dust cover still intact, flips three pages; his eyes light up, "Ah, here it is!" He then reads the perfect passage, usually funny, always with that pregnant Mark Twain finale, and he glances sideways with a childish gleam in his eye, finishing off the ironic close.

As he reads a passage, any number of ancillary people, things, places or events are mentioned, and he parenthetically explains them without so much as a pause.

"You will have to read Dr. Cane..."

Dr. Cane is a report that..."

"Let me read this other letter if I can find it."

That letter was found by Bob years ago and its precise spot in the book is also memorized. He finds letters as he is answering questions. Today he even paged straight to a paragraph from a fellow editor of *Life on the Mississippi*.

He is a joy to watch and hear. All the while his white mane flops around, falling in front of his readings, not nearly as subservient as his page markers. His eyes twinkle, his voice drops at sentence end, just where Twain would probably have whispered, to make everyone strain to catch the dénouement.

"What did he say?" "What was that?"

Sitting in a white rocking chair in the bow of the *Mississippi Queen* just below the pilot house, I watched the sun rise above the river, a glowing red-orange gem, too young in the day to hurt your eyes, or maybe too old from yesterday to be dangerous. Two slim tendrils of cloud pose briefly across the upper half, then waft off to join their plumper cousins in a cotton sky that threatens to absorb the day. "It's gonna rain," I think. That shining orb moves constantly with the river twists, now here, soon there, a random target before the boat at one time, off to starboard with the next shake of the river.

On the shore, killdeer cries don't match the lumbering majesty of a great blue that has just gone airborne, nor the curious neck bobs of a pair of egrets seeking breakfast on the mud flats. The river is low. Aerial specialists, the swallows and swifts, dart above the gray water with their endless energy and skill. Except for their occasional squeaks, the killdeer's plea and the flutter of the Mississippi flag on the mast above me, there is quiet.

The thick woods that line the levees and float fog-bound into the distance are just beginning to awaken, lying momentarily silent, half an hour before the claxon reveille of the locust will wake its natural world and send it scurrying.

Two towboats approach on the port side, one pushing a puny five barges, hardly worth the effort, perhaps heading for a "tow farm" somewhere to join a larger family. The *Anita M*, from the Mid-South Towing Company follows with a respectable eighteen barges in tow, most of them laden with coal, destined for a power plant upstream. "Why does a tugboat *push* a tow?" I mused, a silly thought. They follow the markings of the river, red right returning buoys on the channel, white mile markers and red or green Passing Daymark triangles and square Crossing Daymarks on shore. This mighty water, so capricious and dangerous, is as orderly as man can make it, but everyone in the know is aware that we really have nothing to say in the matter.

It is so calm! The rising sun, now reflected on the barely rippled waters of the Old Man, will soon beckon the rest of the passengers. They won't know what they have missed.

Bang!

We rounded a sharp bend in the river, and I was torn from my reverie back to reality by a man-made world of concrete, steel and neon as the Ameristar Casino "floated" by on the port, "floated" in its coffer dam moat high above the sunken Mississippi. Required by casino law to float on the river, the Ameristar and her sister casinos are "cruising" only in a Jesuitical sense of the term, land-locked and legal, like a little boy's bathtub toy. There is an old saw about the difference between boys and men...

We are late getting into Vicksburg because the *Mississippi Queen* was required to move tentatively downstream on a water level that was a -3' in Memphis. How can a river register a negative number, like the record -12' in 1987? Frank Nicholl had explained that to us back in Cape Girardeau. In 1864, officials decided that they needed standards for measuring the depth of the river. The old timers were asked to recall the lowest water level in their experience. That level was designated as "0," different in every town, on every part of the river. So the 1987 drought level of -3' is relative to pilots' memories in 1864. It might be -3' in Memphis, +7" in New Madrid and -12' in Caruthersville, and none of those numbers relate in any way to sea level, except by accident.

"We used to plough past the lofty hill-city, Vicksburg, downstream; but we cannot do that now. A cut-off has made a country town of it, like Osceola, St. Genevieve, and several others. There is currentless water—also a big island—in front of Vicksburg now. You come down the river the other side of the island, then turn and come up to the town; that is, in high water: in low water you can't come up, but must land some distance below it.

Signs and scars still remain, as reminders of Vicksburg's tremendous war-experiences; earthworks, trees crippled by the cannon balls, cave-refuges in the clay precipices, etc. The caves did good service during the six weeks' bombardment of the city—May 18-July 4, 1863."

What follows is a lengthy description of the siege of Vicksburg, the pivotal battle of the Western Theater of the war, decided, ironically on the very same day as Gettysburg. Then the author continues:

"Vicksburg is a town of substantial business streets and pleasant residences; it commands the commerce of the Yazoo and Sunflower Rivers; is pushing railways in several directions, through rich agricultural regions, and has a promising future of prosperity and importance."
Life on the Mississippi, pp. 375-385

Myra and Betty, our Vicksburg guides, were waiting for us on the levee at Latourno Landing when we arrived, the river being too low for us to dock at the usual place along the Yazoo Diversion Canal. We are the only ones going on tour this morning, because the standard shore excursion tours had been moved to the afternoon.

Vicksburg is an impressive battlefield memorial, recalling the 47-day siege that brought the population to the edge of starvation, and the Confederate Army of the West to dissolution, at the same time elevating General U.S. Grant to hero status and ultimately to the Presidency. For over a century, military strategists and students have been studying Grant's Vicksburg campaign, one of the most imaginative in our history. Grant, with his Army of the Tennessee, had fought his way south from Cairo, past Island #10 to Vicksburg, "the Gibraltar of the West" where he faced a Confederate army of 30,000 under Pemberton, entrenched on the high bluffs of the city. The place was considered by Lincoln to be the key to the West. Heavily fortified on the river, protected by swamps on the north and south, the city was a fortress, defended on the east by a string of nine forts. Grant recognized he couldn't attack from the river, and ferried his army to the Louisiana shore, and marched them some twenty miles south where he again crossed the Mississippi to Bruinsburg, Mississippi. He then moved them over 100 miles east to capture the state capital of Jackson, before turning back west to Vicksburg, defeating Pemberton's army at the bloody Battle of Champion's Hill before arriving at the defenses of the city in May, 1863. Several frontal attacks failed miserably, so Grant ordered his troops into siege trenches surrounding the city, paralleling the Confederate circle of forts about a half-mile distant. Twelve miles of trenches or saps were dug fully to invest the town. His army of 45,000 troops faced approximately 30,000 Confederates along the inner perimeter. Grant had 220 cannons to bombard the city with 25,000 explosive shells, almost double the Confederate artillery. Twenty-eight states sent men to this battle, all eleven Confederate states and seventeen from the north.

"Vicksburg doesn't know how to surrender. We don't intend to learn."

17,000 Union soldiers are buried in Vicksburg National Cemetery; 6,000 Confederates in town.

The battlefield is far different from 1863. The defenders had taken down all the trees, used for fortifications and fuel and to clear their defense lines. They placed thicket barriers called abatis around the fields as hindrances to attack. In only a few spots today can you form a clear picture of conditions and we stopped at one, Battery de Golyer that faced the Great Redoubt half a mile across the valley.

Today the Battlefield Park is a collection of thousands of granite monuments and bronze statues, marking the various regimental positions, blue signs outlining the Union forces, red for the Confederates. Every state except Kentucky has a major memorial or marker, although the Union memorials are understandably more elaborate than the South's. The largest is that of Missouri, a copy of Rome's Pantheon. We climbed the 47 steps (one for each day of the siege), where Myra led us in a rather moving rendition of "God Bless America," most apropos given the events of the past week.

The park loop takes you completely around the Union lines, presided over by a monumental bronze of General Grant riding his rebel horse Kangaroo, and then turning at Fort Hill, the last of the Confederate strongholds, to trace the inner defense line. It is a sad experience to witness the full extent of the killing field of Vicksburg.

Our last stop was at the Museum of the Union Ironclad *U.S.S. Cairo*, which was sunk on Dec. 12, 1862, the first warship sunk by torpedo, an electric mine developed by Zedekiah McDaniel and Francis Ewing. It was detonated by volunteers in "torpedo pits" hidden behind the levee. The Cairo sank in twelve minutes with no loss of life. It was raised exactly one century after it was sunk, Dec. 12, 1962.

There is always an argument about which states seceded, exacerbated by the differing stars on Confederate flags which at odd times have 7, 11 or 13. There are seven original secessionists: South Carolina, Mississippi, Alabama, Florida, Georgia, Texas and Louisiana. They were later joined by North Carolina, Arkansas, Virginia and Tennessee. The south symbolically wanted thirteen states just like the colonies and incorrectly anticipated the secession of Missouri and Kentucky. There were 34 states in 1861, 36 at the end of the war, including West Virginia, whose population seceded from Virginia in order to stay in the Union.

Vicksburg today has 28,000 population, with another 22,000 surrounding. The largest employer is the Army Corps of Engineers' Waterways Experimentation Station operating six labs and employing 1,700 people. There are four casinos that contribute three percent of their gross to city coffers. There are twenty-nine casinos in all along the Mississippi coast, plus one on Choctaw land. Grain, gravel, lumber, natural gas, cotton and catfish are the major products of the region. We drove through downtown Vicksburg. It didn't look terribly prosperous, but it is much improved since my last real visit about ten years ago.

☙ ❧

Bob Ikeda peed! I promised him a sign in neon atop the *Mississippi Queen*, but this is the best I can do. Poor Bob started getting miserable last night with a bladder infection, and by this morning was dancing around in grave discomfort, so he went off to the hospital in Vicksburg. He was back on board tonight considerably relieved, pun intended. I would have said "with a smile on his face" but Bob always has a smile on his face. He was even smiling when he left in the cab for the hospital. It is the most wonderful smile, taking over his whole face, making his eyes squint a bit, overflowing and spreading to everyone near him. I think it is his gift to the world, a world that has by no means always been kind to him. His nation first deposited him and his family in a WWII detention camp and then had the effrontery to ask him to serve her in the war effort. Bob accepted both somehow and returned to pick up the pieces and forge a fine life for himself, in that country that had made such an awful mistake. I don't think there is a resentful bone in Bob's body. He is the most genuinely contented man I have ever met, filled with joy and love of life. Just to be with him and watch him makes you feel great. My life is richer for having known him, and no one who has ever met him would disagree with me.

All the ladies on board are showing their affection by pouring a steady stream of cranberry juice down his throat.

XI

There was a young girl from old Natchez
Whose clothes were all covered in patches.
When questions arose on the state of her clothes
She said, "Wherever I itches I scratches."

Our guide, Betty Lou was trying to teach us how to pronounce Natchez properly, and she would spend most of the time entertaining us with her charming brand of "Suthren," finishing with a flourish over the word "pecan." "It ain't something that you slide under your bed at night."

She and Mac's guide, Lucianne, met us at Natchez-under-the-Hill, that notorious den of iniquity, "hell with bells on," founded around 1716 as Fort Rosalie, and passed around freely from France to England to Spain, to the U.S.

> "Famous Natchez-under-the-hill has not changed notably in twenty years; in outward aspect—judging by the descriptions of the ancient procession of foreign tourists—it has not changed in sixty; for it is still small, straggling, and shabby. It had a desperate reputation morally, in the old keel-boating and early steamboating times—plenty of drinking, carousing, fisticuffing, and killing there, among the riff-raff of the river, in those days. But Natchez-on-top-of-the-hill is attractive; has always been attractive."
> *Life on the Mississippi,* p. 408

By the Treaty of Paris, following the American Revolution, all land west of the Mississippi and north of the 31st parallel was ceded back to Spain. The Spanish claimed the high ground of the city and built on top of the hill, "Natchez Proper" as opposed to the disreputable "Natchez

Improper" below the cliffs. Finally in 1796 after the Treaty of Lorenzo, the Spanish vacated the town in favor of the Americans, who would be perfectly positioned in 1803 to grab Western lands after the Louisiana Purchase. Availability of fertile land coinciding with the introduction of the cotton gin made Natchez the immediate King of Cotton and provided the wealth that would make her one of the wealthiest towns in the Antebellum South.

All of this was delivered to us by Betty Lou in the time it took Gene to drive out of the lower town. These Southern women talk fast!

"Now don't none of y'all git caught in Fat Mama's Tamale House down here. She got those 'Knock-You-Naked Margaritas' there."

Crossing on to the freeway on our way to the Natchez Trace she spotted some kudzu, the neatest field of it I have ever seen, mowed and orderly.

"That there's kudzu, the vine that ate the South. It covers everything, trees, telephone poles, buildings, slow moving tourists. And it doesn't even prevent erosion. It may even speed it up. You don't know 'cause it covers everything up."

I had asked our guides to show us part of the Natchez Trace, a 450-mile path that connected the Mississippi city to Nashville on the Tennessee. Flatboat men, on reaching New Orleans usually sold their boats for lumber and walked back north. The Trace became their avenue, a dangerous one filled with cutthroats and thieves, but the straightest way to get up to the Tennessee River and back ultimately to St. Louis. Later the keelboat would be sailed or pulled back north but it took up to six months to accomplish that task, providing the impetus for the development of steam power.

An old animal path and later Indian trail, the Natchez Trace was prominent from 1780-1810, notoriously known as the Devil's Backbone, racking up more than 10,000 murders and robberies in its three decades of use. Boatmen joined in bands for protection, moving from farm to farm, known as "stands." We visited Mount Locust, the last of the "stands" before Natchez, today part of the Natchez Trace National Park.

Mount Locust is a modest cotton plantation house, too far from the town for the owners to live there. Today it appears far more attractive than it must have been in cotton days, though not nearly as fancy as the town mansions. The mosquitoes are probably little changed from 1810.

"There are two types of mosquitoes here," Betty Lou explained, "those small enough to fly right through the screen, and those big enough to open the door."

We made two brief stops on the Trace after Mount Locust, one to view a loess deposit, "pronounced 'löss' really, but usually 'low-ess', or down heah, 'looow-essss sile.' All three of them are a very fine clay soil with no rocks at all and easily eroded.

Our second stop was at the Emerald Mound, the second largest in the U.S., an impressive pyramid pile from the Mississippian Culture from 1300-1600 AD, covering four acres with two smaller mounds on top. The local tribe was called the Natchez, mound- building, sun-worshiping, family-oriented farmers, who recognized a Great Son ruler, who lived in one of the smaller mounds. The Natchez at first lived in peace with the French, but that happy state gradually eroded, due to French demands. In 1729 they attacked Fort Rosalie, killing and capturing 400 of the inhabitants. The reprisal was swift and the tribe was hunted down and annihilated, killed or sold into slavery. Today many claim descent from the Natchez but consider themselves a clan of the Creek.

We were somewhat late on our schedule heading back to town, but Betty Lou announced that we were on a "free flowin', laid-back Natchez time schedule" and not to worry, as if that had even occurred to any of us.

The Natchez Trace, modern style, is one of the most beautiful roadways in America. Huge live oaks, festooned with Spanish moss and decorated with dried resurrection ferns, dot the land. Dogwoods are spread around mowed lawns along the highway, and red surprise lilies (*lycuris*), a harbinger of fall, have popped up everywhere. For us Californians it is so green! In fact much of the town looks like a garden, with stately magnolias, the state flower and tree, gracing many of the mansions, French mulberry and crepe myrtle (the "lilac of the South") gracing the streets. Every home has a flower garden, and the cotton estates are parks. Natchez has two Garden Clubs, now friendly competitors though that has not always been the case. Betty Lou explained that her family in the old days could never have joined the Natchez Pilgrimage Society, founded in 1931, but nowadays "if you can breathe, follow instructions and pay dues, you're in. I chose the Pilgrimage Society because they have a bigger pool."

Today Natchez has a year-round full schedule, with a four-week Spring Pilgrimage, and a Fall Pilgrimage, two weeks at Mardi Gras, a Balloon Festival, music festivals and a bunch of lesser celebrations. "We'll do it if y'all'll come see it."

I love the use of "y'all" in these parts. You commonly hear, y'all, but in plural it comes out as "y'alls," or even better, "all y'alls." You can add "should" with "y'all'd." That works for "would" too. I'm sure they could come up with "y'all could," but they already have that covered with "might could."

Natchez was spared destruction during the Civil War. The citizens had voted overwhelmingly not to secede but were overruled elsewhere in Mississippi. 1440 of her 6000 citizens joined the Confederate army in spite of their opposition to the war. The town was spared because it wasn't strategically important, and surrendered almost immediately, without a shot being fired. Fort Rosalie served as a most elegant Union headquarters.

We reentered the town on St. Catherine Street, passing a string of historic buildings. Indeed, the whole town seems to date back to the early and mid-nineteenth century. There are 500 ante-bellum buildings, fifty being homes, ten of which are open to the public. Many others are B&Bs. Kings Tavern, the end of the Trace, fights with Hope Farm for the title of the oldest house in town. The latter was the home of the curiously named Don Carlos de Grande Pre. There are exquisite estates: Melrose (1850) is now a National Preservation Society home; Auburn (1812); Dunleith (1856); Twin Oaks (1830); Greenleafs— "they've never knowingly thrown anything away."; Magnolia Hall— "The uther Garden Club"; Linden— "Mt. Locust dressed up"; Monmouth; Stanton Hall; Rosalie; and many more. Completely new to me is the Holy Trinity African Catholic Church, apparently taking a page from the African Methodist Episcopal congregations.

Even with all these estates, houses are not expensive, averaging about $125,000-$140,000. "Over $200,000 you're gonna have a sho' 'nuf fine-style house."

Many of these old places are built of brick but are rusticated to resemble stone. Many are now being restored, as is much of the town. In 1998 Natchez was hit by a series of "un-tornados", fierce straight-line winds that literally ripped the sides and roofs off much of the town. There seems to be downtown construction everywhere. In addition, the river has been fought with a recent Bankside Stabilization Program, with the loess cliffs covered with concrete and elaborate drainage systems. They have given up on kudzu.

In town we stopped at the First Presbyterian Church where Dr. Tom Gandy was waiting in the Sanctuary with a slide show on the history of the steamboat. A man of 80, I surprised him when I entered. He jumped up and hurried into the church, apologizing, "I'm sorry you caught me in my suspenders. I never give a slide show without my coat on." He started his show slowly, forgetting to install his remote control for the projector. Then he dropped the control. Then he dropped the lapel microphone, tripped over the table, talking very slowly. I really feared that he would drop his teeth, or maybe fall completely to the floor, but gradually he righted himself and began clicking, slowly, through his slides, which I reluctantly noticed numbered 110. He started picking up speed around 1807 and Robert Fulton, building up a head of steam, growing comfortable with us and we with him. He recounted the first steamboat on the Mississippi, a trip from hell, beginning with Haley's Comet, getting chased by Indians, shook up badly by the New Madrid earthquake, catching fire, and finally having the captain run off with the maid. Dr. Gandy had wonderful slides of the whole evolution of steamboats, culminating in the massive *J.M. White*, the largest ever built, 320' long, 90' wide with the cotton guards, capable of carrying 10,000 bales of cotton. It had ten steel boilers and a main cabin 230' long. It burned before it took a load. He was a delight, mixing in obvious expertise with a dry sense of humor that often caught us by surprise.

"I don't know why honeymooners need the biggest cabin. It's a waste of space."

"She's pregnant as a jaybird!" he exclaimed focusing on a woman aboard a crowded ship and blowing up her picture to explain how unusual it was to see a photo of a woman in her condition. "The poor woman. She had no idea I would come along 100 years later and expose her."

"There's your evaporation of whiskey," he laughed showing a picture of several drunks lounging on a rail.

"I wouldn't touch that with a ten-foot pole. You never know when you might be running into a relative. This is the most inbred town in the country."

"The cheapest cabins were over the boiler."

The steamboat was largely done in by the railroad. By 1900 there were only seventeen side-wheelers left. The stern-wheeler came about because it was more capable of pushing barges, gradually finding function as a tugboat masquerading as a passenger vessel. But to speed up travel time, the Corps of Engineers started shortening the river by cutting off the loops, lessening the mileage and increasing the river flow, and the steam-driven boats couldn't handle the heavier currents. Diesel-powered tugs took over and the era of steam was at an end, except for the three riverboat Queens.

It was a very entertaining and informative talk, given the shaky start. But even more exciting things would be discovered upstairs in the Stratton Chapel Photo Gallery. In 1960, Tom Gandy bought thousands of old glass negatives from the Henry C. Norman Photo Gallery that operated back to the Civil War days. Norman's son, Earl continued his father's studio work during the 1920s and 1930s. Dr. Gandy has worked for forty years to restore the negatives and print them. The result of his labor is an incredible portfolio of the Victorian life of Natchez, extraordinary portraits of children, of beautiful women, including many women of color, of steamboats and buildings, of small vignettes of town life. Dr. Gandy has brought back to life an entire era that without his labor of love would most certainly have been lost.

We finished this busy morning with a light lunch at the Carriage House Restaurant behind Stanton Hall. Then we completed our tour of the town before returning to the *Mississippi Queen*. I have to admit, I have been to Natchez many times and this was the best visit I have had, due both to a charming woman who talks so fast and a whole bunch of new discoveries, including my first ever sighting of a Blue-gray gnatcatcher.

XII

Today is set aside for what the *Mississippi Queen* folks like to call "Steamboatin'," a form of robbery I would not dignify with the euphemism, but rather a means of converting a six-day cruise into seven without having to pay port taxes or taking a chance with denting the shore in the form of a landing. I was once on a four-night journey from Memphis to St. Louis that stopped in New Madrid, Cairo and Cape Girardeau. Two years later that same cruise was five nights, exactly the same, except they eliminated New Madrid, blaming "river conditions" for the subtraction. Port taxes however remained $45, so river conditions were apparently not severe enough to cause anything so drastic as a refund. I could accept a no-refund policy for deleting Cairo because there is nothing in Cairo and the subtraction of zero should have no deleterious effect on the remainder. Then, in 1986, I took the *Mississippi Queen* from Memphis to St. Louis in seven days! Most of the time we were going backwards, wandering around on the river desperately trying to find a way out, at one point finding ourselves completely blocked off from the Mississippi by Kentucky Dam, which I later found out is on the Tennessee River, separated from the Mighty Mississippi by a little stream called the Ohio. The captain was seen on the Texas Deck asking passengers if anybody had a AAA card so he could order a map, his having fallen overboard when the boat made a sudden U-turn back there on the Arkansas. The port taxes had risen by this time to $75, and we never actually had a chance to spend them, being so busy catching the proper river that we never actually found a port of any sort, missing even poor old Cairo by a state or two, and not being permitted to land at Nauvoo, Illinois, because the kind folks there still remembered kicking the Mormons out back in '46, and they weren't taking any chances. For a week we just wandered around aimlessly hoping against fear that somehow, we would catch a glimpse of that elusive Gateway Arch and sail through to the West, but all we found was that the Mississippi does indeed drain 40 percent of the U.S. A week of "Steamboatin'" is a great way to see America if your aim is to collect towheads, sawyers, sandbars and shoals, none of which extract port taxes, only grief.

Today I knew we were in trouble when Paul, our "Riverborean," announced we were taking a "trial run" at landing at Saint Francisville where we are supposed to be tomorrow, and if we do it well today, we probably will be able to do something similar the next day when all the cards are on the table and we are finally expected to show our hand. It is useless for anyone to be *here* when we all know that *here* is where we will be tomorrow. *There* is where we are going today, with a brief trial stop *here*. I harbor a deep admiration for anyone who can take words and concepts and bend them around the truth like the snake of a river and then having stretched and convulsed the thing to a proper flexibility, snap it back straight and dispense it to all who will listen as the truth. Without embarrassment! Facts are of no use whatever in pulling wool over eyes and truth would be positively dangerous.

As I write, the *Mississippi Queen* is executing a dexterous U-turn, the third today, Captain Muddlemud, now having committed the maneuver to his repertoire, and having received an e-mail from AAA which convinced him that St. Francisville is somewhere behind us. He probably got the same sinking feeling that Huck and Jim experienced when they missed Cairo.

This has now become a thing of considerable concern, I am sure because when he practiced his landing this afternoon, he was going the other way and the landing is now on the wrong side of the Mississippi. "Steamboatin'!" The world was considerably younger when we started.

Bob held forth this morning on fortune tellers, blue jays and burying Democrats. I love it when he has his hands on a reading he really likes, because he changes into dialect, runs his glasses down on his nose and always looks up with a sly conspiratorial smile whenever Mark Twain is being especially clever. There is so much material! And Bob has such a firm grip on it. I am sure that all of us are going to be compelled to start re-reading all the works we read as kids as well as the thousands of pages the Mark Twain Papers Project has released to the public. I think I will print up a copy of a warning for my friends, a card advising them that a funny quote is coming their way, because you can't read Mark Twain quietly, without the irresistible urge to pass it on. I suspect more than a few of us are going to be pretty unbearable.

It would be a disservice to try to shorten his wonderful essay on "What Stumped the Bluejays." As Bob has told us many times, it has to be read out loud. But his essay on Democrats is shorter:

The only man I ever knew who could counteract this passion on the part of Democrats for voting, was Robert Roach, carpenter of the steamer Aleck Scott, "plying to and from St. Louis to New Orleans and back," as her advertisement sometimes read. The Democrats generally came up as deck passengers from New Orleans, and the yellow fever used to snatch them right and left - eight or nine a day for the first six or eight hundred miles; consequently Roach would have a lot on hand to "plant" every time the boat landed to wood - "plant" was Roach's word. One day as Roach was superintending a burial the Captain came up and said:

"God bless my soul, Roach, what do you mean by shoving a corpse into a hole in the hill-side in this barbarous way, face down and its feet sticking out?"

"I always plant them foreign Democrats in that manner, sir, because, damn their souls, if you plant 'em any other way they'll dig out and vote the first time there's an election - but look at that fellow, now - you put 'em in head first and face down and the more they dig the deeper they'll go into the hill."

In my opinion, if we do not get Roach to superintend our cemeteries, enough Democrats will dig out at the next election to carry their entire ticket. It begins to look that way.

Territorial Enterprise, October 21-24, 1865 Quoted in www. twainquotes.com

Reprinted in *The Works of Mark Twain; Early Tales & Sketches, Vol. 2 1864-1865*, (Univ. of California Press, 1981), pp. 313-14

The *Mississippi Queen* hosted a private lunch for us this noon and then Karl the photographer got us all out on the railings for the traditional group photo. That was the extent of our formal programming today, and we went off on our separate quests to track our progress on the river, which does in fact look quite different when viewed from the perspective of both directions.

XIII

I spent a week in St. Francisville today! Where is W.C. Fields when you need him? Just as I feared yesterday, Captain Muddlemud ended up on the wrong side of the river, having committed the term "port" to memory and recalling that the landing was on the left side of the river. Here we are, pointing upstream looking silly when all the world knows we are supposed to be on the other side looking down river.

Even the swallows are confused, being used to following the boat as it churns up mosquitoes; they are not sure which way to follow. I swear I saw one flying backward trying to get its bearings. If I knew its language, I would tell it to back up to Vermillionville and take another pass at it. The mosquitoes have a better grasp of the Mississippi and all its secrets than the captain of our vessel.

Speaking of birds, it takes a dozen swallows to see one, they are so swift. Get one in your sights and follow it to see what it's up to. Just as you are set to make up your mind with an idea about it, zap! it crosses the flight path of another of its kind and you are forced to adjust your scope and start again. One sleek bird veers right in to the next and your head will be swiveling at a rate that belies your age. By the seventh runner in the relay, your neck will have cracked just right, obviating any future need for your chiropractor. By the tenth bird, you will have finally identified the bird's tail configuration and back color, eliminating two species from consideration. Now you need the breast and throat to nail down this critter.

Margaret and I have been arguing about the type of swallow that has been around the river, darting here and there and forever, eluding anything like a good look at them.

"Barn swallow," I say. The tail is forked.

"No, not enough. I might accept rough-winged, but not barn. It doesn't have the russet breast."

I darted from bird to book and back, eleven times, when the twelfth bird I latched on to disappeared right into the ground.

"I'm a bank swallow," he said, "Why didn't you just ask. We can talk you know."

I don't have the nerve to tell Margaret. She only speaks robin.

Where was I? Oh yes, St. Francisville, or whatever it is called on the other side of the river. At 2:11 P.M. the *Mississippi Queen* pulled back out into the river having spent the entire morning trying to talk the ferry boat captain into getting us to the left bank going down. At first the ferry was broken, but a pump was found around noon, and the problem was fixed. But now having a whole ferry, so to speak, the grizzled old operator decided to take the rest of the day off, and departed, leaving Muddlemud high and dry on the wrong side of the river. I just don't believe that ferry captain wanted to sully his reputation by association. Now we are actually *backing* downstream, still trying to separate starboard from port. Even I know that port has four letters, the same as "l-e-f-t" and "r-i-g-h-t" has more than four letters, just like starboard. Pilot, big deal! What's to learn?

We called an emergency meeting this morning, back in the theater, to resume our quest for the real Mark Twain, and restore some order to our lives. This time, Mac and Bob formed a tableau, sitting on the stoop in front, proposing to operate an academic duel, er, duet, for our enlightenment. And they did. We have all been captivated by Bob's bottomless well of knowledge of Clemens/Twain, but Mac is no slouch either. He peppered Bob with a series of very detailed questions that left me most impressed, and of course Bob fielded them all without blinking. It was like a professional tennis match, with 109 mph serves returned just as fast. Wonderful theater! All learning should be that much fun. Mac started:

"Bob and I feel really svelte on this cruise, like lookin' in one of them mirrors that make you look skinny. Look around at t' other guests on board and you really feel svelte."

Q: Can you comment on Mark Twain's financial situation, and his investment in the typesetting machine? And the effect it would have had on him if it had been successful?

A: Twain really bought into the Paige Typesetting Machine, but it just didn't make it. It drained him and Webster Publishing, forcing them into bankruptcy in 1893. Eventually he paid off all the debts, dying in 1910 with about $500,000 in assets.

Q: Is the *Autobiography* a good place to crawl into Clemens' head?

A: The autobiography is the great potpourri of Twain's career. It was written in haphazard order, never chronological, and he insisted it should be published that way. It contains all sorts of excerpts from other works in his attempt to extend the copyright limits. Mark Twain hated planned things and thought that the only way to tell the truth was to have free association thinking.

Q: What was Clemens' relationship with U.S. Grant?

A: They were very close since their first meeting in Washington in July, 1870, when in his "Toast to the Babies," he poked fun at Grant at the Banquet of the Grand Army of the Tennessee.

The fifteenth toast, "The Babies - As they comfort us in our sorrows, let us not forget them in our festivities," was responded to by Samuel L. Clemens in a humorous and highly appreciated speech. His injunction, "As long as you are in your right mind don't you ever pray for twins; twins amount to a permanent riot, and there ain't any real difference between triplets and an insurrection," called forth shouts of laughter. In conclusion, he alluded to the future Farraguts, historians, and Presidents, who are now lying in their cradles, and said: "In still one more cradle, somewhere under the flag, the future illustrious Commander-in-Chief of the American armies is so little burdened with his approaching grandeurs and responsibilities as to be giving his whole strategic mind, at this moment, to trying to find some way to get his big toe into his mouth, an achievement which, meaning no disrespect, the illustrious guest of this evening turned his attention to some 56 years ago; and if the child is but a prophecy of the man, there are mighty few who will doubt that he succeeded."

The New York Times, November 15, 1879

Twain became the publisher of Grant's memories, *Personal Memoirs of U.S. Grant,* earning him posthumously the huge royalty of $400,000 in the first year.

Q: In later years he became a polemicist. What did he attack?

A: He attacked the Spanish-American and Boer Wars. He opposed Czarist Russia. Throughout his life he moved toward a condemnation of slavery, and late in life wrote against it.

Q: Can you tell us about the "Whittier Birthday Speech?"

A: He gave an 1877 speech in Boston in which he virtually roasted Holmes, Lowell and Emerson, using their poetry out of context to the embarrassment of just about everyone including himself. He never could decide whether it was embarrassing or funny.

"They were a rough lot - but that's nothing - everybody looks rough that travels afoot. Mr. Emerson was a seedy little bit of a chap - red-headed. Mr. Holmes was as fat as a balloon - he weighed as much as 300, and had double chins all the way down to his stomach. Mr. Longfellow was built like a prize-fighter. His head was cropped and bristly - like as if he had a wig made of hair-brushes. His nose lay straight down his face, like a finger with the end joint tilted up.

The New York Times, December 20, 1877

Q: Was he a pacifist?

A: Probably not. He did write a very famous piece, published after his death: "The War Prayer," which was popular in the Viet Nam era. The essay concludes with:

"O Lord our Father, our young patriots, idols of our hearts, go forth to battle – be Thou near them! With them, in spirit, we also go forth from the sweet peace of our beloved firesides to smite the foe. O Lord our God, help us to tear their soldiers to bloody shreds with our shells; help us to cover their smiling fields with the pale forms of their patriot dead; help us to drown the thunder of the guns with the shrieks of their wounded, writhing in pain; help us to lay waste their humble homes with a hurricane of fire; help us to wring the hearts of their unoffending widows with unavailing grief; help us to turn them out roofless with their little children to wander unfriended the wastes of their desolated land in rags and hunger and thirst, sports of the sun flames of summer and the icy winds of winter, broken in spirit, worn with travail, imploring Thee for the refuge of the grave and denied it – for our sakes who adore Thee, Lord, blast their hopes, blight their lives, protract their bitter pilgrimage, make heavy their steps, water their way with their tears, stain the white snow with the blood of their wounded feet! We ask it, in the spirit of love, of Him Who is the Source of Love, and Who is ever-faithful refuge and friend of all that are sore beset and seek His aid with humble and contrite hearts. Amen.

(After a pause)

"Ye have prayed it; if ye still desire it, speak! The messenger of the Most High waits."

It was believed afterward that the man was a lunatic, because there was no sense in what he said.

Europe and Elsewhere, Harper & Brothers, 1923, pp. 397-398

These last two questions came from the audience. A few more sessions with Bob and we will get very good at Twainology. This has been a stimulating series of talks, from that noisy hall at the Sheraton Palace in San Francisco to the theater on board the *Mississippi Queen*.

XIV

The river is the lowest in the captain's memory. At Baton Rouge they have a "paper clip dock" for the riverboats. It spirals up from the mud, capable of being tied up to until its lowest rung is itself clear of the water. We tied up to the lowest rung, next to the historic *USS Kidd*, a Fletcher-class destroyer, which is completely naked, propped up on bricks twenty feet high and dry.

Today we get to explore the world of Huey Long. Mary Beth and Willa are our guides, taking us through Huey Long's "new state capitol" and then out to the Louisiana Rural Life Museum. The guides are from Lagniappe Tours (It means "a little extra" in Cajun French), a division of the Foundation for Historical Louisiana, a women's group that seems to run Baton Rouge.

We started in Catfish Town at the Old State Capitol, a structure that comes as a complete architectural surprise especially in the context of the rather modern New State Capital built by Huey Long, a sort of granite trophy that towers above its neighbors. Mark Twain always showed an abiding interest in architecture and he was not blunt in his feelings about this extravaganza on the Mississippi.

> "Sir Walter Scott is probably responsible for the Capitol building; for it is not conceivable that this little sham castle would ever have been built if he had not run the people mad, a couple of generations ago, with his medieval romances. The South has not yet recovered from the debilitating influence of his books. Admiration of his fantastic heroes and their grotesque "chivalry" doings and romantic juvenilities still survives here, in an atmosphere in which is already perceptible, the wholesome and practical nineteenth-century smell of cotton-factories and locomotives; and traces of inflated language and other windy humbuggeries survive along with it. It is pathetic enough that a whitewashed castle, with turrets and things—materials all ungenuine within and without, pretending to be what they are not—should ever have been built in this otherwise honorable place; but it is much more pathetic to see this architectural falsehood undergoing restoration and perpetuation in our day, when it would have been so easy to let dynamite finish what a charitable fire began, and then devote this restoration money to the building of something genuine."
> *Life on the Mississippi*, pp. 416-417

Willa was a bit incensed by the author. "How dare he! I visited Mark Twain's house in Hartford, Connecticut. Have you seen it? It's dreadful."

We passed the old Governor's Mansion, built by Huey as a copy of the White House. "I want to know my way around when I get there," he is reported to have said.

Baton Rouge, normally a city of 500,000 people was virtually empty this morning, still in shock and mourning from the attack in New York. "There *are* people here," Willa assured us, but basically we had the place to ourselves. The "New Capitol" built in 1933, in only fifteen months, is the tallest in the U.S., 450' high with an observation deck on the twenty-seventh floor. Huey's grave and statue face the tower. There are forty-eight granite steps leading up, the first flight of thirteen inscribed with the names of the first thirteen colony-states, then thirty-five in order of their admission to the union, ending with Arizona. Alaska and Hawaii are shunted off to the side of the top stair. Inside is a world of marble, taken from around the globe, including a floor from Mt. Vesuvius. There are four huge statues of past governors inside, not including Huey, a rare omission. The view from the top floor takes in most of the city: the huge

Exxon Refinery, Dow Chemical plant, LSU campus with Tiger Stadium and the Pete Marovich Arena, the Pentagon Barracks and old Arsenal, even the Willow Glen Nuclear Power Plant way off in the distance. The capitol is almost surrounded by a picturesque though very polluted lagoon-lake.

We visited the House of Representatives and Senate rooms in the Capitol wings. In the former, Rudy Budoin, the Sergeant-of-Arms, entertained us with trivia.

"Since these folks sat over there where they ain't supposed to sit, I'll walk over there and make it legal." He reported that the Representatives only make $26,000 a year, that they "cain't raise taxes in an odd year" and that he had been in the movie "Blaze" which was filmed here. "Paul Newman warn't the only star in that movie."

We saw the spot in the hall near the elevator where Huey was gunned down in 1935 by Dr. Weiss, who was then gunned down in turn by Huey's bodyguards, in a fusillade of over sixty bullets. There are lots of stories about this event, "but y'all can believe anything you want."

Leaving the city behind we took I-10 out to the Louisiana Rural Life Museum, a facility, formerly Windrush Plantation donated by Ione and Steele Burden to LSU, intended to be used as an agriculture research facility. It is comprised of 450 acres including the Burden collection of working-class houses and artifacts, and an extensive sculpture garden. I particularly like the statue titled "Uncle Jack", a dignified black worker doffing his hat to welcome visitors. The work was done by a Baltimore artist, Hans Schuler for the town of Natchitiches, LA.

৵ ৵

"Are you two married? Will you join our game of 'He said, She said'"?

Bill let out a "Hell, no!" and ran out of the Grand Saloon, leaving wife Alice sitting there obviously sans mate and laughing, just as relieved as her terrified husband at not being roped into this dangerous game. The incident startled Bill so, that he has not returned to the Grand Saloon since, hiding out in a corner of the Upper Paddle Wheel Bar, sneaking back and forth from his room to the dining room for days.

Today he ventured into the library, a haven of peace and quiet, free from insipid games and prying fools. Just settling in to an illustrated edition of *Thus Spake Zarathustra,* he was jolted again.

"Are you my Floozy?" breathed a bulbous woman in a straw hat with pink leotards, lime green halter, silver patent leather boots and blue hair.

"What the hell is a floozy? What are you talking about? Of course not, hell no I'm not. Are you crazy?"

The color-polluted armadillo was literally blown out of the library by the sheer force of Bill's terror, rolling down the staircase in a wonderful imitation of a kaleidoscope, actually bumping into her real floozy at the landing, snagging him and dragging him back to the Grand Saloon. Bill slid up to the corner of the Paddlewheel Bar, not again appearing until tonight, when the lure of the Ink Spots once again dragged him of hiding.

જે જે

"I know that one!"

Mac, on the last night of the cruise, finally consented to drop into the cesspool of popular music and attended the concert of the Ink Spots. Since they were formed over seventy years ago, this doesn't constitute a foray into modernism for him, but it is a step, and nice to see him perk up when the first words of "To Each His Own" wafted out into the Grand Saloon. It can't be too long before he is grooving to Culture Club and Dead Altar boys and then moving on to Smashing Pumpkins and rediscovering Madonna.

The Ink Spots are long gone but the modern quartet of Morris Stiles on guitar, Sonny Hatchins goofing around, Harold Wendley with that wonderful bass narrative and Herman Denby the trademark lead singer do a great job of recreating the original group. "Gipsy", "Paper Doll" and especially "If I Didn't Care" bring back all the memories. Even Mac's.

જે જે

Jeanne didn't heed our warning. All our suitcases were to be put into the halls late tonight, where they will be picked up by the porters for "debarking" tomorrow. I admonished everyone to be sure to leave something to wear tomorrow, which Jeanne did. Dutifully, clad in diaphanous mauve peignoir, she pushed her large suitcase out into the corridor, only briefly lifting her back foot that was holding the door open. It slammed shut behind her! The word is, she was caught on film by the cruise photographer redressing herself from her packed suitcase outside her locked room. The negatives will be sold on E-bay next month.

XV

Time to go home. Our group fragments into sub-sets to find Virginia, San Diego, Miami or Northern California, with ten staying on in New Orleans for varying periods. All of us are a little nervous about the security procedures at the airports, where everyone is on high alert, confiscating anything sharp, metal or plastic. There are a variety of other precautions, eliminating curbside check-in, prohibiting non-ticketed people at the gates, and picture IDs required at every turn. No one objects.

Angela bounced off the bus that was to take us on a brief tour and then, quickly, to the airport. A vivacious Sicilian-N'yorleean, she reacted barely a second when I told her we had only an hour for our tour, instantly formulating a plan which would prove to be perfect. In a couple of sentences she conveyed the route to our driver, Pascale, a rough-looking Cajun woman whom I instantly respected and feared, the minute I saw her flinging around a box I had filled with rocks and books as though it were a feather. It took Pascale a bit of jockeying to get the coach out of the Delta Queen garage, but once underway, she was dynamite going straight ahead. She won a battle of "Chicken" with a St. Charles St. Streetcar, ran a couple of cement trucks off the road and completely ignored anything less consequential than a Sherman tank. We did our tour and reached the airport precisely as scheduled at 10:30.

Meanwhile Angela was thoroughly entertaining, taking on both Mac and me in playful verbal skirmishes, all the while maintaining a very accurate running commentary sprinkled throughout with one-liners.

***"New Orleans is surrounded 95 percent by water. Keep moving. If you stand still too long, you sink."

***"I always carry an umbrella, for rain, sun or fun. If things get dull, I decorate it and start a parade."

***"It's in our charter that we eat every hour and a half. Nothing bland. Well, no, you can get bland at the hospital and it comes with jello."

***"Those are pec<u>ah</u>n pr<u>ah</u>lines, not pea-can pray-leenes."

***"You can't buy a bird house for $55,000 in California," she commented as she pointed out a double shotgun camelback on Elysian Fields Blvd.

***"We are a gumbo of ethnic groups, French, Spanish, American, black Haitian, Germans and Irish."

***"That house is ultra 1950 ugly."

***"We're not laid back. We can't breathe. It's hot here! People jogging? Those are tourists."

***"An acre of land here is a subdivision."

Of course she hit all the things every guide in the South includes: resurrection ferns, Spanish moss, pecan pronunciation, shotgun houses, neutral ground, kudzu, humidity, etc.

***"Where do we bury Baptists? In gin." When asked again:

*****"Where do we bury Baptists? In California."

***"Creole? You're going to hear millions of definitions, but mine is correct. The real word means an 'original settler' regardless of nationality."

***"Last year, New Orleans was voted the most obese city in America. There is a lot of recreational eating here."

***"The evacuation route? Don't take it! It will take you around in circles and you'll never get out."

***"A hurricane is like a man. It can't make up its mind."

***"I'm not going to say we never sweat. We glow."

In between all of this, Angela talked us around the French Quarter, out Elysian Fields, Claibourne, through Carrollton to Riverbend, back down St. Charles through the Garden District to Lee Circle and past the Superdome to the airport. A great four-hour tour condensed into sixty-three minutes! When God dispensed tongues he sure was in a hurry down South!

We had a teacher at my old high school who got completely fed up one day, walked into the hall and bellowed, "If you took away half the faculty and all the students, this would be a great place to work." If he had said that in an airport, he would be describing New Orleans International today, a cavernous empty box that was a joy to be in.

There was no curbside check-in, but the skycaps were waiting for us. Not a single traveler was in line at TWA and we were screened and checked in twenty minutes. Mac and I got our coffee in a world record thirty-seven minutes. Where is everybody?

"We'll have a special boarding call for your group at the gate," the TWA clerk had volunteered up front and I was duly grateful. At the gate the special call was made, leaving seven lonesome souls remaining in the boarding area.

An empty airport is a thing of beauty, but sadly not at the cost that had to be paid to achieve it. This has been a trip we shall all remember, and hopefully part of that will be attributed to the tour itself.

One final thrill! Our flight to St. Louis took us along the Mississippi, and there below us, in clear sunshine was the New Madrid loop, twisting and turning in its effort to figure out whether it was Missouri, Illinois, Kentucky, Tennessee or Arkansas. Who cares? Our lives are completely fulfilled now that we have collected New Madrid AND the ducks! Mark Twain should have seen his river from this vantage point. He would have loved it, and written it up for sure. And the ducks? They would have inspired him, as they moved from their penthouse suite to the elevator to the red carpet in the hotel to the pond in the lobby. And still could remember how to swim.

> "If you should rear a duck in the heart of the Sahara, no doubt it would swim if you brought it to the Nile."
> *The Gilded Age*, Oxford Mark Twain, p. 201

BOOK TWO

The Homes of Mark Twain

We may be doing something unique!

It is the most overused of clichés, a word almost reduced to no meaning at all, but occasionally, we stumble into its correct use, and this may be one of those times. I am not sure that anyone, except perhaps Sam Clemens himself, has ever participated in a tour that includes Hannibal, Missouri, Buffalo and Elmira, New York and Hartford, Connecticut. These are not necessarily primary destinations by any standards, and even the most avid Mark Twain buff probably never combined them into one event, perhaps never making the mental link centered around the writer's homes. I doubt that Sam Clemens visited all his home bases in a single two-week period. But we are far from normal! Over the years, Bear Treks, the travel arm of the U.C. Berkeley Alumni Association, has chosen a dozen odd itineraries, covering just about all elements of American history. This is just one of the oddest of that bunch.

Of course, our list is far from complete, because it doesn't include the cabin on Jackass Hill or the Occidental Hotel ("heaven on a half-shell") in San Francisco, or the apartments in New York City and London. Or even Stormfield, in Redding, Connecticut, his last residence, where he died on April 21, 1910. Stormfield was destroyed by fire in 1923. But even with those omissions, our list is quite large enough to be able to gather most of the residences that were important to the author. And with Bob Hirst to direct us, those homes will come to life.

I

We negotiated the e-ticket intricacies of American Airlines in San Francisco at 6:00 A.M. today, bound for St. Louis, Missouri. As always, most of our travelers beat Mac and me to the airport, but we were actually on time and quite proud of ourselves. It didn't take long to get everyone settled out at the gate, and without incident, we were soon in the air, twenty-five of our eventual group of thirty-four. Most certainly we are top-heavy in administration on this tour. Once again, our team is led by Bob Hirst, the Director of the Mark Twain Papers Project at U.C. For twenty-five years, Bob has been editing that massive volume of writing, producing six volumes of letters and beginning the huge process of working on the essays and other writings, as well as the huge production of Mark Twain's autobiography. In that process, I think that Bob has just about committed the whole thing to memory, developing an expertise that is unmatched in the world. In setting up the programs I found it very useful to bludgeon our various hosts during the itinerary with the formidable expertise reputation of Robert Hirst, opening many doors that otherwise might be closed.

From the touring standpoint, our adventure as usual is led by Mac Laetsch, former botany professor and vice chancellor at U.C., and my closest friend in travel. Mac and I have teamed up on 21 formal Bear Treks since the initial Santa Fe Trail in 1991. Mac often brags, or moans, about the fact that we have spent more than a year of our lives together. At an average of two weeks per trip, that would be 42 weeks. Throw in set-up trips for most of those, and you easily get another 10-20 weeks. And that doesn't even begin to count the research time spent in restaurants and bars all over the land. I would think we are getting up to a year and a half by now. It has been a very meaningful partnership. On this trip, Mac is going to be in his finest role, as a facilitator and questioner for the group, to bring out the knowledge that is jammed inside of Bob's head. I have never seen anyone as expert in asking good questions as Mac, whose interrogations are based on a formidable knowledge on his own part.

Lastly, we have the casual services of yet another Twain scholar in Bob Middlekauf. Bob, former chairman of the history department at Cal, and nationally acclaimed author on Colonial America and the American Revolution, is also in the midst of major research into Mark Twain. On this tour he is participating as a "normal" passenger, but I have seen Mac in action before, and I am certain that Bob will be called upon here and there for his expert comments. About four times a day, Mac tells us that Bob is the author of *The Glorious Cause*, a fundamental work on the history of the American Revolution. For my part, I have taken dozens of groups throughout New England, but I will most certainly hesitate with my Yankee history in the face of Bob's knowledge. If Mac doesn't call on him east of Hartford, I most certainly will.

We landed in St. Louis right on time, and there was David with his motorcoach, from Arrow Bus Line. David is a very outgoing man, bus-driver portly with an easy laugh and a pot-full of one-liners. In the old days, all drivers were expected to be characters, part of the entertainment on tours, but these days such amateur comedians are becoming a rare breed. Of course we don't really want or need the diversion, since we have plenty to say on our own, but David is refreshing. He is also very professional, having studied the itinerary carefully, and armed with a GPS unit, knows precisely where to go.

Actually, this is our second visit to St. Louis and Hannibal with the Cal Alumni. Five years ago we did our first Mark Twain tour, focusing on his early life in Hannibal and on the Mississippi. It was the tragic year of 9/11. Many of our participants this time were on that trip.

You know immediately when you are nearing Hannibal because whitewashed fences start proliferating and businesses get named things like Huck and Becky Thatcher, Sawyer and, of course, Mark Twain. I quickly noted the Hotel Clemens, Mark Twain Dinette, Huck's Home Stand, Becky's Old-Fashioned Ice Cream Emporium, Mrs. Clemens's Shop, Pudd'nhead Antiques, Clemen's (sic) Landing, Tom Sawyer's Dioramas and the Mark Twain Card Shop. There seems to be a homogenous theme to this place. Downtown I spotted the Twain Yarn Co, but my favorite was the Mark Twain Deli and Italian Pasta Shop. We were first booked into the Hotel Clemens downtown, but on reviewing my notes from our 2001 trip, I discovered that we had used the Hannibal Inn, and everyone seemed to like it. So I changed the reservation and was all set until Henry Sweets, our Hannibal historian, called about a month ago.

"Jack, there is an article in the Hannibal paper today that says the Hannibal Inn has declared bankruptcy. You might want to check it out."

I did check it out and discovered that the inn was in danger of completely closing, that the staff had not been paid for weeks. At Henry's suggestion, I called the Quality Inn and Suites, and with a little scurrying on the director Melanie's part, we got the rooms we needed. Today, driving into Hannibal, we passed the Hannibal Inn, which appeared almost deserted. And the Quality Inn, somewhat out of town, proved to be a very nice property with great service. Thank God for Henry!

Tonight we cruise the Mississippi on the Mark Twain Riverboat. It is always nice to get off the bus and into a different form of conveyance, but dinner cruises on riverboats are usually mediocre in both areas. Food is generally not so hot (no pun intended) and the cruise is usually less than exciting. But the river and paddle-wheelers are so important in the Mark Twain story, and since everything in Hannibal is Twain-labeled, how is it possible not to include this? Actually, the food was passable, and since there is still a shred of daylight-saving time left this fall, we could spend at least a half hour on the upper deck, looking at Lover's Leap and the townscape of Hannibal. In addition, it was a lovely evening, where we could enjoy the air, and with a little bit of jet lag, fresh air always helps. I think that most everyone agreed that this was a nice way to spend our first night in Hannibal, free of sleep-inducing lectures, and unhampered by too much critical thought demands. Tomorrow we start to mine the brain of Bob Hirst!

II

"Did Mark Twain like biscuits and gravy?"

Our quest for the Compleate Marke Twaine has now officially begun! It started with a simple question from me, inquiring of Mac how he liked the biscuits and gravy at the hotel. He always raves about such culinary delights, but this time he was less than enthusiastic, stating that they weren't nearly as good as in Gold Run, "where they make the finest biscuits and gravy in all of California." David snorted at that comment, implying that it would be impossible to find good biscuits and gravy anywhere in California, that you had to come to Missouri to taste the real thing. I think that down deep Mac knew he was right, so he promptly redirected the discussion to Mark Twain.

"Well, he did like biscuits and gravy," Bob said, and then promptly disclaimed the statement. In *A Tramp Abroad*, he made a list of the American foods he missed in Europe.

"I am pretty sure that biscuits are on that list, but I'm not sure of the gravy."

"You can't have one without the other," Mac insisted

Most of us would have objected to that statement, but it didn't matter to Bob at all, because his considerations are far above the gastronomical ones. Simply put, he couldn't for sure place the word "gravy" in any of Mark Twain's writings, and if that is the case, he could hardly pronounce the word itself out loud. Bob lives in great fear of speaking for the author without hard proof. We were all amazed that he could come up with a list of foods our hero liked and were quite willing to adopt Mac's extrapolation to the present conversation. But not Bob! For two weeks he would continue to disclaim about gravy, while Mac and the rest of us (except me) had gone on to far distant subjects. I proposed that we do a "gravy" word search of the Mark Twain Papers Project and settle the matter once and for all.

My guess (God forbid) is that he couldn't possibly have lived in Missouri without having biscuits and gravy, and he wouldn't dare to say he didn't like them. They were probably better than the Gold Run version.

One of the first things I did when I got home was to drag out *A Tramp Abroad* and look for gravy. My admiration for Bob now knows no bounds whatsoever. There in the first column of foods he missed in Europe, the tenth item on the list, is "Hot biscuits, Southern style." He also listed "Hot hoe-cakes…Hot egg bread…hot light bread," all "Southern style." *But there is no mention of gravy.* Now I am sure that Mac will argue that "Southern style" obviously means gravy. But this list, as Bob fully well knew, makes no mention of the word "gravy."

Perhaps more to the point, in a small story about his "war experiences," Twain describes a "Missouri country breakfast."

> "…hot biscuits; hot "wheat bread," prettily criss-crossed in a lattice pattern on top; hot corn-pone; fried chicken; bacon, coffee, eggs, milk, buttermilk, etc.; and the world may be confidently challenged to furnish the equal of such a breakfast, as it is cooked in the South."
>
> *The Private History of a Campaign that Failed,* Rise of Douai Publications, p. 24

Not a mention of gravy!

Henry Sweets was standing on the corner of Center & Main Streets, waiting for our bus to arrive at the Mark Twain Museum. He had agreed to open an hour early for us so that we would have the place to ourselves, free of those pesky critters called "tourists." I always enjoy the mental process that allows you to rationalize yourself out of that tourist role, simply because you were attending a lecture or two, and listening to a person who is not driving the bus. Bears would be positively horrified if someone inadvertently referred to them as "tourists." That's why I like to refer to our adventures as "Bear Treks" or "Field Studies," denominations that are ever so much classier than "tours."

Henry ushered us into a conference room on the second floor where he had set up a PowerPoint show for us, entitled "Hannibal 1819-1860," which introduced us to the society of Mark Twain's day, expanding on the social structure, the economy, religion, school system that could produce this largely self-taught, but world-wise genius. I think it was a well-received background introduction to the author. Henry has compiled a large amount of material on Hannibal and Bob has urged him to put it into a book.

Samuel Clemens was born in Florida, Missouri on November 30, 1835, the fifth child of John and Jane Clemens.

> "My parents removed to Missouri in the early 'thirties; I do not remember just when, for I was not born then and cared nothing for such things. It was a long journey in those days, and must have been a rough and tiresome one. The home was made in the wee village of Florida, in Monroe County, and I was born there in 1835. The village contained a hundred people and I increased the population by 1 per cent. It is more than many of the best men in history could have done for a town. It may not be modest in me to refer to this, but it is true. There is no record of a person doing as much—not even Shakespeare. But I did it for Florida, and it shows that I could have done it for any place—even London, I suppose."
> *Autobiography of Mark Twain,* Vol.1, p. 109

Four years later the family moved from the backwater town to Hannibal, a river community that showed far more promise, Sam Clemens wasn't too sure.

> '
> "Hannibal has had a hard time of it ever since I can recollect, and I was "raised" there. First, it had me for a citizen, but I was too young then to really hurt the place.
> Letter to the *Alta California,* dated April 16, 1867; published May 26, 1867. Quoted in www.twainquotes.com.

Henry Sweets' talk covered the rise of Hannibal as a trading town, focusing on 1847, the year that John Clemens died. It was a year when more than 1000 steamboats called on the town. Henry traced the early town plats, illustrating the growth of Hannibal, and particularly pointing out the rough and tumble river society that was heaven for a young boy like Sam. On the death of his father, Sam went to work as a "printer's devil," his first introduction to the journalistic world.

Henry finished his lecture around 10:30 and we have the rest of the morning scheduled to visit the various elements of the Mark Twain domain in town. There are six museums in the complex overseen by the central museum that Henry directs. These include the Tom Sawyer House, Becky Thatcher House, J.M. Clemens Justice of the Peace Office, Grant's Drug Store, Huckleberry Finn House and the Mark Twain Interpretive Center. I decided to take a look at the statue of Tom and Huck at the bottom of Cardiff Hill and climb the 200+ stairs to the lighthouse on top. The light rain that was falling didn't make for much of a view, but the exercise was badly needed.

At 1:00, we boarded our motorcoach for a ride to Florida, (the Missouri Florida) to visit the Mark Twain Shrine, situated in Mark Twain Birthplace Park, located in the middle of Mark Twain Lake. Nothing here is where it is supposed to be, since the lake was never here at all in Sam Clemens' day; the park is new; and the house was moved to the current location. Of course, Florida itself is supposed to be somewhere south of the Mason-Dixon line, but then again, this is Missouri, and that state has a habit of collecting all sorts of disparate parts. Paris isn't far from Florida in this crazy place, and Mexico is just a bit farther south, with Palmyra to the north. I have been to Nevada, California and Washington, Carthage, Versailles, Warsaw, and Savannah and never once left the state.

The bridge was closed on the road to Florida, so we detoured south and hit the place from the wrong direction. We were met at the Shrine by John Huffman, who was positively thrilled to have us here. This is not exactly the center of tourism in Missouri, and for a whole busload of Twain enthusiasts to arrive is purely heaven for someone like John who is caretaker for a surprising wealth of Mark Twain items. Perhaps most surprising is an amanuensis copy of *Tom Sawyer*, complete with the London editor's proof sheets, a prize that immediately attracted Bob's attention. The preface, hand-written by Twain after the book was finished, is the original. I have been surprised more than once on finding similar treasures in unexpected locations. I recall on our first Lewis and Clark trip, we discovered, in an interpretive center near Fort Mandan, North Dakota, the original Jefferson letter to Meriwether Lewis authorizing the Corps of Discovery. This copy of *Tom Sawyer* neatly fits into that surprise category, just a level below finding half of *Huck Finn* in an attic in Hollywood.

The museum has just produced a new video of the life of Samuel Clemens, which John asked us to review and make comments. The film was quite good, accurate and fairly complete. I commented that the pictures of Nevada were actually of Arizona (Saguaro cactus et al) and California (Sierra forests).

"Oh, those are generic pictures," John disclaimed. "Those places all look the same."

John then invited everyone out to the front of the museum, where they have installed the cabin that was once owned by the Clemens family. It has been moved from its original location, encased in the museum, considerably reconstructed, but looks somewhat like the early pictures of it. No wooden structure could survive long in Missouri weather, and I think they have done the best they could in saving it.

> "Recently someone in Missouri sent me a picture of the house I was born in. Heretofore I have always stated it was a palace, but I shall be more guarded now."
> *Autobiography of Mark Twain*, Vol. 1, p.109

We finished our visit to the home site with a Q & A, featuring Mac and Bob. I feel that this is where both of them shine, with Mac firing a steady barrage of interesting questions and Bob providing fascinating answers. As is his habit, Bob protests that he does not have enough information on the subject, and then proceeds to extemporize for an hour, always capturing our rapt attention. He positively lives for questions, reveling at the sight of multiple hands raised in the audience. Once the questions start, Bob loses all thought of time, finishing an answer a few seconds before responding to the next inquiry. I do believe that he would talk right through the night if the questions kept flowing. We have learned that the statement, "We'll take two more questions," means very little in time, because a single answer could take in a dozen Mark Twain letters, several novels and six unfinished essays. "We have to leave!" is more effective. The problem is, however, that nobody in the audience is any more ready to call it quits than Bob is, because he is such a wonderful speaker with such an attractive delivery. It is a treasure not to be missed when you encounter someone with true expertise in a subject that fascinates you.

We have found that cocktail time is an effective limit to lectures. Since we have a flight tomorrow, Mac and I decided to postpone our room parties until we arrive in Buffalo. The new air regulations against carrying liquids makes it very difficult to transport the essentials for our ongoing cocktail parties. I phoned the hotel, and they agreed to open their bar at 6:00 tonight for an hour icebreaker party for the Bears. That would have worked fine, except they had previously agreed to a 5:00 P.M. party in the same place for a convention of Caterpillar Tractor people, "who have a dinner reservation at 6:00." Our polite Bears did try to get near the bar, but they invariably retreated with tractor tread marks all over their backs, pushed out by a raucous group of guys who could care less about dinner. But we adjourned to another room and finally reclaimed the bar area around 6:30, scarfing down all the munchies the caterpillars had left untouched.

Dinner was at Lula Belle's in town, a nice little restaurant with average food, but a good time was had by all.

"What did I order for tonight?"

Most of these restaurants limit the choice of entrees for group meals. I usually have to take a count, but folks tend to forget what they ordered several days before. I try to identify "wild cards" in the group, people who don't care what they eat, and will take whatever the restaurant has left. Mac and I fit into that category, and several more in the group volunteered. Since the choice is always salmon, some sort of beef, and an anomalous treatment of chicken, I really should simplify the whole thing into Beef, Salmon or Chicken. From my standpoint, on the road they all taste the same anyway, so it really doesn't matter. Someday I am going to have a choice of beef Wellington, veal Oscar, linguini with clams and shark stuffed with Manta ray eggs, and I will really throw the whole selection process into confusion.

III

We are off to Buffalo!

I have never taken a flight of any sort to Buffalo. Why would I? Why would anyone? The poor city suffers more insults than Philadelphia, and never even had the luxury of passing the barbs off as W.C. Fields humor. Even that rotund comic couldn't bring down a place that only has two seasons—winter and the 4th of July. Sam Clemens lived in Buffalo, but he quickly moved on to Elmira.

You can't really fly to Buffalo, not directly that is. I think if you told an airline you wanted to go to Buffalo, they would throw you off immediately as some sort of lunatic. No, you have to feint going to Buffalo, take off on a tangent, to St. Louis or Pittsburgh, or Cleveland as we are doing. Then before anyone realizes what you are up to, you have to jump a puddle and land in Buffalo. Some people call it Niagara Falls and hitchhike south. Others go to Cleveland and catch a freighter across Erie. I had the urge today to just stand up and shout it out, "I'm going to Buffalo!" but I seem to have lost my nerve when I received my Medicare card. Even with cheap hospital care, you may not be able to afford a Buffalo reaction. Mac will defend the place because he once lived in Buffalo, but at the same time he would insist that there are no buffalo around here anyway. Maybe I could just say, in the interest of being academically correct, that I want to go to Bison.

Before we leave the Mississippi, Mac asked Bob to comment on Mark Twain, the river pilot.

Bob reported that Sam Clemens was probably never as happy as when he was a river pilot. He always felt somehow blocked as a writer, to publish exactly what he thinks. You can't give a pilot advice, tell him what to do, talk to him when he is on duty—by law! It is "unfettered independence," far from what he experienced as a writer.

"When Mark Twain starts writing for publication," Bob commented, "he stops being funny." Sam left piloting at the beginning of the Civil War. He was on the last riverboat to run the Union blockade around Memphis and realized that it had become a dangerous business, since the pilot would certainly become a target on any boat on the river. The job would always be in his mind for the rest of his life. Moving west, he launched himself into his career as a writer, picking up his first paycheck with the *Territorial Enterprise*.

The road back to St. Louis was paved with questions. Mac kept up a steady flow whenever the group started to slow down. Bob, of course, armed with $50 worth of overweight book baggage, was ready for anything. Even typical Mac questions:

Q: "Did he remain a lush?"

This started Bob off on the various drinks that Sam Clemens enjoyed, beginning with scotch and certainly including beer. He did drink wine, "as long as it was cheap."

Q: "Did Sam Clemens get part of the Langdon fortune?"

A: Yes, Livy got a quarter of it, and was certainly the money factor in the family. Sam did not personally go bankrupt, probably because of the constant advice of his Standard Oil friend, H. H. Rogers. His publishing company declared bankruptcy, but he felt obliged by honor to repay all his debtors.

Q: "What was his relationship with Olivia's brother, Charlie Langdon?"

A: Charlie was with Sam on the *Quaker City* cruise and they became friends. "It was a funeral excursion without a corpse." It was Charlie who introduced Sam to Livy, although there was a falling out when Sam married her. The relationship seems to have been patched up in later years however. Sam met Livy when the *Quaker City* returned, and then left for the West Coast. Charlie met him when he returned east and objected to the courtship.

Bob described the famous story about Sam and Livy's new home at 472 Delaware Avenue in Buffalo after their marriage in Elmira. The house, far more elegant than anything that Sam Clemens could afford, was a wedding gift of Jervis Langdon, complete with furnishings and staff.

"I remember one circumstance of bygone times with great vividness. I arrived here after dark on a February evening in 1870 with my wife and a large company of friends, when I had been a husband twenty-four hours, and they put us two in a covered sleigh, and drove us up and down and every which way, through all the back streets in Buffalo until at last I got ashamed, and said, 'I asked Mr Slee to get me a cheap boarding house, but I didn't mean that he should stretch economy to the going outside the state to find it.' The fact was there was practical joke to the fore which I didn't know anything about, and all this fooling around was to give it time to mature. My father-in-law, the late Jervis Langdon…had been clandestinely spending a fair fortune upon a house and furniture in Delaware avenue for us, and had kept his secret so well that I was the only person this side of Niagara Falls that hadn't found it out. We reached the house at last, about 10 o'clock, and were introduced to a Mrs. Johnson, the ostensible landlady. I took a glance around and then my opinion of Mr. Slee's judgment as a provider of cheap boarding houses for men who had to work for their living dropped to zero. I told Mrs. Johnson there had been an unfortunate mistake. Mr. Slee had evidently supposed I had money, whereas I only had talent; and so, by her leave, we would abide with her a week, and then she could keep my trunk and we would hunt another place. Then the battalion of ambushed friends and relatives burst in on us, out of closets and from behind curtains, the property was delivered over to us and the joke revealed, accompanied with much hilarity. Such jokes as these are all too scarce in a person's life. That was a really admirable joke, for that house was so completely equipped in every detail—even to house servants and coachman—that there was nothing to do but just sit down and live in it."

"Twain and Cable," Buffalo *Courier*, December 11, 1884, quoted in *Mark Twain's Letters*, Vol. 2, p. 48.

Sadly, within months, Jervis Langdon died. Sam and Livy stayed in Buffalo only a year and a half, then moved to Hartford, where they rented the Hooker house, prior to building their own lavish home in the Hartford development called "Nook Farm."

Somewhere around St. Charles just as we were passing the Mark Twain Hobby Center and the Mark Twain Mall, Bob announced, "I think I've said all I know about it."

I didn't write down what the "it" was, but it was an unequivocal end to Mac's question session and time to get the group ready for the airport.

We are taking Continental Express from St. Louis to Cleveland and then on to Buffalo. CNN reported this morning that there was light snow in Buffalo, so I called Patrick Keyes at the Adams Mark Hotel, where we are staying, to ask about the weather.

"It's great, 60° and sunny."

We were a bit late leaving St. Louis, boarding a cute little Embraer ERJ 145 aircraft, a 50-passenger plane that is most often used for these mid-western city transfers. I noted that the card in my seat announced that the plane was assembled in Brazil, but I thought it best not to mention that until we were all back home. It is always a challenge flying into these northern cities after Labor Day because weather usually plays a major role in your flight connections. But our pilot announced that we would be only five minutes late on arrival in Cleveland. He landed a bit later than that, taxiing over to a non-gate at the end of the terminal. There was no gateway and we had to disembark in a bit of rain, down to the tarmac and up a stairway to the terminal. There was our flight to Buffalo! We literally walked 100 feet to the new gate and right on to the plane. I think it was the shortest, most convenient connection I have ever made, and I am going to give Continental the credit for having deliberately plopped us down in that spot, on purpose. After all we were thirty-four of the fifty seats on both flights. Why make us walk too far, or delay the flight to Buffalo? Does that make too much sense?

Fred was waiting for us in Buffalo in a very attractive motorcoach from Anderson Coach Company. Our hotel tonight is the Adam's Mark Hotel on Delaware Avenue, a very nice hotel, well positioned for our stay in the city. We can relax tonight with dinner at the hotel. Tomorrow we see Buffalo. I am so happy that I decided to add a night in Buffalo. This is a surprisingly attractive city with many historic attractions, not the least of which is the proximity to Niagara Falls. I was shocked to find out that almost half of our group has never been to Niagara Falls, something we would not have been able to do with our original one-night stay.

IV

Sandy met me at the hotel this morning. She is our guide for the day, a bright, optimistic woman who has a genuine love for her city, displayed in an astonishing grasp on the current and past activities in the areas of art, music, history and sports. Sandy began her narrative before we left the hotel at 9:00. She brought her much maligned city alive for us.

We circled the lakefront, a rather downtrodden area like so many of these industrial Great Lake cities, but it is definitely being reborn. We immediately were surrounded by new waterfront condos, which replaced decrepit warehouses that used to line the shore. The Erie Basin is the scene of much activity. The original locks of the Erie Canal are being resurrected, long forgotten when the newer canal entrance was moved north through Lockport. The old lighthouse remains, "the oldest on the Seaway Trail. Grain elevators, invented in Buffalo, give silent testimony to the importance of the city at the time of the Erie Canal, when the grain of the Great Lakes poured into the Buffalo waterfront in preparation for shipment east through the canal. Today General Mills is the main employer in the area, packaging "anything with marshmallows." The *Battleship The Sullivans* is the central venue of what is soon to become a new Naval Museum that will also incorporate the Erie Canal locks. Those locks have been buried for years, and the government wanted to build a replica elsewhere on less valuable land, but the general outcry of the citizens prevailed. The entire project is called the Erie Canal Harbor Redevelopment Project. There are two sports arenas in the district, the HSBC Arena, home of the Buffalo Sabers, and the Dunn Tire Park, where the minor league Buffalo Bisons play. (an interesting name to be sure!) Buffalo Community College, occupying the old Post Office building, fills a major chunk of the area.

Our first stop this morning is at the Buffalo-Erie County library. We were met by Elaine Barone, Manager of the library's Humanities Division.

"Do you pronounce that "Bar-own-ay?"

"Actually it's "Bar-own, but I accept anything. I've even heard "Bar-won.""

The library is the proud owner of the original manuscript of *Huckleberry Finn*, the first half of which was found in an old chest in Hollywood in 1991. The manuscript as well as the chest is displayed, along with many Twain items in the Mark Twain Room. Besides these treasures there is a nice collection of photographs of Buffalo at the time of the Clemens' stay, including several of the fine house that had been given to them as a wedding present. I loved two wonderful envelopes sent by Twain to his friend, C.W. Underhill. Lacking the exact address, he simply wrote elaborate descriptions of the addressee.

> To C.W. Underhill
> "One of the best men there is and tolerably moral and is running the coal business now and very popular."
> Buffalo, New York
> From Mark Twain

Another read:

> "Who is in the coal business in one of those streets there and is very respectably connected and generally decent and is a tall man and old but without any gray hair, and used to be handsome. PS: A little bald on the top of his head."

Both letters were postmarked as delivered. It was a simpler day!

Rob Alessi was a very nervous docent in the Mark Twain Room, not at all sure that he wanted to lecture in the presence of the awesome Mr. Hirst, but Bob as always, was extremely gracious and humble and tried his best to put Rob at ease. The library had many important items on display for us today, including a dozen pages of their prize, the original manuscript of *Huckleberry Finn*.

In 1885, James Gluck, the librarian in Buffalo asked Mark Twain for a gift of one of his writings. That gift was the original manuscript of *Huckleberry Finn*, which was delivered in November of that year. The title page and the second half of the manuscript have been in the library since that date, but the first half was somehow lost. In February, 1991 the missing first half was found in a trunk in the attic of Gluck's granddaughter in Hollywood, California. The manuscript was put up for auction at Sotheby's, but since there was some question as to the ownership, the gallery began investigations of the history of the manuscript. The Mark Twain Papers Project at Berkeley was consulted, with Bob giving a report that they had two letters that stated unequivocally that the manuscript had been given to Buffalo-Erie County Library. Negotiations were conducted and in July, 1992 the first half was finally reunited with the second and now resides where it was donated by the author.

Bob spoke for the Bancroft:

"We never aspired to it. We knew it belonged to the Buffalo Public Library."

As with the *Tom Sawyer* we found at the Mark Twain Shrine in Florida, Bob is thrilled to see these treasures and really doesn't seem to need them at Berkeley, although years later he confided to me that he would most certainly not turn them away. There is a fraternity of owners of Twain's writings that makes them readily available for other scholars. It strikes me that the actual ownership of Mark Twain is America, wherever the individual manuscripts, letters and other writings may be found.

The library also displayed other Twain treasures, including his Memory Builder, patented by the author on Aug. 18, 1885.

The game was a notable failure probably due to the conplicated instructions provided by the author. Twain had a fascination with human memory, and wrote a curious essay, "How to Make History Dates Stick," that was published after his death by Harper's Monthly Magazine in December, 1914. In it he explained how to remember the names and dates of all of the British monarchs from William the Conqueror to Victoria.

We split our group in half for the library, the second half visiting the Rare Books Room, where Elaine Barone and Karen Thomas had laid out some impressive literary and artistic treasures. The most obvious, being the largest, was sitting in the front window of the room, Audubon's double elephant folio of 419 prints. We have seen parts or all this work in other collections, including the Audubon Museum in Henderson, Kentucky and the Magnolia Plantation in Charleston, South Carolina, but in this rare book environment, it seemed even more impressive. But the Audubon prints paled by comparison with other items Elaine would bring to us inside the room.

She started with two original pages of the Gutenberg *Bible*, printed in 1450, which she actually passed around!

"Can we keep this?" Peter asked sheepishly.

What an incredible feeling to handle the most famous printed piece in history!

The next book displayed was the *Hypnerotomachia,* attributed to Francesco Colonna, which Elaine said was one of the most sought-after books in the world, "the oddest book I have ever come across." It was printed in Venice in 1499 and has considerable sixteenth century annotations.

Next, we looked at *de Stirpib*, Fuch's Herbal published in 1542, the first of its kind.

"We heard that one of your group is a professor of botany. We put this book out for him."

"He's in the next group," Janet told her. "Brace yourself!"

Next, we examined Shakespeare's *First Folio*, dated 1623, just seven years after his death. It contains thirty-six plays of which sixteen would have been lost if not for this volume.

The last of these treasures was *The Federalist Papers*, Thomas Jefferson's copy which he received from John Jay. It contains many notes made by Jefferson, whose comments are quite as valuable as the book itself.

We just scratched the surface of the treasures contained in this seemingly ordinary public library. I had allocated about an hour for our program. In fact we used nearly double that time and could easily have taken the whole morning.

After we returned from the tour, I went on the Internet to find out how to spell *Hypnerotomachia*. I found the book on the alphabetical listing of incunabula at the Bancroft Library, well hidden among a horde of at least 430 titles, by definition, all printed before 1501. I also found out that *incunabula* is the Latin word for "swaddling clothes," since these works are from the infancy of Western printing.

From the library, we drove to the site of the Clemens home which once stood on the corner of Virginia and Delaware Streets. Today it is an empty lot, the parking lot of a defunct restaurant. There are brick columns on each corner and a small wrought iron fence. I am told that the carriage house still stands, but it is not at all evident.

In August, 1869, Sam Clemens came to take up the *Buffalo Express*, purchased for $25,000. He only worked there two months and then went off on a lecture tour, returning in January, 1870. On Feb. 2, 1870, he and Olivia Langdon were married in Elmira, returning to Buffalo the next day. They were ushered into sleighs, "driving up and down and all over America," before being deposited at the elegant home on Delaware and Florida, the gift of Livy's father.

On August 6, 1870, Jervis Langdon died. Two years later, Sam and Livy left Buffalo for Elmira and then on to Hartford. Their home in Buffalo burned down in 1963.

Theirs was a marriage that would last. In his courtship campaign, Sam wrote lengthy letters to Olivia in his efforts to win her hand, and perhaps more important, win the acceptance of her family. Both Jervis and Olivia Langdon sought recommendations. Bob tells a hilarious story of Jervis Langdon asking Sam for written recommendations. The "recommendations" were not entirely complimentary.

> "You speak of Mr. Stebbins. He came within an ace of breaking off my marriage by saying to the gentleman instructed by "her" father to call on him & inquire into my character, that "Clemens is a humbug— shallow & superficial—a man who has talent, no doubt, but will make a trivial & possibly a worse use of it—a man whose life promised little & has accomplished less—a humbug, Sir, a humbug"…The friends that I had referred to in California said with one accord that I got drunk oftener than was necessary & that I was wild & Godless, idle, lecherous & a discontented & unsettled rover & they could not recommend any girl of high character & social position to marry me—but as I had already said all that about myself beforehand there was nothing shocking or surprising about it to the family."
>
> *Mark Twain's Letters*, Vol. 3, Letter to Charles Warren Stoddard, August 25, 1869.

Livy's mother, on the other hand, went straight to her newfound friend, Mary Fairbanks, who had formed a friendship with Sam on the Holy Land cruise, and continued to advise him on his writing.

> "I cannot, & need not detail to you the utter surprise & almost astonishment with which Mr. Langdon & myself listened to Mr Clemens declaration to us, of his love for our precious child, and how at first our parental hearts said no. —to the bare thought of such a stranger mining in our hearts for the possession one of the few jewels we have…
>
> You, my dear friend have known Mr Clemens, more or less intimately since your and his embarkation on the 'Quaker City'—you knew him first, as a somewhat celebrated personage next you knew him as a fellow traveler, and as your acquaintance with him increased into the time of weeks & months, you began to look upon him from your higher standpoint of maturer experience & closer estimate & appreciation of men… Now what I am about to write, must be plainly and frankly spoken. I do not ask as to his standing among men, nor do I need to be assured that he is a man of genius that he possesses a high order of intellectual endowments, nor do I scarcely crave your opinion of his affectional nature, but what I desire is your opinion of him as a *man,* what the kind of man he *has been,* and what the man he now is, or is to become."
>
> Letter of Olivia Langdon to Mary Fairbanks, December 1, 1868 as quoted in *Mark Twain's Letters*, Vol. 2, pp 286-87

Somehow, Sam survived the inspection, and he wrote to his family.

> "This is to inform you that on yesterday, the 4th of February, I was duly & solemnly & irrevocably engaged to be married to Miss Olivia L. Langdon, aged 23 ½, only daughter of Jervis and Olivia Langdon, of Elmira, New York. *Amen.*
>
> *Mark Twain's Letters*, Vol. 3, Letter to Jane Lampton Clemens and Family, February 5, 1869.

In the full flush of honeymoon, Sam wrote to his friend, William Bowen.

"For behold I have at this moment the *only* sweetheart I ever loved, & bless her old heart she is lying asleep upstairs in a bed that I sleep in every night, & for four whole days she has been *Mrs. Samuel L. Clemens.*

I am 34 & she is 24; I am young & very handsome (I make the statement with the fullest confidence, for I got it from her.) & she is much the most beautiful girl I ever saw (I said that before she was anything to me, & so it is worthy of all belief) & she is the best girl, & the sweetest, & the gentlest, & the daintiest, & the most modest, & unpretentious, & the wisest in all things she should be wise in & the most ignorant in all matters it would not grace her to know, & she is sensible & quick, & loving & faithful, forgiving, full of charity, —& her beautiful life is ordered by a religion that is all kindliness & unselfishness...

She is the very most perfect gem of womankind that ever I saw in my life—& I will stand by that remark till I die."
Mark Twain's Letters, Vol. 4, pp 51-52.

☙ ❧

This is the extent of Mark Twain's legacy in Buffalo—a library room and an empty lot. But our guide Sandra was by no means finished with her tour. We stopped briefly in front of the Ansley Wilcox house, where on September 14, 1901, Theodore Roosevelt took the oath of office becoming the 26th president. President William McKinley had been shot in Buffalo at the World's Fair Temple of Music on September 6th and died on the 13th. Today the home is a National Historic Site.

Not far from the home, we entered Delaware Park, another of those magnificent urban gardens laid out in 1860 by Frederick Law Olmstead, who roamed our nation from Manhattan to San Diego. The park and its upscale neighborhoods are a view of Buffalo that the outside world seldom sees. It is typically Olmstead-huge, containing a golf course and zoo, lakes and miles of walking and bike paths. It also holds Fairlawn Cemetery, which is the proud possessor of President Millard Fillmore. Sandy mentioned an essay that Mark Twain wrote while in Buffalo entitled "A Curious Dream," which speaks about the moving of two old cemeteries in the city center out to Fairlawn and new digs, so to speak. Bob brought out the essay and read it to us, a lament of sorts decrying the forlorn state of the old cemeteries.

> "Night before last I had a singular dream. I seemed to be sitting on a doorstep, (in no particular city, perhaps), ruminating, and the time of night appeared to be about twelve or one o'clock. The weather was balmy and delicious. There was no human sound in the air, not even a footstep...Presently up the street I heard a bony clack-clacking, and guessed it was the castanets of a serenading party. In a minute more a tall skeleton, hooded and half-clad in a tattered and mouldy shroud whose shreds were flapping in the ribby lattice-work of its person, swung by me with a stately stride, and disappeared in the gray gloom of the starlight. It had a broken and worm-eaten coffin on its shoulder... Before I could collect my thoughts and enter upon any speculations...I heard another one coming..."

(CONCLUDED FROM LAST WEEK'S EXPRESS.)

(In the chapter preceding this, was set forth how certain shrouded skeletons came mysteriously marching past my door after midnight, carrying battered tombstones, crumbling coffins, and such like property with them, and how one sat down by me to rest, (having also his tombstone with him, and dragging after him his worm-eaten coffin by a string,) and complained at great length of the discomforts of his ruinous and long- neglected graveyard. This conversation now continueth.)

"Yes, friend," said the poor skeleton, "the facts are just as I have given them to you. Two of these old graveyards—the one that I resided in and one further along—have been deliberately neglected by our descendants of to-day until there is no occupying them any longer. Aside from the osteological discomfort of it—and that is no light matter this rainy weather—the present state of things is ruinous to property. We have got to move or be content to see our effects wasted away and utterly destroyed. Now you will hardly believe it, but it is true, nevertheless, that there isn't a single coffin in good repair among all my acquaintance—now that is an absolute fact. I do not refer to people who come in a pine box mounted on an express wagon, but am talking about your high-toned silver-mounted burial-case, monumental sort, that travel under plumes at the head of a procession and have a choice of cemetery lots—I mean folks like the Jarvis's, and the Bledsoes and Burling's and such. They are all ruined.,,,"

"A Curious Dream," Mark Twain Collected Tales, Sketches, Speeches, & Essays, 1852-1890, p. 356-361

Buffalo was founded in 1832, after the opening of the Erie Canal. Joseph Ellicott and the Holland Land Co. laid out the city lots and squares. Sandy drove us through the old part of town, around Niagara Square with its McKinley Monument. The Statler Hotel, the first of that chain, sits empty on the square, awaiting renewal. Such was the wealth that accrued to the new city, that Delaware Ave. quickly became known as "Millionaires Row." The Buffalo Club still operates, across from Trinity Church, with its Tiffany and Lafarge windows. Farther along is the Twentieth Century Club, the first private women's club in America. The Midway-Ross House gets the name from the location, halfway between City Hall where you get your birth certificate and Fairlawn Cemetery. We all laughed at a nearby funeral home, called Amigone Funeral Parlor. The cemetery is huge, 269 acres, and still open for new clients. Frank Lloyd Wright designed a mausoleum for Darwin Martin whose house we will visit later today. It is called the Blue Sky Mausoleum, the sky being the roof, and was only recently completed.

"This day is playing with us, isn't it?"

Sandy observed this as we were passing Canisius College. "We started the day with rain, moved to sunshine, which was pushed out by high winds. Now it is snowing! Buffalo was about to live up to the reputation we have been laughing about for the last couple of days. But right now it is lunch time, and the snow isn't important. Sandy drove us around a most forbidding looking insane asylum, designed by H.H. Richardson and surrounded with parks by Olmstead. We passed several Frank Lloyd Wright homes built for the executives of the Larkin Soap Co., skirted around Hoyt Lake in the park and by the impressive Albright-Knox Art Gallery.

Our goal is Wegman's Grocery Store, which Sandy insists is one of her favorite places in all of Buffalo. Wegman's is no ordinary grocery store. Fred let us off, in a light snow, at the entrance to a world class deli. At first glance, it looked like a Disneyland crowd, all jammed near the door of the place, and I think we each let out a silent groan. But then the possibilities began to unfold, once we figured out the system. To the right stretched a long counter devoted to creating just about any type of sub sandwich you could imagine. There was a long, long salad bar. In the center to the right was a soup station. Further investigation revealed a pizza shop, and Wegman's Wok, a Chinese buffet where for $6.95 you could eat to your heart's content. What looked like a butcher shop was really a Meat Table, where you could order just about anything for heating in a bank of microwaves. Next door was a Seafood Bar. Want oysters? Giant shrimp? A whole plate of sushi? I found a counter that sold Artisan Breads, just about any kind you could think of. One island boasted thirty-six different kinds of olives, and another was filled with humus, kibbe, stuffed grape leaves, couscous, orzo, pita bread fixings, and other Near Eastern delicacies. I couldn't even begin to count all the cheeses that were displayed in the Cheese Shop. All of this funneled into a bank of cash registers where somehow the clerks figured out what to charge you. Within twenty minutes, our whole group had made their choices, discovered the soft drink machines and found a table. Amazing!

But they don't have any Polish sausage!

Lunch completed, we turned our attention to Frank Lloyd Wright and the Darwin Thomas House. Thomas was the founder of the Larkin Soap Company and he seemed to have a love affair with the work of Frank Lloyd Wright. We already saw the BlueSky Mausoleum he had ordered for his final resting-place in Fairlawn. All his officers lived in Wright homes, and his personal residence was the highpoint of Wright's Prairie architecture. It was built in 1907, six buildings on 1.5 acres, at a cost of $175,000. With beige-colored bricks, cut narrow and deeply set, the house gives the appearance of being very low slung. As we would discover it was more than appearance. Inside the ceilings are in fact very low by our standards.

It was beginning to snow in earnest by the time we reached the house, so our guide, Peggy naturally walked our half of the group to the corner so we could stand there and freeze while she delayed entrance to give the first group a head start.

"What are we doing here?" I asked very nicely, even though it was obvious what we were doing here—fidgeting and shivering.

"We can't all fit in the house at the same time. I want to give you some background on the exterior."

"Have you noticed that it is snowing? And that we aren't wearing any winter clothes?

"Well, we'll just have to make the best of it."

"No we won't. Get us under some shelter. Now!"

Peggy started to object, but it is possible that some sort of cold sensation had finally percolated into her brain as well, so she led us toward the front door, where she stopped again, still in the snow.

"Take us under that overhang!" It was only about twenty feet away, but far too obvious to be used.

Finally, mercifully, we were allowed into the house. Peggy turned out to be a very fine guide, with a good voice and lots of information, without the usual adoration that docents often have for famous dead artists. The house was abandoned for fifteen years and was nearly destroyed by the elements and vandals. A restoration committee decided to rebuild the whole thing, budgeting the project at $32 million. So far, they have spent $40 million, and they still have considerable work to do, both on the main house and on the other buildings on the property.

I would have found the main house to be completely unlivable even if it were in perfect condition. If I were Mr. Martin, I would have moved out the first day, right after shooting Mr. Wright. The place is claustrophobic, with low ceilings, relatively small windows, even if they are "Chicago Style" with clear middle panes and Wisteria or Tree of Life patterns flanking them. With indirect lighting the place must have seemed very dark, particularly in the Buffalo nine-month winters. Even the "Long Room," a 70' combination of dining room, music room and living room, seemed tightly enclosed. Peggy explained that Wright wanted to "Break the Box," by essentially eliminating the corners of the rooms with elaborate wall formulations. He designed everything inside and outside the house—furniture, lighting fixtures, window treatments, indoor and outdoor plants, all landscaping, even insisting on gecko trees outside the windows.

We were ushered into the reception room, where visitors were first assembled. A large fireplace dominates the room, featuring a two-foot high brick arch and bronze fireboxes on either side (designed by Wright). The Japanese prints he picked out still adorn some of the walls. The ceiling is a "tray ceiling," which Peggy explained is an inverted serving tray, upside down to make the room look shorter. Tree of Life windows adorn the front wall.

The soap company succumbed to the Great Depression, and Mr. Martin died penniless in 1935, probably of architect-induced claustrophobia. Two years later, Mrs. Martin locked the doors and walked away forever. In 1955 the estate was sold, the back lots resold to a developer who converted them into an apartment house. In the mid-1960s, the University of Buffalo purchased the whole thing, using the main house for the president's home. In the late 1980s, the Martin House Restoration Association began the rebuilding. It just opened for tours two weeks ago.

We left the Martin House in a driving snowstorm. By this time, it had started to accumulate, and it was very treacherous even walking to the bus.

"Good afternoon, folks! This is another example of global warming."

Lightning blitzed through the falling snow, and a terrific peal of thunder added to our growing collection of Buffalo weather. Hail, quickly changing to sleet was falling as we pulled away, bound for Niagara Falls. The notorious "Lake Effect" was in full glory. If it's not snowing in Buffalo, it is counted as a sunny day. This was definitely not such a critter.

Mark Twain visited Niagara Falls with the Langdons in 1869.

NIAGARA FALLS is a most enjoyable place of resort. The hotels are excellent, and the prices not at all exorbitant. The opportunities for fishing are not surpassed in the country; in fact, they are not even equaled elsewhere. Because, in other localities, certain places in the streams are much better than others; but at Niagara one place is just as good as another, for the reason that the fish do not bite anywhere, and so there is no use in your walking five miles to fish, when you can depend on being just as unsuccessful nearer home. The advantages of this state of things have never heretofore been properly placed before the public.

The weather is cool in summer, and the walks and drives are all pleasant and none of them fatiguing. When you start out to "do" the Falls you first drive down about a mile, and pay a small sum for the privilege of looking down from a precipice into the narrowest part of the Niagara river. A railway "cut" through a hill would be as comely if it had the angry river tumbling and foaming through its bottom. You can descend a staircase here a hundred and fifty feet down, and stand at the edge of the water. After you have done it, you will wonder why you did it; but you will then be too late....

There is no actual harm in making Niagara a background whereon to display one's marvelous insignificance in a good strong light, but it requires a sort of superhuman self-complacency to enable one to do it.

When you have examined the stupendous Horseshoe Fall till you are satisfied you cannot improve on it, you return to America by the new Suspension Bridge, and follow up the bank to where they exhibit the Cave of the Winds....

Mark Twain Sketches, New and Old, "Niagara," Oxford Mark Twain, pp. 63-65

The weather improved a bit as we headed north. It is only about twenty miles to the Canadian border at the falls. I have never taken a group to the

American side of Niagara, because New York has done little to spruce up their side of the border. From Buffalo to Niagara, the land is filled with industrial plants, the most famous of which created the infamous Love Canal. Even today, with the Buffalo lakefront being rapidly upgraded, Niagara seems to be stuck with rusting machinery and refineries. Our plan was to go to Goat Island, which sits in the middle of the two major cataracts. The great Horseshoe Falls is usually called "the Canadian Falls" while the straight one is "the American Falls."

We got to Goat Island as the snow arrived. Fred pulled us up to the park, where we could see folks dressed in parkas heading for the Maid of the Mist, the boat that takes visitors right up to the base of both waterfalls.

"Do any of you want to see the falls?" Sandy asked naively, assuming that the weather would inhibit the base tourist instincts of a Niagara Falls virgin. The whole bus emptied, into a driving wind, that propelled the snow parallel to the ground, and into our faces. A few made it to Terrapin Point at the eastern corner of the Canadian Falls, but the majority retreated in defeat to the gift shop. Our restaurant, the Inn at the Falls, is right above that gift shop, so I got out my cell phone to contact the manager, Kieran. Our dinner is set for 5:30, designed to be an early dinner with good weather.

"Can we possibly push the dinner up a bit?" I asked Kieran. "We are at the falls, and with this weather, there is nothing we can do."

"I think I can get the chef going."

"Can I bring people up early? Do you have a bar?"

"We do have a bar. I'll get a bartender out there right away."

"Give everyone the first drink. I'll put it on the meal ticket. You probably need some coffee for Irish Whiskeys."

And so we began our Niagara Falls experience at 4:15, drinking away the snow. We had a very nice dinner, efficiently served, a choice of, (What else?) salmon, chicken and beef. The weather cleared a bit before we sat down, so I walked down to Terrapin Point to take some pictures for the group. The sign says that 675,000 gallons pass over the falls every second. The crest line is 250 feet and the drop is 167 feet. The flow is by no means uniform throughout any 24-hour period. Large reservoirs fill with water during the night, reducing the river flow, when tourism is not so important. Those reservoirs are emptied during the day to power the identical turbines that are built on both sides of the border and the river runs with its natural ferocity.

In any weather, at any time of the year, Niagara is awesome. To stand at Table Rock on the Canadian side, or Terrapin Point on the American is breathtaking. The sheer power of the river is scary, and worth the visit. I think that the view is incomparably better from the Canadian side, where you can see the full face of both falls. But you don't feel the power of the river as on the American side. The St. Lawrence Seaway conquers the Niagara escarpment on the Canadian side, with the flight locks of the Welland Canal. The Niagara River is really quite short, less than fifty miles, between Lake Erie and Lake Ontario, and only about twenty miles from the falls to Niagara-on-the-Lake, and Lake Ontario. But it is a treacherous cauldron of roiling water for most of its stretch. Both sides of the border have a very nice park system that runs along the river, from the falls to the whirlpool just before Lake Ontario. The region was very important during the American Revolution and particularly during the War of 1812, when the border was contested, and a naval war was fought on the Great Lakes. Just to give the falls full Twain treatment, I found this in *Following the Equator.*

I had to visit Niagara fifteen times before I succeeded in getting my imaginary Falls gauged to the actuality and could begin to sanely and wholesomely wonder at them for what they were, not what I had expected them to be. When I first approached them it was with my face lifted toward the sky, for I thought I was going to see an Atlantic ocean pouring down thence over cloud-vexed Himalayan heights, a sea-green wall of water sixty miles front and six miles high, and so, when the toy reality came suddenly into view—that beruffled little wet apron hanging out to dry—the shock was too much for me, and I fell with a dull thud.

Yet slowly, surely, steadily, in the course of my fifteen visits, the proportions adjusted themselves to the facts, and I came at last to realize that a waterfall a hundred and sixty-five feet high and a quarter of a mile wide was an impressive thing. It was not a dipperful to my vanished great vision, but it would answer.

Following the Equator, pp. 574-577

All in all, our extra day in Buffalo was everything the city could offer. While the weather held, we saw the former wealth of what was once the third wealthiest city in New York State. And for Californians, a little snow is always exciting, and when you throw in sun, rain, sleet, hail, thunder and lightning, it is elevated to the status of an experience. Who could be blamed for hoping for a tiny tornado, or a quick hurricane? Niagara could have been better, but Kieran and her staff at the Top of the Falls made for a very nice evening. And Sandy was a treasure! Tomorrow in Elmira we resume our Mark Twain theme.

V

Friday, the 13^h of October

None of us saw it coming. Friday the 13th should have told us something, but that is a myth, like perpetual snow in Buffalo. Looking at the date now, I just realized that I also missed my daughter Anne's birthday, which is October 13. But that wasn't something to think about when I looked out the window this morning and saw a land blanketed in white and cars covered with snow. Things went downhill from there when I turned on the TV and found that disaster had fallen on the city during the night. This completely unexpected Lake Effect storm had deposited up to three feet of very heavy, wet snow on the Buffalo area, or more precisely on the trees and power lines of the Buffalo area. Varying estimates put the power outages as much at 80 percent, and the governor had already declared an area wide State of Emergency, and worse yet, slapped a complete driving ban on the whole region. No cars moved in the city of Buffalo, and, even more important, no motorcoaches. We are stuck!

I strolled downstairs to breakfast, trying to look as carefree as possible, but was met by a deluge of hopeful expression. We are scheduled to leave at 8:30 for Corning.

"What's the story, Jack? Can we leave on time?"

I've always wondered at the supposed power of the tour manager. People seem to think that there is an undercover source of information that we can plug into that contains the answer to all travel questions. I have always called it the "Great White Hunter Syndrome," having been raised on the safari stories of Frank Buck, who handled any problem that arose in his wild world.

"Jack, the toilet is plugged in the men's john."—that was Gene in Glendive.

"My cell phone doesn't work here. Can you make a call for me?" That was in Wolong, China.

"What restaurant do you recommend?" That was in Bamberg, a town I had never seen before.

I got Betty to clear the john, Vicky Lee to make the phone call, and the bus driver to find a good restaurant in Bamberg that also served their famous *Rauchbier*. Come to think of it, the problems were solved. I'll be damned.

"What are we going to do?"

Now this is a problem of another sort. With a driving ban, we simply can't leave the hotel. There was not a car on the road when I looked out my window. Most of the hotel staff couldn't even get in this morning. Thinking back, we were lucky that the hotel's power hadn't gone out like the rest of the city, and I think I took breakfast for granted.

"We won't be leaving on time," I said in a brief flash of genius. "Bring your bags down to the lobby at 9:00. There are no bellmen, so we'll have to handle our own. I'll load them on the bus and when we get the word, we'll be ready to go."

Our folks settled in without a negative thought, and I went back to my room to try and interpret the news. It seems that 105 miles of the New York Thruway are closed from Rochester to Dunkirk, with no immediate hopes that it will reopen soon. The snow was extremely heavy, perhaps as much as four inches of water content to a foot of snow, about four times the normal. Since the storm is so early, the trees are still full of leaves, and many have fallen over the power lines. The city is paralyzed. Despite this gloomy report, I felt that the Thruway would certainly be opened soon, since it is the major East-West artery for the whole of eastern U.S. From my room on the 9th floor, I could see the freeways that feed the Thruway. Not a vehicle was in sight.

Fred and I loaded the bus at 9:30, and our departure time was moved to 10:30. Bob and Mac set up a Q & A in the room where we had dinner the night we arrived. They would hold forth for most of the morning, Bob bringing out his heavy artillery library and plumbing the depths of Twain profundity. I don't believe that Mac ever ran out of questions. Four of our folks set up a bridge game in the restaurant. A few slept, some in the lecture room, others in an actual bed. Fred and I finally found an emergency phone number for the State Troopers, but we didn't at all like the information. There was no prediction of anything being opened today. Why don't we have lunch here at the hotel?

Around 11:30 I started seeing movement on the freeway. Random 18-wheelers were slowly moving past Buffalo, a few non-police cars mixed in. Just after noon, two Coach USA buses motored past, bound in the very direction we intended to go. That's it! We're out of here. I went and found Fred and told him I wanted to leave at 1:00, right after lunch. Our normal route would have taken us east on the Thruway to Batavia, and then south to Corning, 115 miles, a couple of hours. But the Thruway is closed, so it made more sense to head directly south, try to get onto Highway 219 to Salamanca, and then take I-86 to Corning. I figured if we could get out of Buffalo, it would take about four hours, and we would arrive in Corning right at cocktail time. Fred was a bit dubious, but when I told him about the two buses heading south, he agreed. 1 P.M. it is!

Folks were ready to do something. I figured that if we waited much longer, the day would run out on us, and I really didn't want to be stuck somewhere in the cold after dark. We loaded up, and just as we were about to leave, two Coach USA buses pulled into the Adams Mark. I walked over to talk to one of the drivers.

"Didn't I see you drive by a while ago?"

"Yeah, we're headed for Manhattan. But the state troopers turned us back at the Thruway. We have to spend the night."

We escaped from Buffalo!

I never told Fred about those two motorcoaches. He was nervous enough without me adding to his discomfort. Off we went, sliding a bit when we first hit the street, dodging around a couple of trees that had been split by the snow, and up onto I-33 bound for the New York Thruway. It was heaven for about five miles, almost no traffic on the entire highway, but just enough so we didn't feel completely alone. It is a bit nerve-wracking to be constantly looking as far ahead on the road as possible, fearful that something unpleasant was bound to show up, such a thing as a long line of brake lights. We were nearly at the Thruway when the traffic came to a stop, maybe a quarter mile from the very exit we were looking for. I noticed that a trickle of traffic was exiting up ahead, and my feeling of hope went up quite a bit. Our single line of traffic soon became two lines, as interlopers cut in ahead of us. But in less than ten minutes, in spite of the outrage expressed by folks in the bus, we reached the state troopers and were waved from the freeway. Most of the traffic retreated to Buffalo, but a few turned south on the frontage road. Fred was right with them. We had agreed that we would just keep moving south until there was no more snow, figuring that it wouldn't be more than ten or fifteen miles of slow going.

And that is precisely what happened. Actually, we never had to leave Rt. 240S as we motored in the general direction of Pennsylvania. We did hit two telephone lines, one breaking across the windshield with a loud snap as our bus continued on. "We can have a party line," Mac quipped to the nervous laughter of a few of us. I looked up the side streets, and saw many of them completely blocked with fallen trees. We seem to have hit the one road that plows had been able to clear. We hit Rt. 219 in less than an hour, and we were off to Salamanca, and freedom. The snow had disappeared. It is hard to quantify the degree of relief we had on our bus having put Buffalo behind us. Maybe Mark Twain said it for us:

> "I have come at last to loathe Buffalo so bitterly (always hated it) that yesterday I advertised our dwelling house for sale, & the man that comes forward & pays us what it cost a year ago, ($25,000,) can take it. Of course we won't sell the furniture, at *any* price, nor the horse, carriage or sleigh. I offer the Express for sale also, & the man that will pay me $10,000 less than I gave can take *that*."
> Mark Twain's Letters, Vol. 4, Letter to John Henry Riley, March 3, 1871

Our ride was extremely pleasant, far more scenic than the one I had planned, but also almost twice as long, time-wise. But there was such exhilaration in the coach that the time simply didn't matter. We made a strategic potty stop at a McDonalds in Cuba and drove into the Radisson Hotel in Corning right at 5:00 P.M., just in time to set up a room party. Life just couldn't be finer! True, we missed our visit to the Corning Glass Factory, but we can do that tomorrow. And we missed the first programs at Elmira College, but we can do that tomorrow. Tonight, we can have a drink, and devise ways to make our escape from Buffalo even more tense and exciting than it really was. I am quite certain that most of us will forget most of what we learn on this trip, but the Buffalo Blizzard of '06 will only become clearer with time. It will be elevated into a fine Mark Twain event.

Mac, Bob and I celebrated our escape at the Three Birds Restaurant on the main street of lovely Corning, New York. It is a very fine restaurant, a nice ending for an unusual day. Happy Friday the 13th! I still didn't remember it is my daughter's birthday.

VI

Today I propose to do half of yesterday as well as most of today. Throughout our delay in Buffalo, and several times during our ride south to Corning, I was in contact with Barbara Snedecor, the Director of the Mark Twain Studies Program at Elmira College. Barbara was my very first contact when I started putting this Bear Trek together, and she literally organized our entire stay in Elmira, including the box lunch and dinner at the campus. When I did my dry run last August, Barbara was away on vacation, but her assistant, Nina, took me to all the Twain sites in the town.

During the bus trip yesterday, we rearranged our day on campus. Yesterday's scheduled visits to the Octagonal Office and the Mark Twain Room in the library will start our day today. We will move our dinner from the Barn at Quarry Farm to Hamilton Hall on campus so our folks can visit the museum and gift shop after the meal. Quarry Farm will remain in the same time slot, but we will drive to the Corning Glass Museum after lunch instead of going to Watkins Glen. In poor weather, Watkins Glen would not be comfortable anyway, and that is the only thing we will miss by the time we are through. We'll sandwich the Clemens/Langdon gravesite after the glass museum.

Mark Twain is still very much alive in Elmira. On the way to the college, I spotted the Mark Twain Motor Inn, the Mark Twain State Park and the Mark Twain Golf Course. Barbara was waiting for us at the Octagonal Office and would stay with us throughout the day. Mark Twain didn't actually ever live in Elmira, but his in-laws, the Langdens did, and he and Olivia visited nearly every summer for twenty years. He and Olivia were married in Elmira on February 2, 1870. They began their married life in Buffalo and moved to Hartford in 1871.

It was in Elmira where he did the bulk of his book writing, penning all or parts of *Tom Sawyer, A Tramp Abroad, Connecticut Yankee, Huck*

Finn, Roughing It, Life on the Mississippi, and *Prince and the Pauper.* The Langdons had a large home next to the Park Church that was torn down in 1930. At Quarry Farm, Susan Crane built an octagonal-shaped study for Sam in 1872, and here he spent his most productive years. The social scene in Hartford was hardly conducive to creative writing. That study was given to Elmira College and moved to its present location on campus in 1952.

From the study, we moved across campus to the Gannett-Tripp Library where we were met by Mark Woodhouse, the Mark Twain Archivist for Elmira College. Mark opened the library especially for us today, since the campus is closed for some sort of holiday. He led us to the Mark Twain Room, a very finely furnished study that for our program was filled wall-to-wall with thirty-five chairs of varying descriptions. The room is lined with the collections of the Langdon family, including many volumes from Sam Clemens' library. Many of the books contain marginal comments written by the author. Mark Woodhouse is a personable man, who admitted to being nervous in the face of a group that includes Bob Hirst, but once again I assured him that Bob is not to be feared because he is such a likeable man and has only occasionally been known to bite, never fatally.

Mark laid out a variety of books from the various collections. The first two bookcases in the room contain first editions, many of them quite valuable. The third case holds Mark Twain in translation, a collection that continues to increase as foreign enthusiasts visit the library. The next two cases are filled with books taken from the family libraries at Quarry Farm, many of which are filled with marginalia written by Twain. The last two bookcases contain the collection of Jules Marron. Mark had samples to show from each of these collections. We particularly enjoyed Mark Twain's comments throughout a work called *Pearl Island,* a book he obviously despised.

From the library we moved to the hills and Quarry Farm. When Jervis Langdon passed away, the farm passed to his daughter Susan and her husband Theodore Crane. Susan was a very important person in Sam's life, always supportive, a very good friend. The Octagonal Study is the symbol of that support. Susan called her house, the "Do As You Please House," and life was very comfortable. Here at Quarry Farm, Sam, Livy and the girls spent their summers away from the very different life they lived in Hartford. His last summer in Elmira was in 1903.

"We have spent the last four months up here on top of a breezy hill six hundred feet high, some few miles from Elmira, N.Y., & overlooking that town….This little summer house on the hill-top (named Quarry Farm because there's a quarry on it,) belongs to my wife's sister, Mrs. Crane…. My study is a snug little octagonal den, with a coal-grate, 6 big windows, one little one, & a wide doorway (the latter opening upon the distant town.) On hot days I spread the study wide open, anchor my papers down with brickbats & write in the midst of hurricanes, clothed in the same thin linen we make shirt bosoms of. The study is nearly on the peak of the hill; it is right in front of the little perpendicular wall of rock left where they used to quarry stone. On the peak of the hill is an old arbor roofed with bark & bloodied with red. The study is 30 yards below the old arbor and 100 yards above the dwelling house—it is remote from all noise."
Mark Twain's Letters, Vol. 6, Letter to John Brown, September 4, 1874

Originally Barbara planned to begin our program with a leisurely talk on the front porch, which has a lovely view of the valley below and the Chemung River. But the weather was changing again, and the wind was virtually howling by the time we arrived at the porch. So we struggled through the mandatory group photo and then squeezed into the library inside the house. Here Barbara gave her introduction, beginning with a series of questions, which probably works fine with school groups:

"What was the name of the ship Sam went on?"

"Whom did he meet on that cruise?"

"What happened next?"

"What….?"

"When…?"

The result was predictable: "You all know more than I do!"

Barbara talked about the importance of that front porch in the family life at the farm. She spoke of the "average" day at the farm, which Sam would write in his office, away from the house, from 8 A.M. to 5 P.M. He came down for dinner, and afterwards would read to the family the pages he had written that day, a thing he called "air space." Sometimes it was Livy who did the reading.

> "The children always helped their mother edit my books in manuscript. She would sit on the porch at the farm and read aloud, with her pencil in her hand, and the children would keep an alert and suspicious eye on her right along, for the belief was well grounded in them that whenever she came across a particularly satisfactory passage she would strike it out. Their suspicions were well founded. The passages which were so satisfactory to them always had an element of strength in them which sorely needed modification or expurgation, and was always sure to get it at their mother's hand.
>
> Autobiography of Mark Twain, Vol. 1, p.349

Barb pointed out a desk in a corner of the living room. "It's called the *Roughing It* corner, because that's where Sam wrote before the office was built." She reported that there was great sadness after the death of Jervis

Langdon, but then Sam started writing again. "He would write one page, then two pages, ten pages, until he was up to... Bob?"

"Thirty-five."

There wasn't even a second of hesitation. The answering machine has struck again!

⇢ ⇣

Today we were startled by the strange apparition of Bob Hirst in a coat and tie. True, he had on his jeans and hiking shoes, but from the waist up he was a vision of sartorial splendor. He even combed his hair. He and Barbara are going to lunch with Irene Langdon, the widow of the recently deceased Jervis Langdon III, the great grandson of Livy's and Susan's father. Bob is curious to know if the Langdons still have more Mark Twain writings—letters, unfinished essays, maybe a book manuscript or two. Surely enough curiosity to warrant a necktie.

There is a generation jump between the three Jervis Langdons. Jervis II was the son of Charlie Langdon. When Susan Crane died, Jervis II inherited the house, expanding it in size, adding the library where Barbara welcomed the group today. He died in 1952 and his widow lived in the house until 1972. Ten years later the house was donated to Elmira College by Jervis III, including six acres of the original 200. The donation bears the restriction that the house never be open to the public, and that it be used as a center for the study of Mark Twain.

Bob and Barbara departed for their luncheon engagement, while we wandered over to the barn for our own lunch, the weather being a bit too blustery for our intended picnic. In the barn, Gretchen Sharlow gave a very fine slide show presentation on "Elmira, Quarry Farm and Mark Twain." She is a bubbly, very well-informed volunteer for the Mark Twain Studies Program. Early on, she started relating a story of the runaway carriage, which we had already heard several times.

"We know that story already," Mac stopped her.

"Tell us again and we'll break your arm," I added.

Gretchen took those comments in good humor, not realizing the seriousness of the situation she had just escaped, and went on to tell us a lot of things we hadn't yet heard, maintaining a lively discussion until I gave her the sign that we had to start thinking about Corning Glass.

She had nice photos of the Park Church, where the Reverend Thomas Beecher held forth. It was quite distinctive, built like an auditorium and without the normal furnishings and artwork of a church. It sits on a holy intersection, with the First Baptist (1829) and Trinity Episcopal (1833) on other corners. The Langdon house occupied the fourth corner. It was torn down in 1930, voted out by the Depression-strapped citizens who didn't want to fund the place, which had largely been deserted by the family. Ironically it now boasts the Langdon Plaza, a strip mall that would certainly have amused Sam Clemens. I can picture his essay vividly, laughing at the imagination of the modern world. The estate once occupied a huge block of land, perfect for a largely under-patronized flock of stores.

Several folks wanted to see the place where the Octagonal Study originally sat. Nick Bontorno, a friendly young grad student who lives on the farm, tends the gardens and maintains security, led them up the hill to the knoll where the study sat before being moved to the present college site. Today it is a level opening hacked out of rampant underbrush, undoubtedly defended by mowers from the luxuriant greenery that has enveloped the farm. Only a few foundation stones, a circle of them, give a hint of the famous building they once supported. The steps that Twain used climbing up to his office are still there, crumbling and overgrown. But the calming spirit of the place, the silence of a woodsy knoll remains. I had a fleeting thought to give everyone a pen and pad to see what they might create. But I once did that with a teacher group, providing paper and crayons at Frederick Church's estate, Olana, on the Hudson, with dreadful results. Teachers can't sketch!

"Susie Crane has built the loveliest study for me, you ever saw. It is octagonal, with a peaked roof, each octagon filled with a spacious window, and it sits perched in complete isolation of top of an elevation that commands leagues of valley & city & retreating ranges of distant blue hills. It is a cozy nest, with just room in it for a sofa & a table & three or four chairs—& when the storms sweep down the remote valley & the lightning flashes above the hills beyond, & the rain beats on the roof over my head, imagine the luxury of it! It stands 500 feet above the valley & 2 ½ miles from it."

Mark Twain's Letters, Vol. 6, Letter to Joseph Twichell, June 11, 1874

We bade farewell to Gretchen and Nick and motored back across town to Horseheads, and then on to Corning and its famous Glass Museum. It sits just off the interstate, a mile or so from the town center and our hotel.

135

The highlight of the collection is a rambling series of rooms that covers the entire history of glass making, from Egyptian times to the present. For serious collectors of American glass, there is the Jerome and Lucille Strauss Study Gallery.

I particularly enjoyed the display of Paperweights of the World. The Corning Glass Factory was founded in 1868 by the Brooklyn Flint and Glass Co. By 1905 it employed more than 2,500 skilled glass blowers, cutters and engravers. The present museum is not connected in any way to the Glass Company.

We returned to Elmira late in the afternoon. I had agreed to meet Barbara and Bob at the Woodlawn Cemetery. We all laughed at the road sign on Walnut St. just before the cemetery, which advised the visitor, "Dead End." There was another on the actual gate of Woodlawn. Inside, little signs lead you to the grave, which is placed in the Langdon family plot, marked by an obelisk bearing the family name. At the end of the plot is another pillar, two fathoms high, a symbol for Clemens' more famous pen name. Erected by his daughter, it also bears the name Gabrilówitsch, Clara's husband Ossip, and the inscription:

> "Death is the starlit strip
> Between the companionship
> Of yesterday and Reunion
> Of Tomorrow.
> In loving memory of my father and my husband — CCG"

Around the two monuments are spread the headstones of the family.

Olivia Susan Clemens (d. March 19, 1872)
Jean Lampton Clemens (d. Dec. 24, 1909)
    "Her desolate father sets this stone."
Another stone says simply, "Clemens son, 1870—1872"
Samuel Langhorne Clemens
Nov. 30, 1835—April 21, 1910.

Olivia Langdon's stone is marked

"Elmira, Nov. 27, 1845
Florence, Italy, June 5, 1904"
Gott sei dir gnadig, O meine Wonne.
"Warm summer sun
Shine kindly here
Warm Southern wind
Blow softly here
Green sod above
Lie light, lie light
Good night, dear heart
Good night, good night"
     ***Robert Richardson

There are lots of Langdons and Cranes, including Jervis I., Aug. 6, 1870 and Jervis III., 1905 - Feb 6, 2004.

It was a last-minute decision to move our dinner from the barn at Quarry Farm to Hamilton Hall. It was a masterstroke on Barbara's part, because instead of a drafty open area, we entered a festive refectory, beautifully decorated, and warm! It was also a way that we could let our folks visit the Mark Twain Welcome Center that occupies rooms in front of the hall. They have a nice 10-minute film, "The Legacy of Mark Twain and Elmira College," on the college and the Langdon's relationship to it. Jervis Langdon Sr. was part of the committee to design and lay out Elmira Female College in 1854, and he served on its first Board of Trustees. Olivia graduated in the class of 1864, having completed the six-year Bachelor of Arts program.

Several couples from Elmira College joined us in a fun evening, opened with a reception of New York State wines. Mike Kiskis is the resident Mark Twain scholar at Elmira. I asked Mac if it would be proper to invite him and Bob for a question session after dinner, a suggestion that was immediately adopted. It proved to be very interesting, getting two viewpoints on each question.

Mac: "Would Mark Twain have been the same author if he hadn't been married to Livy?"

Mike: No, Livy and her family changed his social view of life. His daughters softened him.

Bob: The answer is obvious in a certain sense. But we don't know what he would have done with someone else. His western writing before marriage and children, "are the best writing he ever did." His family and friends constantly moderated him.

Mac: "Did Mark Twain actually swear? What were the words he used?"

Bob: People said he was very colorful, a masterpiece of "invention and volcanic power." Assume that his swearing generally invoked the gods and hell and damnation.

Mike: "We wouldn't understand his curses, because they would be so complicated."

Mac: "What is the funniest thing he wrote?"

I neglected to write down the responses, but I remember Bob saying early in the trip that in his opinion it was his story about the blue jay.

Mac: "His grief increased as his life went on and his humor decreases. Is there a cause and effect here?"

Bob: There is some causal relation, but he could still be funny in old age.

Mike: His major work declines in later years, but other materials, smaller things, are still good. "I never subscribed to the theory that grief shut him down…. I think he was dark all the way through his career."

We missed Watkins Glen and its mighty gorge with eighty waterfalls, but I think we got a good tradeoff with a Buffalo blizzard and an exciting escape. I am so thrilled with the incredible hospitality shown to us by the folks at Elmira College—Barbara, Gretchen, Mark, Mike, Nick. They treated us as though we were visiting royalty, adjusted their entire weekend to our needs, and opened their centers to us on a weekend of a holiday week. We can't thank them enough.

VII

Today we cross New York on the Southern Tier Parkway, passing through some lovely farmland on our way to Cooperstown. Near the town of Sayre, the road dips ever so briefly into Pennsylvania, without so much as a sign from that state. All you see is a sign that says, "New York Border." At Mile 209 we crossed the Susquehanna River, a familiar name if only because it is so poetic. We have some melodious river names in America, and I doubt that one in 10,000 could place them on a map—Rappahannock, Allegheny, Housatonic, Shenandoah, Monongahela, Penobscot, Conshohocken, Pequannock, Kennebec. It would make a great trivia game, not to mention a spelling contest.

I also like all the O-towns in New York, which is another considerable collection: Otsego, Otego, Oneonta, Oswego, Onandago, Onchiota, Oneida, Otisco, Owego, Owasc, Otselic, Ontario, Ottawa and Otto. Has any state ever done more for the letter "O"?

Just past Pennsylvania we saw the Tioga Downs Racetrack, prompting Mac to wonder if there was a relationship with Tioga Pass in Yosemite. Recently I received the following email from Mac:

"You probably noticed we went through Tioga County, N.Y., and I wondered about the connection with Tioga Pass. Here it is. Several counties and rivers in New York and Pennsylvania have the name, which is derived from a Mohawk word. The name came to California via the Tioga Consolidated Mine in Bodie established in 1878. In 1880 there was another Tioga Mine near Mount Dana. The Tioga Pass Rd was started in 1882-83 and abandoned in 1884 due to lack of money. A private subscription campaign bought the road in 1915 and donated it to the government. Now that you have this bit or trivia, the rest of your day should be a breeze."

One can't but be impressed at the inquisitive nature of the university professor!

On the bus, Mac played a CD entitled, "Mark Twain and Music," narrated by Bob Hirst. It wasn't as good as the Grateful Dead or the Stones, which Mac would undoubtedly have preferred, but it was passable music, perfectly timed for our coffee stop at McD in Sydney.

It took about three hours to get to Cooperstown, which really should be famous as the home of James Fenimore Cooper. The town was founded by his father, William Cooper, in 1786. He became the first judge of Otsego County and later a Congressman for the region. He moved his family, to the area four years later. His sixth son, James, was born in 1789. The future writer studied at Yale and spent some time at sea before settling the Fenimore Farm, now the site of the museum that bears his name. Such history should be enough to insure the fame of the village. Instead it is almost universally known as the home of the Baseball Hall of Fame.

Outwardly it is a perfectly beautiful New England style town, with lovely tree-lined streets, a majestic Lake Otesaga (One of the Finger Lakes? Certainly one of the O-words), dense surrounding forest, fine history. But once you arrive you are immediately struck by a baseball bat. The main street is lined with bat shops, souvenir shops, T-shirt shops, and quite a few small restaurants. The Hall of Fame itself sits in the center of this mercantile flotsam, a rather stately looking building in front of Abner Doubleday Stadium.

The Hall of Fame is worth visiting. The Hall of Honor has the *bas relief* busts of all the inductees, beginning with the first class of 1936: Babe Ruth, Ty Cobb, Christy Mathewson, Walter Johnson, Honus Wagner.

This year the first woman was inducted, Effa Manley, owner and manager of the Brooklyn Eagles (1935) and Newark Eagles (1936-48) of the Negro League.

"Baseball is the only game you can see on the radio." — Phil Hersh, *Chicago Tribune*

In the Grandstand Theater there is a very fine film, thirteen-minutes long, of the thrills and meaning of the game. Don't miss the catch where the outfielder stands on top of the fence to make the catch. John Fogarty's song, "Centerfield" makes the film come to life.

The street is filled with memorabilia shops. I stopped at Cooperstown Bats to get a personalized one for my grandson, Josh. With a name like Josh he has to be a baseball player. I love some of the T-shirts:

Cubs—"Any team can have a bad century.."

Red Sox—"1 out of 86 is nothing to brag about."

Yankees—"I only root for two teams, the Yankees and any team who beats the Red Sox."

Six of us decided to spend our time at the Fenimore Museum, a stately place about a mile north of town on the lake, which he dubbed "Glimmerglass." It occupies the land that once was the author's farm and house. There is genuine style to the place, with a definite New England feel, and several very impressive collections. The first exhibit is entitled, "The Transforming Power of Masks," which was heavy into the masks of the Pacific Northwest. I particularly liked an Eskimo mask called *Nepcetat*, a ponderous thing that the shaman laid face down on the ground, wedged his face into it, and lifted it without using his hands. When his strength ebbed in later years and he couldn't raise the mask, he was out of a job. I also noted a Salish mask called, *S'xwaixway*, only because it is one of the oddest spelled words I have seen.

The highlight of the Fenimore Museum is their American Indian collection, with exquisite articles from each of the major "Culture Areas": Northeast and Southeast Woodlands, Plains & Prairie, Plateau, Southwest, Great Basin, California, Northwest Coast, Western Subarctic and Arctic. The Teton Sioux items including a war record hide, and a Buffalo robe were impressive. There was a first-rate basket collection from tribes in California.

I smiled inwardly when I looked at this very fine collection, thinking of several writings of Mark Twain which portrayed the American Indians in a very poor light, but also a blistering pair of essays on James Fenimore Cooper, entitled "Fenimore Cooper's Literary Offenses," and "Fenimore Cooper's Further Literary Offenses."

Lastly there was a temporary exhibit of Grandma Moses, the remarkable Anna Mary Robertson (1860-1961), who became "Grandmother to the Nation."

"Paintin's not important. The important thing is keepin' busy."

There are thirty-eight of her very recognizable works in the exhibit. If we had a little more time in the Berkshires, we could go to the Bennington Museum, which contains her old school house and at least as many paintings.

Bob was asked to report on his luncheon with Irene Langdon. He said that they are all still looking for the manuscript of *Innocents Abroad*. He has hopes of finding it someday, saying that Irene told him, "there are a couple of rooms filled with stuff that we haven't gone through yet." I am amazed that such a thing is possible. How could that woman in Hollywood possibly have an old trunk in the attic that she didn't even open? And how on earth can there be a room anywhere in the world that Mark Twain touched that hasn't been "gone through?" Are there no antiquarians left in the world?

k k

"Can anyone tell us about Herman Melville?"

Of course we asked Bob, who replied, "I don't know much," and then proceeded to talk for half an hour on nearly every facet of the author's life. The subject naturally got around to Mark Twain's place in the pantheon of American writers. Among nineteenth century writers, Bob would place Twain in the top five, along with Hawthorne, Thoreau, Emerson and Melville.

"My early corruption at Harvard makes me put Emerson and Thoreau high on my list." The discussion spread to other centuries, adding Hemingway, Joyce, Steinbeck, Faulkner, et al, with Mark Twain retaining his position in the top echelon.

We left Cooperstown, driving north on Rt. 80 East. Don't ever try to figure out directions in this part of the world. You just have to pick a route number and follow it wherever it leads. You never give directional instructions, but rather a string of numbers: "80W to 20E to I-81N to 2E to 7S." That will get you from Cooperstown, New York to Hancock, Massachusetts, the exact sequence of numbers we are doing this afternoon. I will never grow tired of New England roads. Almost any road takes you through a string of picture postcard towns, each lined with elegant old mansions set back from the road by wide lawns and sidewalks. There is the inevitable Congregational Church and burial ground, and small farms that are defined by stone walls. Lawns lope over the hills unfettered by fences, separating houses only by the style and timing of the mower cuts. The roads defy direction. Suddenly you are driving into the afternoon sun on a road labeled "north" or, less likely "west." The only consolation if you feel lost is that eventually your road is going to run into another number and let you re-identify yourself on the map. You may well be lost, but you can always get home.

We arrived in Hancock in late afternoon, turning off Route 7, which runs down the spine of the Berkshire Mountains, and up to Jiminy Peak and the lodge of that name. We are between seasons for the lodge, summer tourism and leaf-peeping being just about finished and the ski season not yet started. Of all our hotels, this is the one I was most worried about, because when I was here last August, they were very disorganized and almost unresponsive. But we were quickly directed to our rooms, which are all very attractive suites, and the baggage was handled efficiently. Mac and I restocked at the hotel's grocery store, and in nothing we were hosting another room party with everyone quite pleased with the hotel. The dinner was served upstairs in the John Harvard Pub, was beautifully handled and tasty. The whole Jiminy Peak experience was extremely positive. I even saw the red crest of a Ruby-crowned kinglet in the woods outside. It goes to show you how effective a lot of worry can be.

Tonight I learned that the Buffalo Blizzard of '06 had struck us twice. We have another Cal Alumni group going through the Erie Canal. At least they were attempting to transit that waterway, but it seems the snow melt from Buffalo had so raised the level of the Canal that the Grande Caribe boat we had chartered couldn't get under the low bridges. Eighty or so Golden Bears are stuck in Rome, New York for two days now, and the prospects are that the water level would stay high for at least a week. I decided that the only sane thing to do would be to finish the cruise on land and ordered two buses from Boston to drive to the stranded boat and free our people. We put together a three-night tour to get them from Rome to Boston and their flight home. If there is a common theme throughout New York and New England it is the weather. We just experienced a late summer blizzard in Buffalo that resulted in a flood in upstate New York.

"Gentlemen: I reverently believe that the Maker who made us all, makes everything in New England—but the weather. I don't know who makes that, but I think it must be raw apprentices in the Weather Clerk's factory.... There is a sumptuous variety about the New England Weather that compels the stranger's admiration—and regret. The weather is always doing something there; always attending strictly to business; always getting up new designs and trying them on the people to see how they will go. But it gets through more business in spring than in any other season. In the spring, I have counted one hundred and thirty-six different kinds of weather inside of four and twenty hours.

"The Oldest Inhabitant—The Weather of New England," *Mark Twain Collected Tales, Sketches, Speeches & Essays 1852-1890*, p. 673.

Having lived in Massachusetts for ten ears I saw snow in mid-May and Nor'easters in late fall. One day in early fall I had a meeting in Boston at the Museum of Fine Arts. Because the weather was so good, we had our meeting in the garden. Halfway through, the skies darkened, and it began to sprinkle. The mist turned to rain, and then sleet. Within an hour the sleet had turned to snow and the garden was white. The sun was back out before I left the museum that day. Of course, Mark Twain gets the credit for the old saw, "If you don't like the weather in New England, wait a few minutes." It's one of those Twain sayings he never said but it sounds so much like him. He did, however, have a few thoughts on the matter.

VIII

We have the morning to explore the Berkshires, one of New England's most popular regions. This time of year it is a place of autumn beauty, with the changing leaves, pumpkin lots, front door decorations and imaginative scarecrows. In winter it becomes a ski destination, though not nearly on a par with our western slopes. But it is in summer that the Berkshires come alive, alive with music, dance and theater. Of course the most famous venue is Tanglewood, an outdoor concert arena that is home to the Boston Symphony Orchestra, taking a vacation from the city while the Boston Pops occupies symphony hall. There are dozens of other theaters and concert halls from Great Barrington to Williamstown, each with their respective devotees. I made a list of the various music, dance and drama stages and it is indeed impressive, even though it is far from complete.

1. The Aston Magna Festival
   17th,18th and 19th century music on period instruments.
2. Close Encounters with Music
   Internationally renowned chamber music
3. Berkshire Opera Company
4. Williamstown Jazz Festival
5. Tannery Pond Concerts
   More chamber music
6. Music Works in the Berkshires
7. Williamstown Chamber Concerts
8. Mahaiwe Performing Arts Center
9. The Colonial Theater
10. Berkshire Theater Festival
11. Barrington Stage Company
12. Mac-Haydn Theater
13. Berkshire Choral Festival

14. Jacob's Pillow Dance Festival
15. Williamstown Theater Festival
16. Shakespeare & Company
17. South Mountain Concerts
18. The Theater Barn
19. Lichtenstein Center for the Arts
20. Williams College Department of Music
21. Richmond Performance Series
22. Sevenars Concerts
23. Robert Boland Theater
24. The News in Review
25. The Miniature Theater of Chester

Those stages are all dark in October, so our interests are directed elsewhere. There is so much more to enjoy in the Berkshires. Here too are people stories, varied ones of writers and poets, dreamers and artists, music, sculpture, novels, paint and verse. In these old, dignified hills, transient residents are inspired to create, and many of our most prized artists were drawn. Melville, Hawthorne, Robert Frost, Edith Wharton, Emerson, Norman Rockwell and Daniel Chester French all came to the Berkshires and drew inspiration from them.

Perhaps none are so unexpected as Herman Melville. Here, "Looking out of my porthole," his upstairs bedroom window at Arrowhead, he spotted "the leviathan" in Mt. Graylock—Moby Dick in the middle of the land.

Melville did not live a happy life. His early books, like *Omoo* and *Typee*, based on his days at sea, were very well received and made him a reasonably wealthy man. But his masterpiece was unmercifully attacked by critics and as each new creation appeared that criticism increased. His fortune dissipated, he was forced to give up Arrowhead, which he sold to his brother Allan. He moved to New York where he took a job as a customs inspector. He died in complete obscurity in 1892, aged 71, so little regarded that the New York Times misspelled his name in the obituary. Even in the best of times, bipolar and schizophrenic, he suffered extended dark moods, exacerbated by misuse of patent medicines and alcohol.

We were met at Arrowhead by Louise McHugh, Director of the Berkshire Historical Society, administrators of the site. She divided our group and directed us on a tour of the author's home and life. Docents met us in several different spots in the house, the most enjoyable of whom was Bill Mund, who conducted his tour with a wonderfully iconoclastic attitude, voiced in the finest of Boston accents.

"Melville called this a 'piazza'. It looks remarkably like a porch to me."

"He spent too much for the property, $6,600. His father-in-law held the mortgage."

"That's a melodeon. It didn't have anything to do with Melville, but that's a nice place to put it."

"Longfellow used to trot through here."

"These two paintings had nothing to do with Melville. I like them because if you had money, they would put your face on this body. The more you had the more body you got."

"The couch was gone, so they went right out to Sears and got one."

Over the years, I have endured a great many house tours. Often the docents are close to unbearable, as were some of these at Arrowhead. But when you find one like Bill Mund who brings a certain common sense and humor to the job, you have to notice him. Actually, Bill knew a great deal about the writer and his times, but he just didn't take himself too seriously.

Here, in a dwelling that was only half the present size, Melville lived with his wife Lizzie, four children, and four sisters. He was the third of eight children, quitting school at age twelve, ending his formal education. He first visited the Berkshires in August, 1850, when he was introduced to the literati of his day, most importantly, Nathaniel Hawthorne, with whom he developed a life-long friendship. Melville says that when he walked into the house, he fell in love with the ancient fireplace, inspiring a lengthy essay entitled "I and My Chimney."

> "I and my chimney, two grey-headed old smokers, reside in the country. We are, I may say, old settlers here; particularly my old chimney, which settles more and more every day."
> www.onlineliterature.com

The family life was centered in the "Best Parlor," with command performances dominated by Herman on nights when he wasn't shut up in his room. Here they read bible passages, followed by lengthy discourses, and discussions of current events.

One interesting item in the room was a porcelain statue of Benjamin Franklin labeled "George Washington." Intended for foreign sale, manufacturers gave all their different statues that same famous name because it was the only one recognized across the oceans.

In 1850, Melville "had *the book* in his head." Most of it was written in his upstairs room, thoroughly read and discussed with Hawthorne who enthusiastically approved it. But when *Moby Dick* was published, he refused to let his friend write the review, and it was universally panned. Before leaving Arrowhead, he burned his remaining unpublished manuscripts, except for one autobiographical work that was published by Lizzy posthumously. *Billy Budd* was immediately acclaimed.

From Arrowhead, we took a quick look at the Hancock Shaker Village. This impressive historical place was once the largest of the Shaker settlements, that curious Quaker offshoot (first called the Shaking Quakers) founded by Mother Ann Lee in England and transplanted to America just before the American Revolution, in 1774. At its height, Hancock Village in 1829 numbered 247 members, almost evenly divided by gender, the men and women separated in housing, chores and church. Their name derives from their peculiar dance. Today they are most famous for their crafts, which set the standards for simplicity and functionality in furniture, tools, baskets, containers and small artifacts such as wooden hooks, racks and pegs. Originals of any of these command extremely high prices, but reproductions are marketed in Shaker shops throughout the country. Today only a couple of church members still survive at a small home in Maine. At its height, there were six "families" at Hancock—Church, Second (for overflow from Church), North, South, East and West. The community was governed by two men (Elders) and two women (Eldresses.) The Shakers were very industrious, and always alert for new ideas and gadgets, their most famous being the modern broom, which they sold at fairs and with traveling salesmen throughout the region. They quickly adopted steam power, greatly increasing their production. The distinguishing feature of the village was, and still is, a phenomenal round stone barn, which must have stunned the whole of the east when it was first constructed.

Our visit to Arrowhead took longer than I planned, so I decided to stop in Stockbridge for lunch before we go to the Norman Rockwell Museum. There aren't many restaurants in the famous village with the Red Lion Inn, so it is best to get there a bit before noon. The Red Lion itself, one of the cornerstones of the classic New England inns, doesn't open for lunch until 12:00 sharp, and after that the crowds start to form. The village-scape of Stockbridge featuring the Red Lion is one of Norman Rockwell's most famous paintings. His original studio and museum are just a few doors down the street.

Bob, Mac and I sneaked in the back door of the Red Lion to the Widow Bingham's Tavern, a place I discovered years ago. It is a nice warm place and you can always get a fast sandwich at the bar. Mac did a quick inventory.

"I would say you sell more vodka than anything," he observed to the bartender, noticing an entire row of vodka bottles. It is a modern phenomenon among the younger set. I remember when all you needed to know was Smirnoff. Then some guy brought in a bottle of "Stoli", Stolichnaya, and the vodka call craze was on. Now you need a notepad to order your vodka: Gray Goose, Kettle One, Absolut, Finlandia, Chopin, Cristall, Belvedere. Not only do you need one of these yuppie names, you need to have a flavor—lemon, orange, vanilla. Zygo is vodka laced with caffeine. Blavod is black vodka, a concept that ought to be banned. Maybe that's how they came up with a "Black Russian." Heaven help you if you just ask for "vodka."

"I serve fifteen vodka martinis to one with gin," our bartender told Mac, who nearly exploded with indignation.

"A martini is made with gin! There's no such thing as a vodka martini."

Just then two women, middle aged, draped with bling and looking a bit too young for their present station, sat down at the bar next to Mac.

"I'll have a Beefeater martini," one ordered with a very certain voice. Mac immediately was impressed with this woman who obviously was well educated, at least in barroom lore, and congratulated her on knowing that a martini demanded gin.

"Would you like to see my fuzzy navel?" the woman next to Mac asked in a very pleasant voice.

Mac was now completely hooked into the conversation, and I could hear his research voice appear. "What's a fuzzy navel?" he asked, already formulating the data for his next motorcoach editorial.

"It's peach schnaps and orange juice."

"I usually have a hairy navel," Ms Beefeaters joined in. "That gives you a much better result." Before Mac could inquire as to the nature of her hairy navel, she added, "It's a fuzzy navel with vodka."

I wanted in the worst way to ask her if she poured Absolut or Stoli on her navel, but Mac was so thoroughly engaged in conversing that I just shut up and took notes. Bob just sat there and smiled. I wonder what Mark Twain would say about a woman with a fuzzy navel.

We adjourned to Main Street to sit in rockers on the front porch of the Red Lion and watch the world go by. The Mass Pike empties right into the town, creating a steady stream of traffic that destroys the ambience of this otherwise lovely place. Lunch finished, we boarded the bus for the Norman Rockwell Museum, just a couple of miles from the village.

Is there any American artist who extracts emotions quite like Norman Rockwell? Anyone over sixty remembers the wonderful vignettes of his *Saturday Evening Post* covers, each telling in comic detail a precise moment in time—sitting at the principal's office, waiting for the doctor, running away from home. Can you remember the umpires deciding on a rainout? Or dad telling you the facts of life? Norman Rockwell filled our lives with loving memories, touched the precise chord of nostalgia, defined perfectly his common American who lives just down the street.

His memories aren't always happy ones. Can anyone forget that tiny black girl following Federal Marshals into school integration? Or the poignant war scenes of the 1940's? In the core of his humor is a serious look at our strengths and our failings. The finest room in the museum is the central hall displaying his "Four Freedoms":

Freedom from Want
Freedom from Fear
Freedom to Worship
Freedom of Speech

In your mind's eye, can't you see that gigantic Thanksgiving turkey; hear that roughshod man standing proudly to voice his opinion in town meeting; picture wartime parents tucking their child into a warm bed? If there is a tear in your body, you will shed it somewhere with Norman Rockwell.

Twenty years ago, visitors jammed into the Rockwell studio in West Stockbridge, a tiny room guaranteed to frustrate everyone. Now there is a world-class center out of town, 120 acres of flowing natural terrain. The artist's red barn-studio was moved there in 1986. The gift shop is larger than the entire center was in town. Downstairs is a gallery with every one of Rockwell's 300+ *Post* covers.

❧ ❦

On the way to Hartford, we discovered that Jeane is coming home. She was raised in Windsor and went to school at Mt. Holyoke. She took the mike to tell us about picking tobacco as a child, as well as a bunch of other stories of growing up in Tobacco Valley. Today the region is still a producer of cigar wrapper tobacco, but the school kids are no longer recruited to do the picking and stringing. Jeane is in for a shock when we get to Hartford and she gets a look at how the inner city has changed, for the good.

By 3:00 we were on the Mass Pike, heading for Springfield and eventually Hartford, Connecticut, the last of the Mark Twain home sites we will visit. We settled in for three nights at the stately Goodwin Hotel, on Asylum Street in downtown Hartford. Originally built as an upscale apartment house, the Goodwin went into a state of deep decline, until converted into a hotel in recent years. The whole inner city of Hartford has been reborn in the last decade, fine restaurants and shops encircling the convention center. Many of the historic buildings are there as well, including the Old State House, designed by Charles Bullfinch, the imposing State Capitol and the Christopher Wren style church that dates back to the founding of the city by Thomas Hooker in 1635.

Dinner tonight is at Joe Black's, a fine restaurant newly opened last month, a restaurant that is filled with class, a beautiful grouping of rooms that exude the atmosphere of a string of Irish pubs. Irish it is, the proprietor being one Michael McEveney himself. In rainy weather, we pretty much had the place to ourselves. This was one of the better parlays of beef, chicken or salmon that we have encountered thus far on the trip. We are becoming experts.

IX

Mark Twain on Hartford, years before he built his house there:

> Hartford
>
> I have been about ten days in Hartford, and shall return there before very long. I think it must be the handsomest city in the Union, in summer. It is the moneyed center of the State; and one of its capitals, also, for Connecticut is so law-abiding, and so addicted to law, that there is not room enough in one city to manufacture all of the articles they need. Hartford is the place where the insurance companies all live. They use some of the houses for dwellings. The others are for insurance offices. So it is easy to see that there is quite a spirit of speculative enterprise there. Many of the inhabitants have retired from business, but the others labor along in the old customary way, as presidents of insurance companies. It is said that a citizen went west from there once, to be gone a week. He was gone three. A friend said:
>
> "What kept you so long? You must have enjoyed yourself."
>
> "Yes, I did enjoy myself, and that delayed me some but that was not the worst of it. The people heard there was a Hartford man aboard the train, and so they stopped me at every station trying to get me to be president of an insurance company!"
>
> But I suppose it was a lie.
>
> The *Chicago Republican*, August 23, 1868. Quoted in www.twainquotes.com

Today we visit the Mark Twain House, the one home of the author that still exists, essentially as he knew it. I have tried repeatedly to get the folks who run the home and visitor center to put together a special program for our group, but in the end I gave up, settling for a standard house tour and the concession that we could use the auditorium at the visitor center. In the past couple of years, the Mark Twain House has constructed a magnificent center to go with the house, a construction that has nearly put them under financially. It features a theater that plays a reduced Ken Burns' film on the author, an auditorium that is equipped with the latest in AV systems, a fine museum on Twain, and upstairs a second museum area that presently offers a display of Tiffany and the Gilded Age. There is also a large, well-stocked gift shop and a café that never appears to be open. The only things that seem to be missing in the place are visitors. Rebecca Floyd met us in the lobby of the center with a big smile and a warm welcome. She quickly sent us off in two groups to tour the home and took me around to the auditorium to show me where we would be meeting after the tour.

A series of Twain sayings are etched into the walls of the new center.

** "A man cannot be comfortable without his own approval."
** "Do your duty today and repent tomorrow."
** "Always do right. This will gratify some and astonish the rest."
** "There is nothing in the world like persuasive speech to fuddle the mental apparatus."
** "If you tell the truth, you won't have to remember anything."
** "Always respect your superiors, if you have any."
** "Near his fateful Compositor he advises, "My axiom is—to Succeed in business, avoid my example."
** On his speaking tour: "Mrs. Clemens and Clara and I started on the 15th of July, 1895. We lectured and robbed and raided for thirteen months. I wrote a book and published it."
** "Do good and you will be lonesome."

I wonder what Sam would say about his brand new, mostly empty visitor center? I also wonder if he would object to being encapsulated in a long string of one-liners. The new center is a sort of albatross right now, dragging down the Mark Twain Foundation. The house by itself didn't draw many visitors, because Hartford is more a business destination than a mecca for tourism, and the Twain house is hard-pressed to support itself alone from entrance fees. Now they also have a major visitor center to worry about. There was an article in the Hartford newspaper this morning reporting that many of the financial problems had been overcome, but from the flow of visitors we saw during two days at the house, it is difficult to believe.

His house is a wonder, built in 1873-74 by Edward Tuckerman Potter, a distinctive example of Victorian-American "Stick Style," high gabled, red-bricked, with an expansive "umbra" or porch. The architect labeled it "High Victorian Gothic." The exterior brick bears geometric designs, achieved by painting in red and black patterns. Inside, the house is dark by our standards, and probably was even darker in the gas light days. The walls and ceilings display a maze of linear designs in moldings, with intricate stenciling throughout the entry, mostly done by Tiffany Associates. The home is remarkably modern in many ways because the author was much in tune with any technological developments in his day. As a result, there is central heat, an alarm system and two phone lines, where he could push a button to contact a "hello girl." In the visitor center is the only remaining example of the Paige Compositor, that automated typesetting machine that drained Samuel Clemens of his fortune, only to be superseded by the Linotype Machines. In his Autobiography, Sam describes the machine:

> "Here was a machine that was really setting type; and doing it with a swiftness and accuracy, too. Moreover, it was distributing its case *at the same time.* The distribution was automatic: the machine fed itself from a galley of dead matter, and without human help or suggestion; for it began its work of its own accord when the type channels needed filling, and stopped of its own accord when they were full enough. The machine was almost a complete compositor; it lacked but one feature—it did not 'justify' the lines; this was done by the operator's assistant.
>
> I saw the operator set at the rate of 3,000 ems an hour, which, counting distribution, was but little short of four case-men's work."
> *Autobiography of Mark Twain,* Vol. 1, p. 101

The family lived here for seventeen years before hard financial times forced them to Europe to resume Sam's lecture career. The house was sold out of the family in 1903. Subsequently it served as a boy's school, a library and an apartment house. In 1929, the Mark Twain Memorial Trust purchased the house and property.

Twain loved this Hartford home which reflects his personality in many ways, from the witty days to the dark. Above a fireplace is an Emerson inscription: "The ornament of a house is the friends who frequent it." There was a steady stream of friends and relatives in a busy parlor and library. Downstairs is the Mahogany Room, dubbed by Twain "the Royal Chambers." Stairs rise to the bedrooms above, where the author's famous Angel bed resides. He slept in the bed backwards, facing the headboard, because "for what I paid, I want to see more of it." His office was on the third floor around a billiard table, where he could let down his hair and his language without the disapproving looks of Livy. "If I cannot swear in heaven, I shall not stay." On one occasion, when his language was particularly blue, he didn't realize that Livy was in the room. To his great shock, without expression she repeated everything he had said, with the comment, "And that's what it sounds like."

When his beloved butler George Griffin would announce an unwanted visitor, Sam would leave the room for the balcony and tell him to say that Mr. Twain had "stepped out."

෫෫ ෫෫

In 1891 the Clemens family left for Europe. He declared bankruptcy in 1895, but within about five years had repaid all his debtors. To their great sorrow, daughter Susie fell ill with spinal meningitis that year, and died in their old house before they could reach her. Sam never recovered from her loss. Jean died of an epileptic seizure in December 1909, followed in April, 1910 at Stormfield in Connecticut by her father.

The house tour finished, we adjourned to the auditorium for another Mac and Bob question session.

Q: "How does Mark Twain rank with other literary figures?"

A: "You can hardly find a twentieth century writer who does not recognize Mark Twain as the father of the literature they want to write."

This is a subject we already covered somewhat in the bus. Bob mentioned here that a major difference between Mark Twain and other very popular writers, such as Hemingway or Faulkner is that Twain is also an industry, his characters inspiring everything from comic books to dolls to Disney. I would add that he is also far more recognizable today than any other writer in our history.

The subject came up of U.S. Grant's memoirs, which Mark Twain published as a two-volume book. Bob reported that the general/president made much more money because Twain understood the publishing business from a profit point of view.

Q: "What are Twain's best and worst books?"

A: "Mark Twain is not the kind of author who practiced perfection." He seldom edited or rewrote after publication.

"*Huck Finn* and *Connecticut Yankee* are his best books."

Bob puts *Huck* and *Yankee* at the top of his list, the first level of writing. Slightly below those, come *Roughing It, Tom Sawyer, Life on the Mississippi, A Tramp Abroad, Pudd'nhead Wilson,* and *Following the Equator.*

"*Prince and the Pauper*" is checkers; *Connecticut Yankee* is chess."

Bob hesitated a bit on a "worst" book, but he clearly doesn't like *Joan of Arc.*

"Mark Twain loved Joan of Arc but had no idea how to write a book about her."

I must admit that my granddaughter Kasey gave me a copy and told me to read it, and even a Papa's sense of duty couldn't get me to finish it. Twain's family however thought that *Joan of Arc* was his masterpiece. That is why Clara gave that manuscript to Yale. Bob heaved a great sigh of relief at that thought.

Q: "Would Mark Twain be a philanthropist?"

A: "Yes!" He gave money to support Black education and to several charities during his life.

Mac is beginning to train us in questioning. I do believe that we could have held Bob in the auditorium the entire day, but sooner or later we would have to eat. I have noticed with Bear groups that eating usually comes "sooner," so we left the Mark Twain center and retreated to the hotel and lunch.

Our afternoon program is in the historic town of Wethersfield, settled in 1634 by John Oldham, one of the three founding settlements of Connecticut colony along the Connecticut River. It is a lovely town, with its Main Street preserved as a historic district. Most of the houses date to the mid-eighteenth century, with at least one claiming to date into the 1600s. Unfortunately, the weather wasn't cooperating this afternoon, putting a damper on my plans to let people stroll down the tree-lined street, enjoying the distinctive New England architecture. Instead, we drove from town center to the Cove at the end of the street. This large pond was once part of the Connecticut River, extending out in a great ox-bow. Eventually the river cut itself off, leaving a fine town waterfront. Two colonial warehouses still grace the banks, testimony to the early days when the river actually came to Wethersfield, bringing trade goods and supplies.

At 3:00 we began a tour of the Webb-Dean-Stevens houses. These three old homes witnessed the meeting of Washington and Rochambeau prior to the Yorktown Campaign. Today they have been largely restored to the 1740-80 era. Lisa and Ellen were our guides, proposing to drag us through all three houses in about an hour, a task I thought to be highly ambitious. The Joseph Webb House is probably the most important of the three, being the one that "George Washington slept in." It is furnished "of the period," with two rooms returned to the time when the house was owned by art critic and collector, Wallace Nutting. He commissioned a series of mural wallpapers in what he called "the Yorktown Parlor," that almost destroy any beauty that might have been in the room. Even in the interest of preserving history, some things should be left buried.

"Which one of you is the historian?" Lisa inquired, a bit unsure of herself. "I was told there was an historian in this group."

"Oh, Professor Middlekauf is not with us today," I assured her.

"Oh, I thought so. Historians always look alike. They have a sort of airy look about them."

I made a note to pass this on to Bob. He has been looking a bit airy lately, now that I think about it.

Of course our guides ran short of time, and each had to rush through the final house so that I could collect the group, but with good will and a bright smile, both Lisa and Ellen finished on time. It is not that we were late for anything, as this is the last program of the day, but I have learned that you never fool around with "Bloody Mary time."

X

This morning we visit the Harriet Beecher Stowe House, the immediate neighbor of Mark Twain. Both houses were part of Nook Farm, probably the earliest "modern" housing development in America, with lots laid out to create a definite social and intellectual community. The Beechers are well represented in that community. There were 180 acres in Nook Farm originally. Only six houses still stand. The Mark Twain house, Harriet Beecher-Stowe house, and the Franklin Chamberlain house share the same block, three elaborate and quite different structures. The last of those is probably the most intricately designed. It became the home of Catherine Seymore Day, the grandniece of Harriet Beecher-Stowe, who established the foundation that administers the property today. The Chamberlain-Day house is now the office of the Stowe Foundation. Across Forest Ave. from these three is the home of the Smith Family, presently being restored by the Mark Twain Foundation. Mid-way on Forest Ave. is the Burton House, a cute "little" gingerbread structure that has recently been renovated. And at the far end of Forest Ave., well hidden behind a modern housing development, is the John and Isabella Beecher- Hooker home, the one that was initially rented by Sam and Livy while they were building their own house. Driving over to Nook Farm, we also passed the Asylum Hill Church, the "Church of the Holy Speculators," which is still a very active parish. Mark Twain's friend Joe Twitchell was the pastor of that church.

> "Set a white stone—for I have made a friend. It is the Rev. J.H. Twichell. I have only known him a week, & yet I believe I think almost as much of him as I do of Charlie. I could hardly find words strong enough to tell how much I do think of that man"
> *Mark Twain's Letters*, Vol. 2, p. 267

When I was setting up our visit to the Harrriet Beecher-Stowe house, I despaired of ever actually talking to someone to make the reservation. Finally in August, I actually visited the home, hoping to find a live body to confirm an appointment.

"Do you have someone who handles groups?" I asked the young lady behind the desk.

"Tell him he has to talk to Patrick," a woman's voice rather bellowed from behind an open door to the left.

"Is Patrick here?" I asked the young woman.

"He's on vacation," retorted the disembodied Voice.

"How do I reach him? Do you have his card?"

"No," answered the young woman, getting just a tiny word of her own in before the Voice could interfere.

"They are in the drawer on the left," declared the Voice. "No, the left, not the right."

"Yes, here they are!" said the young woman delighted, pleased for once to be able to voice a verb of her own.

"Patrick Burgess. Can you at least take my reservation?"

"No," croaked the Voice. "He has to phone him."

"Are you people taking lessons from the Mark Twain House?" I asked, floating just a tiny bit of disdain around the room.

Both the door and the desk were strangely silent. Sarcasm seldom translates.

But I did reach Patrick Burgess and I did make a reservation, and here we are!

"I wrote what I did because as a woman and as a mother, I was oppressed and broken-hearted with the sorrows and injustice I saw, because as a Christian, I felt the dishonor to Christianity—because as a lover of my country, I trembled at the coming day of wrath."

Uncle Tom's Cabin or Life Among the Lowly appeared as a serial in the *National Era*. It was published as a book in 1852, selling a million copies in the first year, making Harriet Beecher-Stowe an instant international celebrity. It has been published in at least sixty different languages. "So you're the little lady that wrote the book that started this Great War," legend has Abe Lincoln asking a decade later.

The group was divided into three parts this time, with strict orders not to touch anything and not to take any pictures and to inhale no more than three times per minute. We could however keep our shoes on. Our guide, Cherie, was a happy woman with a casual demeanor and a good tour voice. Coming to a room blockage in the house she whispered, "We'll cut through here to the front hall of the cottage. Don't look at anything!"

Harriet Beecher-Stowe was a painter as well as a writer, not a bad painter at that. The house has more than a dozen of her works, which are mostly floral subjects. One of eleven children, she had seven of her own.

"She looks very dour," Mac observed standing in front of a photograph. "Did she have a sense of humor?"

Cherie assured us that she did but didn't cite any evidence to support that statement. But the parlor was filled with a bunch of pictures of dour-looking people, not the least of them Henry Ward Beecher. Mac and I agreed that he looked like a guy who probably fooled around a bit, but then we have inside information. Harriet lived in her "cottage" with husband Calvin and twin daughters, Hattie and Eliza. The two shared an upstairs bedroom. The dining table was always set for four. The house had indoor plumbing, the bathroom equipped with tub, sink and pull-chain toilet.

As we were going upstairs, I noticed Alice sitting demurely in a chair in the entrance hall, looking exactly like she belonged in this house. I look out my camera to take her picture when all hell broke loose in the minds of our guides.

"No pictures in the house!" Ms Bullmoose bellowed from around a wall, sounding suspiciously like the Voice I had heard on my first visit. "How does she do that?" I wondered, "...see around corners and behind walls." The other two guides were equally appalled that I would even consider taking a picture.

"But she is Alice. She's not a part of the house."

"It doesn't matter. No pictures in the house!"

I am embarrassed to say that the gauntlet was hurled, and I fear that I am in possession of several illicit photos of the Harriet Beecher-Stowe house. Right at this moment I am looking for their e-mail address to send the pictures back to them, because I feel so guilty about having them in my possession.

Harriet Beecher-Stowe was indeed the Martha Stewart of her generation. Her house was very functional, and by Victorian standards, quite livable. Especially in her kitchen is her organization evident, with every item neatly arranged to permit the most efficient use of time and energy. She even wrote a manual on household tips for women.

I must say that I enjoyed the Stowe house. It was well furnished, with many of the original tables and couches, and felt right, for the period and the woman. It contained her original art works, her piano. Windows are still draped in ivy rather than the cumbersome curtains so often seen in Victorian mansions.

જ∾ ◌ఠ

We returned to the auditorium for our final session with Bob and our final program at Nook Farm. The folks at the Mark Twain center showed me how to operate their AV system and we were able to watch the Ken Burns film as a group.

Mac asked Bob to tell us about the Mark Twain Papers Project. There is an enormous amount of material that was gifted by Clara. Bob explained the path the papers took to get to Berkeley and spoke of his goal of publishing the writings in as complete a fashion as possible. The original goal was a twelve-volume "selected edition," of letters, notebooks, his autobiography, things that Mark Twain never intended to publish. An Iowa group was already publishing and annotating the books. In 1980, Bob became the editor of the Mark Twain Papers Project. The Iowa project was brought to Berkeley, and Bob set a new goal to publish everything that Mark Twain ever wrote. They have now published the letters up to 1875, filling six volumes. Bob expects it will take another fifteen volumes to complete, just the letters! They presently count about 11,000 letters among their papers and are finding two new ones a week. Bob estimates that Twain wrote about 50,000 letters in all. He does not want to do any more selected editions, but rather, "Make it right the first time." There is no other edition of any other author quite like this one.

Much of the funding has come from the National Endowment for Humanities, who has supported the Mark Twain Papers Project since 1967. Other funding has come from a few large donors, from the Mark Twain Foundation, about $25,000 a year from Clara's estate. The Mark

Twain Luncheon Club, established by Bob Middlekauf, Mac and former chancellor Mike Heyman, has been a big contributor. The University supports the program in a different way, by "forgiving indirect costs." And lastly the U.C. Class of '58, with Roger Samuelson in a leading role, is building a Class Gift aiming for a $1 million endowment. Bob says he needs funding of $400,000 every two years in matching funds. Several members of our group belong to the Mark Twain Luncheon Club.

Bob reported that the Mark Twain Papers Project is now about 40 percent done. He sees his job as training the next generation of editors. "I'm aiming at actually getting back to editing myself."

Q: "If you are finding two new letters a week, how do you fit them into your already completed volumes?"

Bob: This is easier to do now that the work is being done electronically. For the hard copy books, adding an addendum in future volumes is accepted practice.

Q: In the Burns film, Mark Twain is said to have said, "I am not an American. I am *the* American." Did he really say that?

Bob: "He never said that about himself. The Burns film is wrong."

We have had a good time with the "Did Mark Twain actually say that?" syndrome. Bob says that they get dozens of such inquiries at the Project, and that they have many of them catalogued with pat answers. In the world of one-liners, attribution is far too easy.

This afternoon, we are scheduled to visit the Wadsworth Athenaeum, Hartford's prestigious fine art gallery. They are presently hosting an exhibit called "American Splendor," the Athenaeum's collection of Hudson River Painters, which is drawn from the private collections of Daniel Wadsworth and Elizabeth Hart Jarvis Colt. This is America's first modern school of painting, which "evoked the Edenic purity of the New World." Wow! I am not sure exactly what that means, but I do know that, inspired by the opening of the Erie Canal, Thomas Cole started a movement of landscape painting that drew artists to the Hudson River Valley, Upstate New York and Northern New England. John Kensett (1816-72), Frederick Church (1826-1900), Jasper Cropsey (1823-1900), Asher Durand (1796-1886), William Trost Richards (1833-1903), Martin Johnson Heade (1812-1904), and many more artists brought wild landscapes of the American west to the attention of the world. The Yosemite work of Albert Bierstadt (1830-1902) sits at the top of those wild vistas. The Wadsworth Atheneum is only one of several large Hudson River School collections to be found in the east, others that we have visited being in the New Britain Art Museum and the Fruitlands Museum in Harvard, Massachusetts.

One of the most impressive rooms of the Wadsworth is filled with the huge panels of John Trumbull, whose historical paintings are familiar to most American school kids. "The Declaration of Independence" (1832), "Death of General Warren" (1834), "Death of General Montgomery, the "Battle of Trenton" and "Battle of Princeton" (all done in 1843) are all executed on monumental canvases.

On the main floor is a large exhibit entitled "Samuel Colt, Arms, Art and Invention." It is a tribute to one of Hartford's major industrialists and most interesting personalities. "He viewed the mention of his name— no matter the context—as advertising, and he viewed all advertising as positive." Born in 1824, he was kicked out of school for firing a cannon on the 4th of July. His stepmother shipped him off to sea to India, hoping to straighten him out. His guns became famous throughout the world, undoubtedly due to his "advertising." At one point he hired western artist George Catlin to paint a series of Wild West subjects using his rifles and pistols. We passed the Colt Arms Factory yesterday on our drive to Wethersfield, unmistakable with a sky-blue onion dome that has become one of Hartford's landmarks.

Of all the treasures in the Wadsworth, the one I was most pleased to discover is a letter from Abraham Lincoln to editor Horace Greeley on August 22, 1862. The letter was a response to Greeley's bombastic and quite insulting open letter, "The Prayer of the Twenty Millions" published in the *New York Tribune* three days earlier. It was 2,200 words of political invective. Lincoln responded in a fashion that must have infuriated the editor.

> Dear Sir. I have just read yours of the 19th addressed to myself through the New York Tribune. If there be in it any statements, or assumptions of fact, which I may know to be erroneous, I do not, now and here, controvert them. If there be perceptible in it an impatient and dictatorial tone, I waive it in deference to an old friend, whose heart I have always supposed to be right.

As to the policy I "seem to be pursuing" as you say, I have not meant to leave any one in doubt.

I would save the Union. I would save it the shortest way under the Constitution. The sooner the national authority can be restored; the nearer the Union will be "the Union as it was." If there be those who would not save the Union, unless they could at the same time save slavery, I do not agree with them. If there be those who would not save the Union unless they could at the same time destroy slavery, I do not agree with them. My paramount object in this struggle is to save the Union, and is not either to save or to destroy slavery. If I could save the Union without freeing any slave I would do it, and if I could save it by freeing all slaves I would do it; and if I could save it by freeing some and leaving others alone I would also do that. What I do about slavery, and the colored race, I do because I believe it helps to save the Union; and what I forbear, I forbear because I don't believe it would help to save the Union. I shall do less whenever I shall believe what I am doing hurts the cause, and I shall do more whenever I shall believe doing more will help the cause. I shall try to correct errors when shown to be error; and I shall adopt new views so fast as they shall appear to be true views.

I have here stated my purpose according to my view of Official duty: and I intend no modification of my oft-expressed personal wish that all men everywhere could be free.

Yours,
A. Lincoln

Source: "Abraham Lincoln: His Speeches and Writings" edited by Roy Basler

To read that letter alone is worth visiting the Wadsworth Athenaeum.

We have our Farewell Dinner tonight, in the Avery Room of the hotel. I am very pleased with the Goodwin Hotel, which has lived up to its boast of quiet elegance. It feels different from other 5-star hotels in that there is very little commotion, almost like a Park Avenue apartment house. Champagne is served every evening in the lobby, to the accompaniment of a grand piano. Breakfast is as elegant as a buffet can be. The dinner was delicious (only filet mignon and salmon this time) and professionally served. A fine end to our last hotel stay.

XI

We are on a tight schedule today, an hour drive to Lexington and Concord, a quick visit to the Battle Green of Lexington and the Old North Bridge at Concord, and even quicker lunch at the Colonial Inn and Mass Pike to the airport for a 2:35 P.M. flight home.

We are now fully into Bob Middlekauf territory and Mac asked him to give us an introduction to the American Revolution, which is the subject of his best-selling book, *The Glorious Cause*.

"I am going to talk to you as I would my students at Cal, on the assumption that you are all ignorant geniuses." It was the nicest thing anyone has said to us the whole trip.

The American Revolution is unique among modern revolutions, in that both sides came from the same stock, with no major differences of race or ethnicity. Economically, there were no trade restrictions within the British Empire. And politically the thirteen different colonies were not dominated by the British government. Colonists enjoyed the rights of all Englishmen.

After the 7 Years War, England tried to change the circumstances of Empire. The 1765 Stamp Act brought immediate and angry reaction, part of which was the creation of the Sons of Liberty. Tax collectors were subject to considerable abuse, including one in Connecticut who was buried until he resigned. While the Stamp Act was repealed in 1769, Parliament retained the right to bind the colonies. Events moved quickly from objection to taxes to the Boston Tea Party to the closing of Boston harbor, quartering of troops, revocation of the Mass Bay Charter, to a line of British troops arriving in Lexington on the morning of April 19.

The Green at Lexington is approximately the size it was in 1775 because three of the buildings that were there are still standing—Buckman Tavern, the parsonage and the Jonathan Harrington house. We stopped for a short visit to the green, on a perfectly beautiful fall day. Lexington Green is 18 miles from the Boston Common, and the British arrived at dawn, having been mustered out the night before and delayed for hours by low tide. Revere and William Dawes and Samuel Prescott had plenty of time to alarm the countryside, before the redcoats came drumming down the Monotomy Road toward legend. Outside of Buckman Tavern at Lexington Green, Colonel Parker lined up his weary Minute Company to watch the Brits walk by. A monument today recites his famous exhortation: "Stand your ground men. Don't fire unless fired upon, but if they mean to start a war, let it begin here." (That may not be exactly the way he phrased it!) The British did fire, and the colonials ran, but sadly eight fell, mortally wounded, including Pete Zischke's ancestor, Jonathan Harrington. It would not be their fault that this would indeed be the start of a war. "The shot heard 'round the world" would be fired a couple of hours later at Concord Bridge, but the inspiration for that shot must certainly be ascribed to Harrington and his Lexington mates who died in a battle accident.

At Lexington Green there is an old monument dated 1799, perhaps the first to commemorate the events of 1775.

> "The die was cast. The blood of these martyrs In the Cause of God and their Country was the Cement of the Union of the States, then Colonies and gave the spring to the Spirit, Firmness and Resolution of their fellow Citizens. They rose as One Man to revenge their brothers' Blood at the point of a Sword to assert and defend their native Rights. They nobly dared to be Free! The contest was long, bloody and affecting. Righteous however approved the solemn appeal. Victory crowned their arms and the Peace, Liberty and Independence of the United States was the glorious Reward."

It is eight miles to Concord, and we followed what is now "The Battle Road," into that pleasant village. We passed the Wayside, home to the Alcotts, Margaret Sydney and Nathaniel Hawthorne; and the Orchard House, where Louisa May Alcott penned *Little Women*. Across the street is the home of Ralph Waldo Emerson. Emerson's father, Minister of Concord, lived near the North Bridge in what Hawthorne called "The Old Manse." Henry David Thoreau lived in town at the Colonial Inn where we are having lunch. Walden Pond is just four miles out, not a great distance to get to the "wilderness."

We stopped at the Old North Bridge, a beautiful spot these days, spanning the Concord River. The Visitor Center now sits on Puncatassit Hill above the river. It was on this hill that the Concord Minute Company, and other Alarm Companies had assembled, unaware of the events that had occurred in Lexington. At Concord Center, the British had piled up what little war materiel they could find and set it on fire, the smoke rising above the town, visible from the bridge area. Another detachment of soldiers was sent on into the country to follow up on a report that the colonials had arms stored beyond the North Bridge. Those Regulars encountered the Concord Minute Company at the bridge, but the British crossed without incident. Smoke was seen rising from town as they returned and the colonials blocked the bridge, lined up in battle formation.

"Will we let them burn down our town?" yelled the militia leader. "Fire, for God's sake, fire!" Here is that famous shot heard 'round the world, as penned on July 4, 1837 by Concord resident, Ralph Waldo Emerson in his "Concord Hymn":

> By the rude bridge that arched the flood
> Their flag to April's breeze unfurled,
> Here once the embattled farmer stood,
> And fired the shot heard 'round the world.
>
> The foe long since in silence slept;
> Alike the conqueror silent sleeps;
> And time the ruined bridge has swept
> Down the dark stream which seaward creeps.
>
> On this green bank, by this soft stream,
> We set today a votive stone;
> That memory may their deed redeem,
> When, like our sires, our sons are gone.

Spirit, that made those heroes dare
To die, and leave their children free,
Bid Time and Nature gently spare
The shaft we raise to them and thee.

In the ensuing running battle back to Lexington the British suffered 273 casualties, the colonials 98. Twenty-seven Minute and Alarm Companies answered the alarm, augmented later by men as far away as Western Connecticut. It was the first time that colonials had fired on the King's army. It would be followed two months later, on June 17 with General Gage's horrible losses at Bunker Hill that would ultimately result, on March 17, 1776, in the wholesale evacuation of the British from Boston. The die was indeed cast.

We took a quick picture at the bridge, admired Daniel Chester French's famous "Minuteman" sculpture, and then hurried into town for lunch. I love the Colonial Inn. It is an historic building, has great food and actually knows how to handle a group on the run. I had alerted them that we were going to be pressed for time, and when we arrived, they had the soup ready for us. An impressive chicken potpie soon followed, and then a very nice dessert. Imagine, 35 people fed a three-course lunch, in just a smidge over 45 minutes!

BOOK THREE

Mark Twain In The West

He wrote so much! This is the third of our Cal Alumni tours on Sam Clemens and we still haven't gotten to Europe, the Holy Land, India, or even Hawaii for that matter. Come to think of it, we still haven't even gotten to New York. But we have made it to San Francisco, Hannibal (twice), Buffalo, St. Louis, New Orleans, Elmira and Hartford. Now we are following our favorite author to places closer to home, in Nevada and Northern California.

In the popular mind, Sam Clemens/Mark Twain is forever associated with the West. In the popular mind, this includes his writings centered in Hannibal and along the Mississippi, which include *Huckleberry Finn, Tom Sawyer, Pudd'nhead Wilson, Life on the Mississippi,* and of course, *Roughing It,* the bridge between Hannibal and Nevada/California. And yet, the author spent only about five and a half years on the West Coast, from August 14, 1861 to December 15, 1866 with a brief return to the lecture circuit in 1868, when he arrived in San Francisco following a Panama passage on April 2, 1868.

> When I had finished the business that brought me home, I lectured for the mutual benefit of the public and myself. It affords me great satisfaction to be able to say that there were eighteen hundred people present, and that sixteen hundred and five of them paid a gold dollar each to get there. Such is the thirst for reliable information in California. It is pleasant to have greenbacks in the State, but somehow it seems pleasanter to handle only gold and silver.
>
> The *Chicago Republican,* May 19, 1868. Quoted in www. twainquotes.com

He left California for good on July 6, 1868. From that date on, his life was centered in the East Coast and on his extensive lecture tours that literally took him around the continent and the world. Although his time in California and Nevada was so limited, it was nevertheless vitally important to the young Sam Clemens. It was there, in the *Territorial Enterprise,* Feb. 3, 1863, he first signed his writing by the pen name, Mark Twain.

Sandwiched between his two stays in California, from June to November, 1867, he was occupied with his famous Holy Land cruise on the *Quaker City.* That cruise would result in his first book, *Innocents Abroad.*

I

Today we commence a new Sam Clemens adventure, entitled "Mark Twain in the West," fully intent on adding Angels Camp and Virginia City to our check list, with a little footnote for Gold Hill, Silver City and Dayton, all in Nevada, as well as Copperopolis, Grass Valley, Nevada City, Red Dog and You Bet in the Gold Country. For most of us, Sam Clemens/Mark Twain has become a significant part of our consciousness. We have followed him down the Mississippi and last year visited him in most of his homes east of California and Nevada. We have been blessed with the great treasure of his papers at Berkeley, a treasure enhanced by the formidable expertise of the General Editor of those papers, Bob Hirst. Through Bob, we have come almost to terms of familiarity with this great American writer.

We are not embarking on this trip without a tiny bit of trepidation. On our first Mark Twain tour for Bear Treks, we awoke at the Embassy Suites in St. Louis to the horrors of September 11. Last fall in Buffalo we were marooned in the Adams Mark Hotel when the "Buffalo Blizzard of '06" closed the entire city to all vehicles, taking out almost three-fourths of the city's trees and power lines. It was as though old Sam Clemens was brewing up things that were truly worthy of reporting, events that we wouldn't even have to conjure up in our imagination. What can we expect on this journey to the land of the *Territorial Enterprise*, where many, if not most, of the exciting tales were pure fabrications?

Motorcoach travel is sure to catch on with the U.C. folks. It has become such an effort to fly these days, that the chance to drive on a tour is very attractive. The Clark Kerr Campus at Cal affords a great meeting place this morning and forty-two of us are boarding our Preferred Motorcoach there, bound for the gold country. Our driver is Theron Brown, a calm, well-built man with a wonderful, deep conversational voice and a nice smile in his eyes. He is driving a brand-new MCI coach, which is very comfortable and smooth.

We don't go far before our first stop. Bob has arranged for a visit to the Mark Twain Papers, now temporarily housed in a "surge" building on Oxford and Hearst, while their permanent quarters at the Bancroft are being remodeled. There isn't a lot of room in the collection area, but we had no problem scrunching in to get a view of the special items he had laid out for us, which included one of Orion Clemens' scrapbooks containing some original Territorial Enterprise articles, and "the most important letter that Sam Clemens ever wrote."

It was a tortuous path that the author's papers took to Cal. Most were in the hands of his "official biographer" Paine in NYC. Bernard De Voto then took them off to Harvard, but De Voto argued frequently with Clara Clemens and ultimately resigned. The new director, Dixon Wecter, brought them to the Huntington and in 1949 the papers finally arrived at Cal. In Clara's will, however, the papers were gifted to Yale, but at Wecter's suggestion, she finally changed that bequest to Cal, placating the Yale folks with the manuscript of *Joan of Arc*, which the family considered to be among her father's finest works. Bob simply says it was "probably his worst book," and gets a mischievous smile on his face when he thinks about Yale's "prize." Clara died in 1962.

Cal's prize consists of 500-700 manuscripts, unpublished and/or unfinished; 46 notebooks; files of checks, bills, photos, deeds, etc; 11,000 original letters from Sam Clemens and his immediate family; 17,000 letters to them; twenty scrapbooks. Bob said that the collection averages two new letters per week through purchase or gift. The Mark Twain Papers are a growing child. In 2010, Bob will begin the publishing of the author's autobiography, dictated by him to be published between 100 years and some parts 500 years after his death. 100 years is quite enough! Bob expects the edited, definitive edition to be three volumes, just about enough to absorb a month or two of the most rabid Twain devotees.

The materials that Bob laid out for us are all important for our tour. The key is one of the scrapbooks of his brother Orion. Most of the originals of the *Enterprise* writings were lost in the Virginia City fire of 1875 and the fire in San Francisco in 1906. A descendant of Sam's sister, Anita Moffett, had a dozen or so of Orion's scrapbooks, which contain the biggest cache of *Enterprise* articles known to exist, as well as at least 100 letters. Bob also had several of Sam's mining stock certificates, and one of his pilot's notebooks.

"The most important letter he ever wrote," at least from the standpoint of those who want to understand his life, was written from San Francisco at the end of 1865, after he returned from Angels Camp.

> "I have never had but two powerful ambitions in my life! One was to be a pilot, & the other a preacher of the gospel... But I have had a 'call' to literature of a low order, i.e.—humorous."
> *Mark Twain's Letters*, Vol. 1, Letter to Orion and Mollie Clemens, October 19-20, 1865

Someone asked if there were other collections in the U.S. besides Cal's and Yale's. Bob listed other materials at the Berg Collection (New York Public Library) in New York, the University of Virginia, Vassar College, Elmira College, and of course at the Buffalo City Library, which holds the complete manuscript to *Huckleberry Finn*.

We left Berkeley around 10:00, bound for Sacramento, a place through which Sam passed a few times in his wanderings and lecture series. We decided to stop at the Sterling Hotel for lunch, a most elaborate Victorian establishment near the capitol.

Bob began his lectures on the bus by discussing *Huckleberry Finn,* which he considers the finest of Mark Twain's works. He did several readings from the book, passages that included the dread "N-word" that has so upset the censors in our public schools, making *Huck* the most banned book in the nation. It is Bob's opinion that it should probably not be taught to students until they are in college when they are old enough to understand it. The objectionable statements on slavery in the novel are Huck's words, those of a young, uneducated redneck southern boy who was parroting the prevalent ideas of his day and region. They are not Mark Twain's words. In fact, in the dialogues between Huck and Jim, it is Jim who always wins the arguments.

While he was reading and talking, I was a bit concerned that our driver, Theron, a black man, might be offended by Huck's language, and I broached the subject to him after we reached the hotel.

"No, I wasn't offended," Theron said with a smile. "People used to say a lot of bad things. I think I'm going to have to read that book."

Mac voiced an objection to Bob's observation about withholding Huck until college, feeling that everyone has read the book in high school and that it is the teachers who have to understand it better and teach it better. There was a lively back-and-forth banter that Mac labeled a "polite academic discussion." "Super classics," they agreed are "praised for the wrong reasons and condemned for the wrong reasons."

We are staying the first two nights at the Murphys Hotel, one of the few extant inns that date back to Sam Clemens' time in the gold country. In fact, the hotel proudly boasts a Mark Twain signature in their guest book, and have restored a Mark Twain Suite, the one he is supposed to have used during his stay. The only problem is that the signature is dated 1883, a very difficult proposition because Sam left California for good in 1868. But hope springs eternal and the new owners assured me that there was a logical explanation to the thing, having already ruled out the possibility of a forgery. They are equally confident of the U.S. Grant signature in their book. They have a Grant Suite too.

We are taking over just about the entire hotel for the next two nights. We have used up all the twenty modern motel rooms and four of the eight historic rooms as well. Bob and Margaret are in the Daniel Webster Room. Mary and Les are in the Grant Suite, while the Ryders are down the hall. Of course the suites do not feature *en suite*, so everyone must do their ablutions in the WC at the end of the corridor. The rest of us are forced to operate in the unromantic modern way.

Except for Mary and Florence that is. We were all pretty much settled into our rooms for the afternoon, when the ladies came down to complain that there was no water in their room. I reported the problem to the management and accompanied them to their room to see if I could help. They pointed out the defective sink and I tried the faucet, one of those that you pull out to activate. Water flowed freely into the sink.

"How did you do that?" they asked in unison and I showed them. But neither of the ladies was able to pull out the faucet, it being just too stiff for their wrists. I tried lubricating the thing with some soap, but it didn't help much.

"I have some graphite," Mary volunteered.

"You have graphite? With you?"

"Oh yes, we always bring graphite with us in case we have a squeaky door."

I have never in thirty-five years of group touring known a traveler who packed graphite. Mary had never opened the tube, but they also carried scissors so in no time I was squeezing the black stuff all over the sink, which made a lovely, ugly paste that seemed to enter every crack in the bathroom. To no avail. That faucet was still too tight for their strength. But we experimented and discovered that if they twisted at the same time as they pulled, they could get the water on. It wasn't a complete fix, but it was better than having them wash their hands in the shower. The next morning the manager of the hotel completely replaced the faucet. The ladies were thrilled with their conventional turn handles, vowing to wash their hands just as often as they could. Of such triumphs is a fine tour made!

It was fun to be at Murphys Hotel. There is a very nice outside area with tables, so we set up the first of our casual cocktail parties tonight, something that Mac and I have been doing for years. It is an easy way to get the group together, always effective in building the group dynamic that is so necessary on a bus tour. Dinner tonight is in the Mark Twain Salon (what else!) on the second floor of the old hotel, a good place to talk about our favorite author.

Brian at Murphys Hotel was kind enough to set up a microphone for Bob, whose voice is very gentle, so he did a variety of readings after dinner, and gave us the background behind Sam Clemens arriving in the Mother Lode country, and Jackass Hill in particular. Sam's friendship with Steve Gillis got him in trouble in San Francisco. Gillis got into a fight and Sam picked up his bail. When Steve jumped bail, Sam had no choice but to leave as well and ended up near Angels Camp in the gold country, staying with Steve's brothers, Jim and Billy. He would stay only eighty-four days in the gold country, from December 4, 1864 to February 25, 1865. From the Gillis brothers he would hear story after story, told around the fire or in Frenchman's bar in Angels Camp. Out of this experience came the jumping frog and the blue jay, and many other tales that have entertained readers for more than a century.

I asked Bob to give us the story of the Jumping Frog, since we have a quiet room and a P.A. system. The story of Coleman's frog was told many different ways, but it was Mark Twain who gave it fame, in "Jim Smiley and His Jumping Frog." In the Mark Twain Museum in Angels Camp they have a book with five variations of "The Only True and Reliable Account of the Jumping Frog of Calaveras County." Urged to do so by his friend Artemus Ward, Twain sent the tale east, for the first time introducing him to the market where he would thrive. I think the story also helps to identify Mark Twain inexorably with the Wild West. Reading in the Pike's County dialect, Bob read us the tale, which he protested, "no one any longer thinks is funny." But few are lucky enough to hear the tale in spoken form as it was meant to be read. And few are fortunate enough to have it explained that the frog was named Daniel Webster because that eminent statesman's face did in fact look like a frog.

Tomorrow we will visit Jackass Hill and Angels Camp.

II

After breakfast, with the microphone again, in a private room, Bob gave us the story of Angels Camp before we arrive in the town. He passed out two old pictures of the "cabin" on Jackass Hill, dated 1895 and 1906. The older picture features ten men, including Billy Gillis, and two children, sitting in front of a ramshackle New England style saltbox with sagging roof, broken windowpanes and fractured clapboards. The pictures are more than interesting in view of the "Mark Twain cabin" that now graces Jackass Hill, a structure that has been rebuilt at least three times with the restorers' mental picture of what a proper period cabin is supposed to look like.

The men didn't spend their whole time at the cabin, but rather freely wandered around the hills in their pocket-mining search for gold. Bob surmised that most of Mark Twain's travels in the mountains was done by walking. He visited Vallecito in late December, 1865 and spent almost a month with Jim Gillis and Dick Stoker at the Frenchman's in Angels Camp. Later, when we drove to the top of Jackass Hill, we got a sense of the distances involved, including the walk both ways to the Frenchman's Hotel in Angels Camp about nine miles away.

'Beans & coffee only for breakfast & dinner every day at the French Restaurant at Angel's—bad, weak coffee—J told waiter must made mistake—he asked for café—this was day-before-yesterday's dishwater."
Notebook 4

"Dined at the Frenchman's, in order to let Dick see how he does things. Had Hellfire soup & the old regular beans & dishwater. The Frenchman has 4 kinds of soup which he furnishes to Customers only on great occasions. They are popularly known among the Boarders as Hellfire, General Debility, Insanity & Sudden Death, but it is not possible to describe them."
February 3—*Notebook 4*

Here Sam first heard the story of the blue jay, from one of the Gillis brothers, Jim. Bob told us that the stories were common in the mountains, a way of filling time around campfires and bars, but they were verbal creations. Mark Twain's genius is that he was able to put them into writing.

Before we left our breakfast room, Bob read the wonderful story of the blue jay, a tale he says is his personal favorite, and which he told us is "buried" in *A Tramp Abroad*. Listening to him read the story, I closed my eyes briefly to get a sense of what it must have sounded like with a beer in my hand at the Frenchman's. Bob can truly recreate the scene in his readings.

There is not much left of Mark Twain sites in the Gold Rush country. The best is Jackass Hill. This doesn't really leave us much of a program for today, especially when Bob said that the cabin we are going to visit is "the wrong cabin in the wrong place," but lack of material has never been much of a problem for Mac and me in the past and it certainly won't impact our day today. This is especially true in the Gold Rush region, which abounds in stories, many relating to the dozen "Trail Trips" that we have done over the years. That will be true this morning because we can't just drive to Jackass Hill. The road up to that beautifully named place can only be approached on Highway 49 from the south because of the sharp turn involved. Since we are coming from Angel's Camp, we will have to pass the hill, make a U-turn and approach it properly. I decided to make that turn at Mormon Creek, or Mormon "Crick" as Mac calls it.

"Where did you learn to say, 'crick'?" someone asked Mac from the back of the bus.

"Why, when I was livin' in the holler."

There is a monument at the creek or crick, dedicated to the Mormon Battalion, several of whose members staked out a claim in the area. In 1848, Mormon men on their way to Salt Lake were pressed into service to fight in the Mexican War. They marched all the way from the Missouri to San Diego, the longest infantry march in U.S. history. Of course the war was over by the time they reached California. A good story, but the real kernel of interest is that one of their guides was Jean Baptiste Charbonneau, the son of the famous Sacagawea, the young Shoshone maiden who "saved the Lewis and Clark expedition through her keen knowledge of the west." Young Charbonneau was ultimately educated in Europe, returned to become a mountain man, was *alcalde* of San Diego for a while, a clerk in Auburn, California and finally returned to the mountains where he died.

Mac talked about Charbonneau and then we finally retreated to Jackass Hill. On the way down the Murphy Highway, Mac had already spotted a jackass on a hill, and I suppose that paved the way for the real thing. In the mining days, mules were often used in the camps and at times even down the shafts. Here, in pocket mining country, they were most often grazed, and their braying gave the name to the hill where the Gillis cabin once stood. Here Sam Clemens spent 84 days, beginning December 4, 1864. His friend Steve Gillis had jumped bail in San Francisco, leaving Sam, who had posted ten percent of the bail, to come up with another $450. Sam worked for the *Call* in 1864 but had been fired. Lacking the funds, and without a job in San Francisco, he fled to Jim Gillis' cabin near Tuttletown. There he lived with the Gillis brothers on a diet of beans and coffee.

"I'm surprised that when they smoked their pipes, they didn't blow up the place because of the gas," Mac observed.

Clemens' earnings from his Sandwich Islands lectures would later be attached to pay the remaining bail money.

The original cabin, which was on a different spot, burned down long ago. Another one was built in 1922 and also burned down, leaving only the chimney. The present cabin was constructed by the Sonora Sunrise Rotary between 2002-2005.

Because of the size of the group and the lack of any place to sit on the hill, we decided to let Bob talk on the bus, out of the wind and where everyone could hear. He gave a brief summary of Sam Clemens' affairs during this important period of his life, which although rather short in time was of major importance for his later writings. Bob reported that there is very little in the Papers or anywhere else about Sam in 1865, only four letters. The men wandered to Vallecito in late December, 1865. Sam spent almost a month with Jim Gillis and Dick Stoker in Angels Camp where they hung out in the French Hotel saloon.

Here Sam listened to the stories of the miners, the details of which he wrote down in his journal. Of course, the important tale was that of the Jumping Frog, which he first heard during this time. He decided to write up the story himself, but Bob said he had a difficult time getting it together. Finally he decided to send the story to Artemus Ward in New York. It would be his first major success.

> "...Coleman with his jumping frog—bet stranger $50—stranger had no frog, & C got him one—in the meantime stranger filled C's frog full of shot & he couldn't jump—the stranger's frog won.
> Wrote this story for Artemus—his idiot publisher, Carleton gave it to Clapp's Saturday Press."
> February 6—*Notebook 4*

We followed the miners' route from Jackass Hill down to Angels Camp, no easy walk. On the bus we measured it at almost nine miles, but they would have gone overland in the old days and it was probably somewhat shorter. There is almost nothing left from the 1860s in the town today. It would have been nice to have a beer or two, and maybe some beans, at the Frenchman's Hotel, but it is long gone. It once sat on the corner where Highway 4 meets Highway 49, the site of a small inn today. We have lunch scheduled at Crusco's, an Italian restaurant that is just across the street.

Lining the sidewalks of the town are bronze plaques of the various winners of the Jumping Frog Contest that, since 1928, has been held annually at the Fairgrounds. We smiled at the first medallion, dated 1865,

"Owner Jim Smiley,
Daniel Webster
0',0"—World Record."

In the middle of Angels Camp is the town museum, which deceptively appears to be quite small. It has the only "Mark Twain display" in the region, something that Bob's staff helped them to produce. I had asked the manager, Naoma, if she could get someone to tell us a few stories about the annual jump-off. Waiting for us was Anne Mastacero, a former Frog Jump Queen, who did a fine job. The first county fair was held in 1893, but the first frog jump was not until 1928, held downtown with a rope ring. Frogs got one jump. The contest was suspended during the depression and World War II but resumed after 1945. It is held on the third weekend in May, these days with 300-500 entrants. Frogs must be a minimum of 4" head-to-toe and a maximum of 8". They have outlawed the African Goliath species from a few years ago, which was huge and had the unhappy habit of consuming the other contestants. Frogs today get three jumps, the distance measured from start to the point where they finish, which a time or two was the same. The owner may not touch them once they are placed. The current world record is 21'5 ¾", set by Rosie the Riveter in 1986.

Tonight we have dinner in the Columbia City Hotel, on Main Street in that restored mining town. Gold was discovered in Columbia in 1850, more gold gathered there from the gravels than any place on earth. The signs of the hydraulic mining surround the town, where forty feet of topsoil were removed to get at the gold. The town was chosen by the State of California to be the example of the full-blown mining town of the gold rush era, many of the buildings being brought in from the surrounding area. The City Hotel is opening for our group tonight. They served a wonderful meal, almost unexpectedly good, with a happy, well-trained staff.

III

We go over the mountains today. Originally, I had wanted to take Highway 4 over Ebbetts Pass, since Murphys is on that highway. But Mac, Bob and I drove that route in our exploration trip a few months ago, and we discovered that a bus couldn't possibly make the turns or the grade, so we settled on Highway 88 out of Jackson, which runs over Carson Pass. I later learned it is the only route south of Highway 50 that a motorcoach is allowed to drive. Sam Clemens' experiences in the gold country were pretty much confined to Angels Camp and Jackass Hill. He visited Vallecito and stopped in Copperopolis on his way down to Stockton and back to San Francisco. He didn't seem to do too much other exploring during his eighty-four days in the mountains. On the other hand, his time in Nevada was more varied, as he moved from Virginia City and Carson City through Genoa and Minden and south to try his hand at mining around Mono Lake.

Our route today takes us into Gardnerville, where a stop at a Basque restaurant is a Mac Laetsch requirement. Most of these Nevada towns have such restaurants, since the Basque sheepherders pretty much spread around the entire Sierra region. It is a five-hour ride into the Carson Valley, a drive filled with mountain scenery, Bob's Mark Twain tales, and Mac's unlimited supply of "important things."

We found out that Sam Clemens didn't wear a white suit until 1906, which came as a great shock to all of us. "The vanilla suit is an anodyne..." Bob told us, and everyone nodded, though I suspect that none of us knows exactly what that means. Mac mentioned that Sam liked his honorary doctoral robes bestowed on him by Oxford University and Bob agreed that he often walked around the house wearing that gown, and even went to Clara's wedding in it. Other than the pictures of the young Sam Clemens,

I can't think of any that doesn't have him in his white suit. Bob asserted that the earlier pictures are far more interesting but are seldom used.

Bob read one of Sam's letters to his mother from Virginia City. It is not easy to imagine receiving letters that are filled with a combination of fact, fantasy, sarcasm and pure wit. I doubt that Sam developed his talent in a vacuum, and that his mother fully understood the nature of his letters. I asked Bob if letters exist coming back from Sam's mom and whether she had a similar wit in her writings. He reported that there are no such letters from her, but that she did have a wit like that of her famous son.

> "My Dear Mother: I hope you WILL all come out here some day. But I shan't consent to invite you, until we can receive you in style. But I guess we shall be able to do that, one of these days. I intend that Pamela shall live on Lake Bigler until she can knock a bull down with her fist—say about three months.
>
> "Tell everything as it is—no better, and no worse" 'Well, "Gold Hill: sells at $5,000 per foot, cash down; "Wildcat" isn't worth ten cents. The country is fabulously rich in gold, silver, copper, lead, coal, iron, quicksilver, marble, granite, chalk, plaster of Paris, (gypsum,) thieves, Chinamen, Spaniards, gamblers, sharpers, cuyotes (pronounced ki-yo-ties,) poets, preachers, and jackass rabbits… Our city lies in the midst of a desert of the purest—most unadulterated, and uncompromising sand—in which infernal soil nothing but that fag-end of vegetable creation, "sage brush," ventures to grow."
> *Mark Twain's Letters*, Vol. 1, October 25, 1861

Mac for his part waded through a potpourri of topics, from magnolias to trees of heaven, to quaking aspens to sagebrush and polecats. We are driving this road at the perfect fall time, the aspens literally glowing in the sun in full autumn gold.

Gardnerville has a couple of Basque restaurants, but everyone seems to agree that J.T.'s is the better of the two. It didn't make much sense to me to order a puny lunch when they are so famous for their dinners, so today is going to be a double supper experience. We were about an hour late coming over the pass, but they didn't care. They basically cook the same thing every day, adding a tongue or a leg of lamb as supply dictates. The fare is as plentiful as it is simple, with a few constants—soup, French fries, fried chicken, and the most common of red wines, always served in a drinking glass. Today they opened with lamb stew, which was a big hit, especially with Mac's wife, Sita.

"That stew was good! That's just like my mother used to make. I didn't know it was Basque food. I thought it was just stew."

Sita was on her third glass of wine by that point. To that *vino mio*, we added the traditional pecan punch, a sort of Basque firewater made with pecan liqueur, grenadine, soda water and a brandy floater. After a couple of those, the wine starts to taste good.

We were a bit behind schedule by the time we finished at J.T.'s. I had wanted to stop and look around a bit at the old Mormon Station in Genoa, but we satisfied ourselves with a drive-thru on the way to Carson City. We are due to meet a local city guide, Lori Hickey, behind the Gold Nugget Casino. She was there waving as we pulled up, and without so much as an introduction, she commenced her tour of 1860-Carson City before the bus door was even closed. We drove across Highway 395/50 to the old part of town, where there are still a few buildings that date back to the days when Sam and his brother Orion were walking around. Orion's house, on the northwest corner of Spear and Division Streets., is still standing, now a lawyer's office. We drove past the governor's mansion, traditionally decked out in jack-o-lanterns for Halloween. Lori said we had time, so we drove out to the Old Stewart Indian School on the edge of town. It was built in 1890, intended to educate the Shoshone, Paiute and Washoe children, who were brought in from all over Nevada. It was run by the Baptists, but the children hated it. Eventually it was converted into a high school, closed in 1979, and today is the Highway Patrol Academy, a battered women's shelter and a variety of other state offices. Many of the original buildings are still standing, all built of stone by the students, between 1890-1920. Lori said that the Gatekeeper's Museum houses a huge collection of very fine Nevada Indian baskets.

In late afternoon, we climbed the hill to Virginia City, checking in for two nights at the brand-new Ramada Inn at the far end of town. After the huge lunch at J.T.'s, I had hesitated to order a big dinner, but the hotel doesn't yet have a restaurant, and the late afternoon winds are way too strong for our folks to walk around town looking for dinner, so I contracted with the Virginia City Jerkey Company to cater a "casual"

BBQ. Originally, they were going to set it up outside, but the Washoe Zephyr was so strong, a few of our ladies could barely make it from the bus to the lobby. It was an easy decision to move the meal indoors. It proved to be a huge success, as the buffet of brisket, ribs and pulled beef was positively delicious. So much for a light supper!

That wind is perfect for our tour, because the "Washoe Zephyr" was discussed at length by Sam Clemens as he arrived in Carson City.

> "But seriously a Washoe wind is by no means a trifling matter. It blows flimsy houses down, lifts shingle roofs occasionally, rolls up tin ones like sheet music, now and then blows a stage coach over and spills the passengers; and tradition says the reason there are so many bald people there, is that the wind blows the hair off their heads while they are looking skyward after their hats....
>
> The "Washoe Zephyr" (Washoe is a pet name for Nevada) is a peculiarly Scriptural wind, in that no man knoweth "whence it cometh." That is to say, where it *originates*. It comes right over the mountains from the West, but when one crosses the ridge he does not find any of it on the other side! It probably is manufactured on the mountain-top for the occasion and starts from there. It is a pretty regular wind in the summer time. Its office hours are from two in the afternoon till two the next morning..."
>
> *Roughing It,* p. 139-140

IV

"Virginia City was the center of gravity for lying in the whole world."

With that declaration, Ron James opened his talk this morning at the Virginia City Museum, which sits across the parking lot from our hotel. Ron is the Historical Preservation Officer for the State of Nevada. He is also the finest guide I have met in all my years of travel. He combines a profound expertise on the history of the state, particularly Virginia City, with a wonderful sense of humor, delivered in the most pleasing of manners. This will be the third time I have heard him speak in Virginia City, and each time he seems to adapt his program to the interest of the audience.

Ron set the background for Sam Clemens' arrival in town. He said that the *Territorial Enterprise* was a very important newspaper, even without Mark Twain. "95 percent of their work was an attempt at good reporting; only 5 percent was lies." He produced two old maps of the town, one an 1863 map done by a local African-American, Grafton Brown, which identifies all the major buildings at the time, including that of the *Territorial Enterprise*. The whole block burned down in the great fire of 1875. Clearly that is not the present building that now purports to have housed the newspaper. We will visit the basement of that building later this morning, and though Ron is certain it is not where Mark Twain worked, he did admit that the building was a fire survivor, as well as the desk which Ron feels was the one that Twain actually used. The *Gold Hill News* took over the presses of the *Territorial Enterprise* and moved to the present site.

Most of Twain's work at the *Territorial Enterprise* was lost in the 1875 fire. There was a collection of the paper's issues in the courthouse, but that also burned. What remains comes from private collections or from other newspapers who reprinted some of his stories.

Ron gave a brief history of the mining in the region. The first placer miners were "rebounds" from the Sierras, but they soon left, unable to pick out a living. But in the winter of 1859, an outcropping of a mother lode was discovered, attracting over 3,000 men in a single year, converting placer mining to hard rock mining. "Virginia City defined hard rock mining for the world," he said, pointing out methods of the "Hot water plugs" as the local miners were known, methods that soon spread across the oceans. Ron said that in their quest for gold, the miners encountered an obnoxious "blue mud" which they spread across the roads as paving. That mud was high grade silver, hardly valued until the Big Bonanza of 1873.

"Silver is the slut of precious metals; sleeps around with everything," Ron laughed. The Comstock began to peter out in 1878, and Virginia City went into decline. But Ron pointed out that in its heyday it was hardly the typical mining boom town. The buildings were extremely elaborate, several still standing four and five stories high. There were four political wards, each having a major school. We will dine tonight at the elaborate 4th Ward School. The town had four International Hotels, one of which still stands in Austin, Nevada whence it was moved. At the height of the mining, the only water was the "best of the tunnel" water, noxious at best, poisonous at worst. A water system was built, bringing lake water from Tahoe, a system still in use.

The 1875 fire came down Main Street to Taylor and then turned down the hill. The original Piper's Opera House, where Mark Twain had spoken, was dynamited as a fire break. Ron said he is 99 percent certain that the Catholic Church was also destroyed, but the church doesn't want to accept that idea. He's probably no more welcomed there than at the Territorial Enterprise building.

"It was a dignified town that had its moments of uproar," Ron laughed. There were about 100 bars, which he said was "normal" for a place of that size. Today, the new Pipers Opera House, the monumental courthouse and the Knights of Pythias building all rise majestically on B Street, a block uphill above the main street, all built a year after the fire. Neighbors of the Pythians are Odd Fellow Hall, E Clampus Vitus and the Miners Union Hall, testimonial to the sophistication of the town. The house where Twain lived with Dan DeQuille was next to the Miners' Union Hall. About 50' beyond that was the Old Boston Saloon, where Ron James said, he could be certain that the writer was a customer.

"The "city" of Virginia roosted royally midway up the steep side of Mount Davidson, seven thousand two hundred feet above the level of the sea, and in the clear Nevada atmosphere was visible from a distance of fifty miles! It claimed a population of fifteen thousand to eighteen thousand, and all day long half of this little army swarmed the streets like bees and the other half swarmed among the drifts and tunnels of the 'Comstock' hundreds of feet down in the earth directly under those same streets...

The mountain side was so steep that the entire town had a slant to it like a roof. Each street was a terrace, and from each to the next street below the descent was forty or fifty feet. The fronts of the houses were level with the street they faced, but their rear first floors were propped on lofty stilts, a man could stand at a rear first floor window of a C street house and look down the chimneys of the row of houses below facing D street. It was a laborious climb, in that thin atmosphere, to ascend from D to A street, and you were panting and out of breath when you got there...."

Roughing It, pp. 282-283

For the rest of our morning program, we split into two groups, the first going to the pressroom of the *Territorial Enterprise*, where Sam became a local reporter; the second doing a walking tour of the town with Ron. That tour began at the *Enterprise* parking lot, looking down on D Street. Ron pointed out the site of the original McGuire's Opera House, opened on July 2, 1863. Sam Clemens attended the grand opening. That opera house burned down in the 1875 fire. A new one was built by Piper on B Street. Ron also pointed out the Boston Saloon, owned by a Black man, William Brown. "It was a 'two-bit bar,' where beer, whiskey or a cigar could be had for 25¢."

We walked up C Street, through what Ron called "the Fire Zone." The 1875 fire gutted only the center of the town, roaring down off the mountain blazing a swath to the bottom. Fulton Street was the eastern boundary of the fire. Many of the present buildings have wrought iron pilasters, some dated 1875 and others 1876. There are several different foundries stamped on the pilasters: the Union Iron Works; Fulton Foundry. The Bank of California, set up by the "California Rock Sharps," once occupied the Sharon House. William Sharon, "the worst Nevada Senator ever," was the local agent for the Bank of California, which collapsed in the Depression. The Old Washoe Club, "The Millionaire's Club," which Sam Clemens probably knew well, occupied the second floor above another 2-bit bar. A couple of familiar names were found in Mark Twain's Virginia City. Roos Atkins was founded here, and Levi Strauss occupied one of the stone buildings. Virginia City probably doesn't look terribly different from Mark Twain's day. There are still lots of saloons around, with some colorful new names: Bucket of Blood Saloon, the Red Garter, the Ponderosa Saloon, but Piper's Opera House, the Territorial Enterprise and the Washoe Club are still to be found.

> "The paper was a great daily, printed by steam; there were five editors and twenty-three compositors; the subscription price was sixteen dollars a year; the advertising rates were exorbitant, and the columns crowded. The paper was clearing from six to ten thousand dollars a month, and the "Enterprise Building" was finished and ready for occupation—a stately fire-proof brick..."
> *Roughing It*, p. 292

Beverly was our guide at the pressroom of the *Territorial Enterprise*, where Sam first started his western newspaper work. Don had said earlier that he was "an adequate liar, the cub liar." The pressroom is found down a steep flight of stairs, today filled with old presses, the walls covered with old posters and pictures. Beverly is a Mark Twain enthusiast, and readily spreads her enthusiasm to her audience. She talked about "Flapjack" Henry Comstock, whose name graces the famous silver strike. "Evil always wins out," she laughed. He had several wives who ran away from him. He sold his claim for $10,000 and died penniless. It was John Mackay who founded the new Bank of Nevada, taking over the Comstock wealth.

Beverly talked about dueling, a common event in Mark Twain's day. "They just wanted to wing them. It would ruin your day if you killed someone." It was a fun half hour with Beverly.

We rejoined our two groups back on the bus for a short ride up to Piper's Opera House. The place is undergoing considerable renovations, much of it funded by Ron's office as State Preservationist. Piper's was originally built on D Street, built by Thomas McGuire from San Francisco in 1863. In Christmas of that year, Artemus Ward spoke at the theater; Sam Clemens was in the audience. Jenny Lind appeared there, as she seemed to have done on every stage in the West. Ditto for Lily Langtree. Two of the Booth brothers, (not John Wilkes) showed up there as well, and John Phillips Souza directed in the theater. Mark Twain gave his Sandwich Island lecture in McGuire's and his "Pilgrim" talk in 1868 in Piper's. Piper bought the old theater in 1867 only to lose it in the great fire. He used the stones from the old place as the façade for his new theater on B Street, which he built in 1877. It burned down again in 1883 and he rebuilt it again two years later. The fabrics and paintings are original. The canvas that covers the ceiling was installed in 1970. Today the theater is active, administered by Bill Beeson and Dick Stole, who opened it for us today.

Bob, sitting casually on the stage steps spoke on a variety of Twain subjects. He spoke of the writer's attitude toward blacks, commenting that there was a black barkeeper almost across the street, whom Twain would certainly know and interact with. There are almost no documents from 1853-1863 that deal with racism. In San Francisco, he had a black friend, Peter Anderson. There is a description of him and Anderson "promenading Montgomery Street arm-in-arm." When in July, 1865, blacks wanted to march in the 4th of July parade, Twain wrote of the shortsightedness of regarding them as inferior beings.

> "The damned naygurs" - this is another descriptive title which has been conferred upon them by a class of our fellow-citizens who persist, in the most short-sighted manner, in being on bad terms with them in the face of the fact that they have got to sing with them in heaven or scorch with them in hell some day in the most familiar and sociable way, and on a footing of most perfect equality.
>
> *Territorial Enterprise*, July 7-19, 186 Quoted in www.twainquotes. com 5

Bob discussed Mark Twain's history in Virginia City. He arrived in Carson City with his brother in 1861, hanging about there for a while, looking around for loose gold. Unsolicited, he sent letters to the *Territorial Enterprise,* signed "Josh" and was offered a job. At the end of 1862, out of money, he accepted. In October he wrote a famous piece about the "Petrified Man," a thinly veiled taunt of Justice Sewell.

A petrified man was found some time ago in the mountains south of Gravelly Ford. Every limb and feature of the stony mummy was perfect, not even excepting the left leg, which has evidently been a wooden one during the lifetime of the owner ... The body was in a sitting posture, and leaning against a huge mass of croppings; the attitude was pensive, the right thumb resting against the side of the nose; the left thumb partially supported the chin, the fore-finger pressing the inner corner of the left eye and drawing it partly open; the right eye was closed, and the fingers of the right hand spread apart. This strange freak of nature created a profound sensation in the vicinity, and our informant states that by request, Justice Sewell or Sowell, of Humboldt City, at once proceeded to the spot and held an inquest on the body. The verdict of the jury was that "deceased came to his death from protracted exposure," etc. The people of the neighborhood volunteered to bury the poor unfortunate, and were even anxious to do so; but it was discovered, when they attempted to remove him, that the water which had dripped upon him for ages from the crag above, had coursed down his back and deposited a limestone sediment under him which had glued him to the bed rock upon which he sat, as with a cement of adamant, and Judge S. refused to allow the charitable citizens to blast him from his position.... Everybody goes to see the stone man, as many as three hundred having visited the hardened creature during the past five or six weeks.

The Works of Mark Twain; Early Tales & Sketches, Vol. 1, p. 159

In 1864, probably drinking he heard about the Carson City Sanitary Ball, reporting "money to be stolen and sent to a miscegenation society." The story was left on his desk and published by accident, causing a considerable storm. He began feuding with James Laird, editor of the *Union* newspaper in town.

> "He was hurt by something I had said about him — some little thing — I don't remember what it was now — probably called him a horse-thief, or one of those little phrases customarily used to describe another editor."
> Autobiography of Mark Twain, Vol.1, p. 296

Three times he challenged Laird to a duel, until finally it was accepted. Dueling was illegal and Twain had to get out of town, leaving for San Francisco in May, entering what he calls his "slinking days.'" He wrote for the *Call*, and later sent stories back to the *Enterprise*. His last major visit to the West was in 1868, when once or twice he repeated his Sandwich Islands lectures from two years earlier, but generally gave a new one based on the *Quaker City* cruise to the Holy Land. Again the lecture series moved from San Francisco to Virginia City.

For lunch, most of us ended up at Sawdust Corner in the town center. There we laughed at a blue-aproned waitress who handled most of the tables as though they were in an assembly line. No matter what the order, she bellowed out "French fries, potato salad or cold slaw?" ringing up a dozen tables in mere minutes. She delivered the orders with the same loud efficiency. Mac went to use the men's room and came back with the biggest smile I have seen him wear. Sita had given him three quarters to gamble away and he won $10. It could have been a Comstock fortune and he wouldn't have been any prouder.

Around 2:00 we all met Ron James again for a bus tour of the region. During his lecture series, Mark Twain spoke at Gold Hill, Silver City, Dayton and of course, Virginia City. Ron took us out of town, past the 4th Ward School where we will be having dinner tonight. It was built in 1877 and at its height, boasted 1,000 students. It was finally closed in 1936. We took the steep road to Gold Hill, past the spot where in 1866, Mark Twain had been "held up" by some of his friends as a practical joke. According to Bob, he didn't much enjoy the experience. Bob later mentioned that Sam was more tolerant of verbal jokes as time went on, but that he detested practical jokes. *Roughing It* virtually ends with this story, told in great detail, and ending with Twain's firm resolution:

> "However, I suppose that in the long run I got the largest share of the joke at last; and in a shape not foreseen by the highwaymen, for the chilly exposure on the "divide" while I was in a perspiration gave me a cold which developed itself into a troublesome disease and kept my hands idle some three months, besides costing me quite a sum in doctor's bills. Since then I play no practical jokes on people and generally lose my temper when one is played on me."
> *Roughing It*, Univ. of California Press, 1995, p. 541-42.

In the final tally, however, he got the best of his friends, as he wrote on his departure from San Francisco:

SO-LONG. EDITORS ALTA:

I leave for the States in the Opposition steamer to-morrow, and I ask, as a special favor, that you will allow me to say good-bye to my highway-robber friends of the Gold Hill and Virginia Divide, and convince them that I have got ahead of them. They had their joke in robbing me and returning the money, and I had mine in the satisfaction of knowing that they came near freezing to death while they were waiting two hours for me to come along the night of the robbery. And at this day, so far from bearing them any ill will, I want to thank them kindly for their rascality. I am pecuniarily ahead on the transaction. I got a telegram from New York, last night, which reads as follows:

"New York, December 12th.

"Mark Twain: Go to Nudd, Lord & Co., Front street, collect amount of money equal to what highwaymen took from you. (Signed.) A.D.N."

I took that telegram and went to that store and called for a thousand dollars, with my customary modesty; but when I found they were going to pay it, my conscience smote me and I reduced the demand to a hundred. It was promptly paid, in coin, and now if the robbers think they have got the best end of that joke, they are welcome — they have my free consent to go on thinking so. (It is barely possible that the heft of the joke is on A.D.N., now.)

Good-bye, felons — good-bye. I bear you no malice. And I sincerely pray that when your cheerful career is closing, and you appear finally before a delighted and appreciative audience to be hanged, that you will be prepared to go, and that it will be as a ray of sunshine amid the gathering blackness of your damning recollections, to call to mind that you never got a cent out of me. So-long, brigands.

MARK TWAIN.

San Francisco *Alta California*, December 14, 1866 Quoted in www.twainquotes.com

🙠 🙢

The road makes a treacherous S-turn at Grider's Gulch leading into Gold Hill. The mines were primarily manned by Cornish miners in the heyday of the Comstock. The Gold Hill Depot dates to 1869 as does the old Bank of California and the Gold Hill Hotel. Today the Plum Mine is the only one still operating. Most of the mines were closed after 1942, when the government outlawed private gold. We drove through Devil's Gate at the bottom of the grade, and into Silver City, continuing through the modern prostitution center of Mound City to Dayton, where Twain also lectured. The old theater where he probably spoke is undergoing extensive restoration.

Dinner tonight was at the 4th Ward School, catered by the Café Del Rio in town. Ron James had suggested the site, and we were all thrilled to be here. The Washoe Zephyr had turned into a mini tornado by the time we arrived, and several of our people had to be assisted to get up the stairs and into the safely of the school. But once inside, what a treasure! There were four political subdivisions in Virginia City in 1877, when this school was built, intended to hold a maximum of 800 students. It was the first high school in Nevada. The place is monumental, a four-story edifice built in Empire style, boasting the very latest in amenities. It even had Philadelphia Flush Toilets, which flushed when you got up off the pot. It was one of many such schools, built exactly after a pattern book of the times. Today it is the only one remaining. There were in all sixteen spacious classrooms. Barbara Mackay is the director these days, operating an extensive museum, trying very hard to keep the doors open. She had one of her assistants, Chic, on hand to operate one of the old presses. We had a very fine dinner in the Wiegand Room, perhaps the first Mexican cuisine buffet I have ever attempted with a group. It was a delicious meal, as Ron had advertised.

This has been one of the best touring days I have ever experienced, due almost entirely to the expertise and good will of Ron James. He has made Virginia City come alive for us through several outstanding programs. He even satisfied Bob in his Mark Twain knowledge, which is no mean feat, and he left Mac without a rebuttal the next day. I can't recall in more than twenty trips with Mac, that we have had a better, more knowledgeable local guide.

V

We have a very easy day today, beginning with a drive to Lake Tahoe. In *Roughing It*, Twain talked about his adventures at Lake Tahoe, where he set the forest on fire.

> "While Johnny was carrying the main bulk of the provisions up to our "house" for future use, I took the loaf of bread, some slices of bacon, and the coffee-pot, ashore, set them down by a tree, lit a fire, and went back to the boat to get the frying pan. While I was at this, I heard a shout from Johnny, and looking up I saw that my fire was galloping all over the premises!
>
> John was on the other side of it. He had to run through the flames to get to the lake shore, and then we stood helpless and watched the devastation.
>
> The ground was deeply carpeted with dry pine-needles, and the fire touched them off as if they were gunpowder. It was wonderful to see with what fierce speed the tall sheet of flame traveled! My coffee-pot was gone, and everything with it.
>
> In a minute and a half the fire seized upon a dense growth of dry manzanita chaparral six or eight feet high, and then the roaring and popping and crackling was something terrific. We were driven to the boat by the intense heat, and there we remained, spell-bound."
> *Roughing It,* pp. 154-156

He also described the fire in a letter to his mother.

...The level ranks of flame were relieved at intervals by the standard-bearers, as we called the tall dead trees, wrapped in fire, and waving their blazing banners a hundred feet in the air. Then we could turn from this scene to the Lake, and see every branch, and leaf, and cataract of flame upon its bank perfectly reflected as in a gleaming, fiery mirror. The mighty roaring of the conflagration, together with our solitary and somewhat unsafe position (for there was no one within six miles of us,) rendered the scene very impressive. Occasionally one of us would remove his pipe from his mouth and say,—"Superb! Magnificent! Beautiful!—but by the Lord God Almighty, if we attempt to sleep in this little patch to-night, we'll never live till morning!

Mark Twain's Letters, Vol. 1, Letter to Jane Lampton Clemens, September 21, 1861.

Prior to the blaze, Sam gives a great description of the lake. Throughout *Roughing It*, he proves himself to be a very observant traveler, often giving detailed descriptions of the natural sights he is observing.

"At the border of the desert lies Carson Lake, or the "Sink" of the Carson, a shallow, melancholy sheet of water some eighty or a hundred miles in circumference. Carson river empties into it and is lost—sinks mysteriously into the earth and never appears in the light of the sun again—for the lake has no outlet whatever.

There are several rivers in Nevada, and they all have this mysterious fate. They end in various lakes or "sinks," and that is the last of them. Carson Lake, Humboldt Lake, Walker Lake, Mono Lake are all great sheets of water without any visible outlet. Water is always flowing into them, none is ever seen to flow out of them, and yet they remain always full, neither receding nor overflowing. What they do with their surplus is only known to the Creator."

Roughing It, p. 130-131

Lake Tahoe was originally named Lake Bonpland by Fremont after a French botanist. Mark Twain refers to it both as Lake Tahoe and as Lake Bigler named for John Bigler, the third governor of Nevada. Finally it became Tahoe from an Indian word for grasshopper soup (according to Mark Twain). This last is courtesy of Mac's book on California place names, an indispensable reference for all our field studies.

࿓ ࿔

Our destination is Grass Valley and Nevada City, both sites of his Sandwich Island lectures in 1866. And nearby are the remains of two gold camps that have since disappeared, Red Dog and You Bet. We will talk about them tomorrow.

We have lots of time on the bus for questions. Last night, Mac asked for questions from the folks figuring they would be useful to pepper Bob during our drive.

"What was Mark Twain's view of the Indians?"

Mac amended the question slightly to specify native American Indians, since Mark Twain had traveled rather extensively in India and very much enjoyed the people and the culture. Back at home, however, was a different matter. Bob explained that Twain disagreed completely with James Fenimore Cooper's idealized view of the Indians and felt he should counter that vision. In the west, he came across the Paiutes and some of the Costanoans, whom he regarded as uncouth. He considered the Nevada tribes to be crude and backward, as per his description of Chief Hoop-dee-doodle-doo who found the vermin dropping from his head quite good to eat.

> Now, Ma, you know what the warrior Hoop-de-doodle-doo looks like—and if you desire to know what he smells like, let him stand by the stove a moment, but have your hartshorn handy, for I tell you he could give the stink-pots of Sebastopol four in the game and skunk them. Follow him, too, when he goes out, and burn gun powder in his footsteps, because wherever he walks he sheds vermin of such prodigious size that the smallest specimen could swallow a grain of wheat without straining at it, and still feel hungry. You must not suppose that the warrior drops these vermin from choice, though. By no means, Madam—for he knows something about them which you don't, viz, that they are good to eat. There now. Can you find anything like that in Cooper? Perhaps not. Yet I could go before a magistrate and testify that the portrait is correct in every particular. Old Hoop himself would say it was "heap good."
>
> Letter to Jane Lampton Clemens, 20 March 1862
> *Mark Twain's Letters, Volume I, 1853-1866*, p. 177

He is at times almost crude in his descriptions of the tribes he encounters.

> "On the morning of the sixteenth day out from St. Joseph we arrived at the entrance of Rocky Cañon, two hundred and fifty miles from Salt Lake. It was along in this wild country somewhere, and far from any habitation of white men, except the stage stations that we came across the wretchedest type of mankind I have ever seen, up to this writing. I refer to the Goshoot Indians. From what we could see and all we could learn, they are very considerably inferior to even the despised Digger Indians of California, inferior to all races of savages on our continent, inferior even to even the Tierra del Fuegans, inferior to the Hottentots, and actually inferior in some respects to the Kytches of Africa. Indeed I have been obliged to look the bulky volumes of Wood's "Uncivilized Races of Men" clear through to find a savage tribe degraded enough to rank with the Goshoots."
>
> *Roughing It*, pp. 126-127

Sam Clemens had almost no contact with Indians in his early life, other than in reading, especially Cooper. He later wrote a scalding essay entitled "Fenimore Cooper's Literary Offenses" which not only ridicules the writer's Indian heroes, but calls into question every aspect of the writing itself

> "Cooper's art has some defects. In one place in "Deerslayer," and in the restricted space of two-thirds of a page, Cooper has scored 114 offenses against literary art out of a possible 115. It breaks the record….
>
> Cooper's gift in the way of invention was not a rich endowment; but such as it was he liked to work it, he was pleased with the effects, and indeed he did some quite sweet things with it. In his little box of stage-properties he kept six or eight cunning devices, tricks, artifices for his savages and woodsmen to deceive and circumvent each other with, and he was never so happy as when he was working these innocent things and seeing them go. A favorite one was to make a moccasined person tread in the tracks of the moccasined enemy, and thus hide his own trail. Cooper wore out barrels and barrels of moccasins in working that trick. Another stage-property that he pulled out of his box pretty frequently was the broken twig. He prized his broken twig above all the rest of his effects, and worked it the hardest. It is a restful chapter in any book of his when somebody doesn't step on a dry twig and alarm all the reds and whites for two hundred yards around. Every time a Cooper person is in peril, and absolute silence is worth four dollars a minute, he is sure to step on a dry twig. There may be a hundred other handier things to step on, but that wouldn't satisfy Cooper. Cooper requires him to turn out and find a dry twig; and if he can't do it, go and borrow one. In fact, the Leatherstocking Series ought to have been called the Broken Twig Series."
>
> "Fennimore Cooper's Literary Offenses," *Mark Twain Collected Tales, Sketches, Speeches and Essays, 1891-1910*, pp. 180-182.

"Did Mark Twain ever campaign for one of the presidents?"

Generally Sam Clemens was cautious about expressing his political opinions. But he campaigned for Grant in the 1872 election, perhaps because the opponent was Horace Greeley. He and Grant had a number of interesting encounters over the years. Bob said that Sam liked Grant a great deal, and knew he was a good writer. They first met at a reception in Washington D.C. in 1868. In 1871, he met him again at a White House meeting. In 1879 at an Army of the Tennessee Reunion, Twain was a speaker, talking on the "The Babies." He said that soldiers were once babies in their cradles, and he imagined the future supreme general of the army "doing his best to get his big toe into his mouth." And he added, "If the child is father to the man, we know that he succeeded." There was universal applause and Grant smiled for the first time that night.

On greeting Clemens later, Grant said, "I'm embarrassed, Mr. Clemens. Are you?" It was a "quote" from what Clemens had said to him in the White House in 1871. Later, when the *Century* offered Grant $8,000 for his memoirs, Sam talked him into publishing them with his own publishing company. The book was finally published in 1885, earning Mrs. Grant $450,000.

In 1884, Twain was one of the "Mugwumps" who bolted the Republican party to support Grover Cleveland against James Blaine.

He was not a fan, however, of Teddy Roosevelt, opposing his stance on imperialism in Cuba and the Philippines.

Bob was not willing to accept a comparison of Twain and Lincoln, except that both went down the Mississippi. He did say that William Dean Howells, editor of the *Atlantic Monthly*, called Twain "the Lincoln of our literature."

"Did Mark Twain write out his speeches?"

Yes, he wrote the "Sandwich Islands" and "American Vandal" speeches but adjusted them frequently, often on the spot. Every lecture "should be a board with square pegs and round pegs." The square pegs were serious points; the round ones, humorous, pegs that he would adjust during the lecture to match the audience.

"How much did he make on these lectures?"

Bob said that initially he was paid about $100, which in today's terms is about $2,000. Lecturing was an accepted institution in those days, common to all communities. Twain was not among the highest paid at first. That level was awarded to such speakers as Artemus Ward, Dickens, etc. But as his fame grew, he was receiving $2,000 for a lecture, once $10,000 for a series of five. In Austria he attempted a few parts of lectures in German, but was not terribly confident of his pronunciation, although from his essay "The Awful German Language" in *A Tramp Abroad*, it is clear he had a good grasp of the language.

"Who set up all of these lectures?"

Denis McCarthy was a "pseudo manager" who helped to set up his California tours. Mark Twain did his own ads for the first lectures. Bob passed out a couple of examples which are hilarious, more like circus promos. For his first lecture in 1866, Twain hired the opera house in San Francisco for half price, printed the ads, and sold the tickets. "The trouble begins at eight."

Bob pretty much filled our ride with interesting details about every subject under the sun. I have never seen him stumped, no matter the topic.

We arrived in Nevada City just after noon, dropping the folks off for a lunch break while Larry and I drove over to Grass Valley to check out the Holbrooke Hotel where we are staying. I was told that there is a night market on Thursday where they close down Main Street and we won't be able to get in. As it turns out, the market is in the evening, so we are able to get in before they set up. The Holbrooke is an old hotel, dating back before Twain's day, though he probably talked up the street at one of the town halls. We got in nicely and took the afternoon off to explore a bit. Dinner was at the hotel, another very fine meal. They even let me set up my own cocktail party in the room, something few hotels would even consider.

VI

Red Dog and You Bet—two historical names that are about as esoteric as can be if you like to explore California. It seems hard to fathom how Mark Twain came to be speaking in those two places, but it seems that in their prime both towns had around 5,000 inhabitants, tribute to the power of mining, which at that time had become hydraulic. In this part of the gold country, they channeled water in from the high Sierras to operate huge water guns, monitors, which literally tore down mountains. Just north of Grass Valley is Malekov Diggins, the most sickening of these forced erosion sites, and in the mountains south of the city one finds the Tom Brady cuts which washed the hills down into the Greenhorn or Bear rivers.

Six months ago, Mary and I drove up to find Red Dog and You Bet. What we discovered was the Red Dog-You Bet Calvary Baptist Church, a fairly new structure sitting about in the center of where the old towns used to be. There was a pastor's name, Joe Ramey, but no phone number. At a nearby mailbox we stopped to ask a man if he knew Joe Ramey.

"Oh, he's my pastor. Do you want his phone number?"

Through Joe, I made arrangements to have a picnic lunch and lecture at the church. I asked him if he knew any of the pastie shops, where they make these meat pies that the Cornish miners took to work every day. Joe agreed to order a bunch and put a lunch together.

Two weeks ago Mary and I were invited to a potluck dinner at the church. Of course we accepted but ended up missing it because my GPS unit sent us to Red Dog Road instead of You Bet Road. One works; the other doesn't. But we did get there as the brunch was ending and met Joe and his friendly congregation. He drove us down to the Red Dog cemetery assuring me that there would be no trouble getting a bus down there. That may well be true, but it would be impossible to get it back out. We scratched the idea of cemeteries. Besides the burial grounds for the two towns, there is nothing left of either community, save a single worn barn building and a couple of stone footings. Otherwise the towns survive in the name of a single Baptist church.

Regardless of all of that, today we are having our pastie lunch and talk from Bob about the Sandwich Island lecture. In addition, there is a local man, Dave Comstock, who has written about the two mining towns and will give us a bit of background history.

We got up to the church, situated in the mountains south of Grass Valley, around 10:30. Joe Ramey and his fellow pastor Guy Prudhomme, with their families, were there to meet us. Dave Comstock was also there, a very interesting man, author of a pair of books on the gold rush, and interestingly, a former employee at the U.C. Press. He and Bob exchanged names of several mutual acquaintances. He opened our morning with a brief history of the two camps. Much of Red Dog had been destroyed by fire shortly before Mark Twain arrived. It was a city in the mid-1850s of around 5,000, employed exclusively in placer mining. There was no hard-rock mining in the region. You Bet was a later settlement, introducing hydraulic mining on a large scale. The eroding diggings washed out much of Red Dog, whose population gradually moved over to You Bet. And they moved many of the buildings with them. The hydraulic mining continued as late as 1930, when it was finally outlawed.

Dave told us he moved from the city to this area 35 years ago, a time when they were off the grid, with no phones, and generators to provide electrical power.

"Anyone within five miles was a close neighbor." Every evening at 7:00 they all got on their CB radios and talked together. "As utilities arrived, it destroyed the tightness of the community."

Bob took over from there. He related a story about one of the Red Dog miners being forced to introduce Mark Twain as speaker.

> "I don't know anything about this man," the miner announced, "At least I know only two things. One is, he hasn't been in a penitentiary, and the other is (after a pause and almost sadly), *I don't know why.*"
>
> Autobiography, V.1, p.153

Bob got into a detailed discussion of the nature of the "Sandwich Island lecture". In March, 1866, Mark Twain left for Hawaii, or the Sandwich Islands. He stayed four and a half months and sent twenty-five letters to the *Sacramento Union*. In August, he was back in San Francisco, went to Sacramento to collect his pay, and then lounged around for a while. He suggested that maybe he should give a public lecture about the Sandwich Islands. Warned by friends against it, he rented McGuire's Opera House at half price, wrote the advertisements and sold the tickets, urging several friends to attend to support him in the audience. Though he was extremely nervous, it was a great success, and launched him on his career, which would see him give more than 1000 talks, speeches and lectures, across the nation and in dozens of countries around the world.

From October to December, 1866, he spoke throughout Northern California, a lecture of "random construction." Bob said that this was very fine writing, because he had to have a serious thread somewhere in the content. There is no complete copy of the speech, but Bob constructed much of it from excerpts found in Paine, newspaper reports and other sources. He read several of those passages, which once again, must be appreciated as examples of spoken rather than written language.

MARK TWAIN'S LECTURE. - This lecture, delivered in San Francisco on the night of October 2d, appears by the comments of the press of that city to have been a success. The Bulletin says:

The Academy of music was "stuffed," to use an expression of the lecturer, to repletion last night, on the occasion of the delivery of "Mark Twain's" (Samuel Clements') [sic] lecture on the Sandwich Islands. It is perhaps fortunate that the King of Hawaii did not arrive in time to attend, for unless he had gone early he must have been turned away, as many others were who could not gain admittance. Nearly every seat in the house had been engaged beforehand, and those who came last had to put up with the best they could get, while many were obliged to stand up all the evening.

The appearance of the lecturer was the signal for applause, and from the time he closed, the greatest good feeling existed. He commenced by apologizing for the absence of an orchestra. He wasn't used to getting up operas of this sort. He had engaged a musician to come and play, but the trombone player insisted upon having some other musicians to help him. He had hired the man to work and wouldn't stand any such nonsense, and so discharged him on the spot.

The lecturer then proceeded with his subject, and delivered one of the most interesting and amusing lectures ever given in this city. It was replete with information of that character which is seldom got from books, describing all those minor traits of character, customs and habits which are only noted by a close observer, and yet the kind of information which gives the most correct idea of the people described. Their virtues were set forth generously, while their vices were touched off in a humorous style, which kept the audience in a constant state of merriment. From the lecturer's reputation as a humorist, the audience were unprepared for the eloquent description of the volcano of Kilauea, a really magnificent piece of word painting, their appreciation of which was shown by long and continued applause. Important facts concerning the resources of the Islands were given, interspersed with pointed anecdotes and side-splitting jokes. Their history, traditions, religion, politics, aristocracy, royalty, manners and customs, were all described in brief, and in the humorous vein peculiar to the speaker... The lecturer kept his audience constantly interested and amused for an hour and a half and the lecture was unanimously pronounced a brilliant success."

Daily Hawaiian Herald, October 23, 1866. Quoted in www.twainquotes.com.

આ ✎

Somewhere along the way back to campus, Bob again brought up the subject of *Innocents Abroad* and the *Quaker City* voyage.

"*Innocents Abroad*?" a voice came from the rear. "When are we doing that trip, Mac?"

"How about Hawaii?" another voice volunteered. "Let's trace his lectures in the Sandwich Islands."

Bob's eyes lit up on that last one.

"What do you think, Jack? Hawaii?"

By the tone in Mac's voice, I already knew that we would be doing Hawaii with Mark Twain soon. I doubt that anyone has ever done such a tour, excepting Sam Clemens himself. I suspect it will be a huge success.

But before we even get to Hawaii, our plans are veering off greatly as we intend to *Follow the Equator* across the Pacific.

BOOK FOUR

Mark Twain In India

"This is indeed India! The land of dreams and romance, of fabulous wealth and fabulous poverty, of splendor and rags, of palaces and hovels, of famine and pestilence, of genii and giants and Aladdin lamps, of tigers and elephants, the cobra and the jungle, the country of a hundred nations and a hundred tongues, of a thousand religions and two millions gods, cradle of the human race, birthplace of human speech, mother of history, grandmother of legend, great-grandmother of tradition, whose yesterdays bear date with the mouldering antiquities of the rest of the nations—the one sole country under the sun that is endowed with an imperishable interest for alien prince and alien peasant, for lettered and ignorant, wise and fool, rich and poor, bond and free, the one land that *all* men desire to see, and having seen once, by even a glimpse, would not give that glimpse for the shows of all the rest of the globe combined.
Oxford Mark Twain, *Following the Equator,* p. 348.

It seems that we at Cal can never get very far away from Samuel Clemens. We have done three trips to date, following the wonderful storyteller around America. This coming November we will add a fourth in Hawaii. But Mark Twain also came to India, telling his experiences as only he can in *Following the Equator.* He came to Calcutta, ruled of course in those days by the British, and he followed them into their old hill station in Darjeeling, just as we will do. It was part of his world lecture series in 1895-96, and he spoke in both cities as well as in many other parts of India. So I suppose we can put an asterisk on this tour and call it yet another Mark Twain experience. The author, known everywhere for his humor, was a wonderful travel writer. His description of Hawaii through letters back to Sacramento is considered the most accurate and informative of his day, one of the primary sources on mid-19th century island culture. His description of India, which fills a large portion of the *Following the Equator,* is also filled with a wealth of accurate descriptions, cleverly couched, sometimes well hidden, in his always imaginative ramblings. Over the next four days, we are not going to be very far removed from the itinerary he followed in Calcutta and Darjeeling, the biggest difference being the plane flight which eliminates the bone-wearying train challenge between those cities in Twain's day.

Twain spent three months in India, traveling to the north after he left Calcutta. In the course of his stay he visited much of the country, traveling as far as Lahore, (now Pakistan) and even as far as the Afghan border region, and marveling along the way at the major sites in Delhi, Agra, and Jaipur. His praise of the country, its people and culture, is lavish at times.

Two years ago, we did a first trip to India with Bear Treks, visiting Delhi, Agra, Jaipur, and Jodhpur, as well as other areas not on Mark Twain's itinerary. Looking back now with a view to his travels, it is easy to understand his enthusiasm for the country. Curiously he compares the Taj Mahal both to Niagara Falls and to an ice-storm, both apparently compliments.

> "I mean to speak of only one of these many world-renowned buildings—the Taj Mahal, the most celebrated construction in the earth. I had read a great deal too much about it in the daytime, I saw it in the moonlight, I saw it near at hand, I saw it from a distance; and I knew all the time, that of its kind it was *the* wonder of the world, with no competitor now and no possible future competitor; and yet, it was not my Taj. My Taj was built by excitable literary people; it was solidly lodged in my head and I could not blast it out... I knew that I ought to do with the Taj as I was obliged to do with Niagara—see it fifteen times, and let my mind gradually get rid of the Taj built in it by its describers, by help of my imagination, and substitute it for the Taj of fact....
>
> I suppose that many, many years ago I gathered the idea that the Taj's place in the achievements of man was exactly the place of the ice-storm in the achievements of Nature; that the Taj represented man's supremest possibility in the creation of grace and beauty and exquisiteness and splendor, just as the ice-storm represents Nature's supremest possibility in the combination of those same qualities.... If I thought of the ice-storm, the Taj rose before me divinely beautiful; if I thought of the Taj, with its encrustings and inlayings of jewels, the vision of the ice-storm rose. And so to me, all these years, the Taj has had no rival among the temples and palaces of men, none that even remotely approached it—it was man's architectural ice-storm."
> *Following the Equator*, 577-578

I

This tour is really labeled as "Bhutan," where we will spend two weeks after we leave India. Bhutan is a favorite place of Mac Laetsch and his son, Krishen because several members of the royal family of Bhutan matriculated at U.C. Berkeley, and Mac was a major figure of welcome and hospitality for most of them. Krishen is our guide for the trip, which of necessity will begin with a few days in Calcutta (Kolkata today) and Darjeeling.

We fly to Kolkata this morning at 9:40 on Jet Air, one of India's privately-owned airlines. That means a 5:30 wake-up call, breakfast at 6:00 and a hotel departure at 7:00, all of which should not be too bad, because most of us will be wide awake long before that phone rings. I figure one more day, living the clock schedule we have at home, and we will be adjusted to the Indian time zone. Of course, that is even more difficult to figure out, because India is 12 time zones different from San Francisco, but it is much further away than say China, which is 15 zones different, or Japan which can be as much as 17 hours different. After crossing the International Date Line, places get closer, so to speak, as they get further away. I never did very well in math in school. Actually, as we neared Kolkata, the pilot set our clocks a half hour forward, which really messes things up if you are precise in your outlook on life, but for most of us, after all day in the air yesterday/day-before, a half hour one way or the other doesn't matter. I dutifully reset my watch, while Mary sat there contentedly on good old San Francisco time.

Two years ago we used Ventours as our tour operator on a lengthy trip to India, so it was easy to contact them again this time for our brief stay in Kolkata. We were met at the airport by Vanesh, the manager of Ventours, and Asif, our guide for the two days in the city. Ventours has farmed out the touring to a local company and my friend Vivian Peres is here to see if the service is up to their standards. We are staying in the Oberoi Grand Hotel, one of India's finest hotel chains, one which we used extensively on our last trip. We landed on time at Netaji Subhas Chandra Bose International Airport (Isn't that a name!) It is named for one of the prime movers of the Indian Independence Movement, during World War II, imprisoned eleven times by the British. His battle cry was "Give me your blood and I will give you your freedom!" He died mysteriously in an air crash in 1945. As we exited, we were officially greeted to Kolkata and to India with beautiful and aromatic flower leis, making even us guys perk up a bit. The weather is hot, but not nearly as humid as I feared it would be.

Our route to the hotel took us through the rather new IT and condominium section of Salt Lake. Asif gave us a bit of background on the city, named by the British "Calcutta," but recently reclaiming its old name of Kolkata. The city was formed in the area of three early villages: Kolikata, Sutanuti and Gobindopur on the banks of the Hooghly River that flows into the delta of the Ganges and the Bay of Bengal. Kolkata is the capital of the province of West Bengal. The British East India Co. arrived on August 24, 1690, led by Job Charnoch, whose arrival is regarded as the city's birthday. Fort William was begun in 1698. Today the population of the city itself is about 4.5 million, with another 10 million living in the greater urban area, making it India's third largest city. Bengali is the mother tongue while English is the official language. Our route from the airport took us past the impressive Victoria Memorial, probably the best-known symbol of the British Raj and the city itself. Nearby is the largest racecourse in India, built in 1817. In the distance we could see the Howrah Bridge, connecting Kolkata to its twin sister on the other side of the Hoogley. The old, steel Howrah Bridge (1943), a city landmark, is the longest cantilever bridge in the world at 645 meters. Also in the distance is the more modern Hoogley Bridge, built in 1992.

It does not seem that Kolkata is as dirty and cluttered with litter as was Delhi and most of the country along the Grand Trunk Highway on our last visit. That is not to say that Kolkata is clean, but everything in India is relative. There aren't nearly the cows that you find in Delhi, and certainly not the monkeys, but as we drove along the Maidan, the large central park, we did see that they use goats, a few cows and some horses as lawn mowers. We briefly saw old Fort William, now the Headquarters for the Eastern Command of the Indian Army.

It took only about forty-five minutes to get settled into our beautiful Oberoi Grand Hotel on Nehru Road in the Esplanade, a standard of excellence for over 130 years. It is certainly a wonderful way to begin our stay in India. Mary and I discovered immediately how good the service is, when a waitress in the Chowringhee Bar dropped a glass of wine all over me. The place positively erupted in apologies, amazement, shock and a dozen other emotions, all of which I considered rather humorous. The Hotel Manager materialized from somewhere, assuring me that the hotel would launder my clothes and offered us anything we wanted for lunch. I assured him that a glass of wine for Mary was quite fine. We had no sooner hit our room when the phone rang from the Housekeeping Manager, advising me that a man would arrive shortly to retrieve my pants and shirt. Then the doorbell rang, the Floor Manager, with his apologies. I was delighted finally to get rid of the clothes, before the Mayor or the Chief of Police called. That evening, even the Catering Manager had heard of the incident and tendered his apologies. Those pants could have been washed clean using only the tears shed by the staff.

At 4:00 we left for a boat ride on the Hooghly, driving through the city to the strand along the river. There we trudged through the mud, over the rails, (where a commuter train positively roared by only inches from our noses), over a bunch of big chains and onto the *MV Panchanan*, a rather dirty, cluttered river boat that proposed to take us for a ride. Off we chugged, downstream, past the old East India Co. warehouses, looking at some of the notable buildings of the city, including the large dome of the old British Post Office. We cruised under the Howrah Bridge, where we saw a sign on the Calcutta side which said, "Welcome to the City of Joy," a name bestowed on Kolkata by writer Dominique Lapierre. Further along, we saw the buildings, largely skeletons these days, of the old jute mills, their high stacks now crowned by encroaching bushes and trees. Once there were 150 of these mills along the river, turning Bangladesh jute into mats, rope and coverings. We noticed a great many ferries all jammed with people, which our guides said was because of the New Year's Holiday today. It was almost dark by the time we turned around, but we made a stop at the Dhakneshwar Kali Temple, the destination for all those boatloads of people. It was an exciting thing to "walk the Pilgrims' Way" with hundreds of the faithful, bound for the temple. We took a brief look at the historic buildings and then quickly returned to our boat and back to the dock. It was after 7:00 by the time we reached the Oberoi.

This evening, we did not officially have anything scheduled, but for most of us it will be our second night together and we have not yet had a Welcome Dinner. I decided we needed one, and earlier Krishen contacted the hotel's Managing Director, gave him my budget, and arranged to have our Welcome Dinner in the elegant Gharana Room. It would prove to be one of the best meals we had on the entire trip, a great sampling of Indian cuisine, beautifully presented in a buffet, and professionally hosted and served by the staff. For Mac's sake I list the dishes:

Chanar Dalna
Shukno Karoushuti
Aar Phulkopi
Jhungh Aloo Poshto
Shorshe Dharoush
Cholar dal Narkel Diye
Murgir Johl
Bekti Macher Paturi (fish in banana leaves)
Paneer Chat
Paapri Chat

The desserts included a Sandesh platter, Mishti doi ("most popular dessert in Bengal), Gulab jamuh, chocolate mud pie and vanilla ice cream.

II

"There was plenty to see in Calcutta, but there was not plenty of time for it., I saw the effort that Clive built; and the place where Warren Hastings and the author of the Junius Letters fought their duel; and the great botanical gardens; and the fashionable afternoon turnout in the Maiden; and a grand review of the garrison in a great plain at sunrise; and a military tournament in which great bodies of native military exhibited the perfection of their drill at all arms, a spectacular and beautiful show occupying several nights and closing with the mimic storming of a native fort which was as good as the reality for thrilling and accurate detail, and better than the reality for security and comfort; we had a pleasure excursion on the *Hoogly* by courtesy of friends, and devoted the rest of the time to social life and the Indian museum. One should spend a month at the museum, an enchanted place of Indian antiquities. Indeed, a person might spend half a year among the beautiful and wonderful things without exhausting their interest."
Following the Equator, p 522

Calcutta rose near a trio of villages, Kalikata, Govindapur and Sutanuti, under the rule of the Nabob of Bengal Sinaj ad-Dauhah, when the British arrived in 1690 in the form of the British East India Company. In 1702 they finished Fort William to protect their interests in a very competitive part of the trading world, a fort they continually reinforced as threats loomed from the French and Portuguese. In mid-century the fort was attacked by the Nabob, protesting the actions of the British in his land, an attack that led to the infamous "Black Hole of Calcutta," a prison cell which was jammed with British captives, most of whom died in the crush. The following year, 1757, Robert Clive counterattacked and ended the rule of the Nabob, destroyed the prison, and cemented the rule of the British East India Company. In 1772, Calcutta became the capital of British India, which it remained until 1911, with summer respites after 1864, when the government moved to the mountains at Shimla.

The city was formed out of the three villages along the banks of the Hooghly River. Swamps were drained, and under the rule of Governor General Richard Wellesley (1797-1895), Calcutta became known as the "City of Palaces." During the 18th and 19th centuries it was the center of the opium trade, operated by the British East India Company. By the early 19th century the city was effectively divided in two, the British "White Town," and the Indian "Black Town." Calcutta suffered dreadfully during World War II, bombed by the Japanese, and enduring a devastating famine in 1943, when millions in Bengal perished following the effects of drought, warfare and misrule. Today the name has changed to Kolkata, which generally implies not only the inner city but the surrounding suburbs, creating India's third largest city, depending on who did the counting and when. The metropolitan area of 15 million people is the 8th largest in the world.

We began this morning with a walk of the region of the British Raj, the BBD Bag (Binay Badal Dinash Bag), once known as Dalhousie Square. The bus took us to St. John's Church on Council House Street, built in 1784, a stately old building with a wealth of monuments surrounding it. Most of us were drawn to the monument to those who died in the infamous Black Hole of Calcutta in 1756. The plaque says that 143 were imprisoned in a tiny cell, and only 23 survived, although there is quite a bit of difference in the numbers reported by various historians. This is not the actual site of the prison; it probably was somewhere around the Post Office. Twain had a great time with the Black Hole:

"When India is mentioned to the citizen of a far country it suggests Clive, Hastings, the Mutiny, Kipling, and a number of other great events; and the mention of Calcutta infallibly brings up the Black Hole. And so, when that citizen finds himself in the capital of India he goes first of all to see the Black Hole of Calcutta—and is disappointed.

The Black Hole was not preserved; it is gone, long, long ago. It is strange. Just as it stood, it was built as a monument; a ready-made one. It was finished, it was complete, its materials were strong and lasting, it needed no furnishing up, no repairs; it merely needed to be let alone. It was the first brick, the Foundation Stone, upon which was reared a mighty Empire—the Indian Empire of Great Britain. It was the ghastly episode of the Black Hole that maddened the British and brought Clive, that young military marvel, raging up from Madras; it was the seed from which sprung Plassay; and it was that extraordinary battle, whose like had not been seen in the earth since Agincourt, that laid deep and strong the foundations of England's colossal Indian sovereignty.

And yet within the time of men who still live, the Black Hole was torn down and thrown away as carelessly as if its brick were common clay, not ingots of historic gold. There is no accounting for human beings.

The supposed site of the Black Hole is marked by an engraved plate. I saw that; and better that than nothing. The Black Hole was a prison—a cell is nearer the right word—eighteen feet square, the dimensions of an ordinary bed-chamber; and into this place the victorious Nabob of Bengal packed 146 of his English prisoners.... Before the dawn came, the captives were all dead but twenty-three..."

Following the Equator, p 520

Another impressive monument is the Mausoleum of those from the East India Co, who died in the Romilla War, in 1794. The church itself is quite picturesque, with rows of caned chairs instead of pews, many of which are original. Five columns line each side of the nave, leading to a vaulted Romanesque sanctuary with a blue niche behind the altar. The most famous element of the church is a large painting of the Last Supper, which certainly brings to mind the Da Vinci code, since the apostle John looks very much like Mary Magdalene. In the rear of the church is a small room, the office of Warren Hastings, who orchestrated the growth of the East India Co. His chair, wash basin and table are still being used.

The British section of the inner city is most imposing. We walked past the High Court, very stylish in red brick with yellow trim, and a rather modern-looking Moorish design to the windows on the façade. The Town Hall (1813) could have been taken right out of London with its massive white columns. There are blocks of buildings that hearken back to the Raj: the City Library, the National Insurance Co., the Reserve Bank of India, Hong Kong House, Royal Insurance Co., and of course, the massive domed block of the Post Office, the largest in India. Our group immediately invaded the last of these in search of post card stamps, while I occupied myself in the center of the rotunda with a wonderful bronze of Sanatun Rudra Pal, the first postman, armed with spear, lantern and mail sack.

In the midst of all of these historic buildings, modern Kolkata is very evident. A car drove by, loudspeaker blaring, "on election duty." India is in the midst of elections, and they do it in a curious way, holding about five different elections at different times across the country. There are not enough security police to oversee every polling place, so they hold the elections on different dates, allowing the police to move from spot to spot. West Bengal's election will be held soon, with all of them complete by May 18. I asked about the problem of exit polls affecting the outcomes of the later votes and was told that such poles were illegal. However the news this evening was filled with the "results" of voting across the nation. The province was split after independence, East Pakistan being lopped off over religious reasons, later becoming the nation of Bangladesh.

At this time of the morning, the city is beginning to come alive. A few merchants had opened their stores already, and many of the vendors had set up shop on the sidewalks. I took a picture of a young teaboy with a large cauldron of boiling milk. Nearby, Krishen spotted the vendor, filling the traditional pottery cups with hot tea, something he had discussed last night. Mac always talks about the "disappearing India," using these pottery cups as evidence, since they have largely been replaced by Styrofoam or plastic cups. Krishen immediately bargained for 18 of the cups, so everyone could take home a souvenir of this vanished India. Mary took three.

We reboarded the bus and drove around the square near the Post Office. Asif pointed out the Writer's Hall, a huge building that housed the scribes of the East India Co. "All big shots now have to come here to begin their company." There was a "Dead Letter Office" in the old days, where letters written for deceased soldiers were collected and forwarded to next of kin. The building is now the CTO, Central Telephone Office.

We drove across the 2nd Hooghly Bridge, the new one, built in 1992, more importantly, looking down at a spot pointed out by Krishen, where in 1956, Sita waved goodbye to Mac from the Port of Calcutta. "She had been sent to India to meet someone of means and title. She met someone with title and little means." The Port is the largest river port in India, about 200 miles from the Bay of Bengal.

On the other side of the bridge is the city of Howrah, founded in 1657 and older than Kolkata. It is an industrial city, with steel plants, and jute mills. It also boasts the Botanical Garden, which was on Mark Twain's list of sites to see. The garden was founded in 1773 by a Col. Keith over 270 acres. It seems that everywhere the British went they established a hotel, of course with a bar, and then a Royal Botanical Garden (to grow plants necessary for their empire), and a bunch of private clubs. At this time of year, the garden looks dry and rather empty, but we only had one thing to see really, the world's largest banyan tree (*ficus bengalensis*), a giant that is 250 years old, and spreads over 1.5 hectares, with more than 2,800 air roots propping it up. Actually the tree has no central trunk, it having become diseased and cut out in 1925.

The town around the garden is alive with people, on bikes, mopeds, in pedicabs or trucks, or just lounging around. The men are mostly nondescript; the women light up the day with their bright saris. One such was walking down the street, brilliantly dressed in bright purple, carrying a regular old black umbrella to shield her from the sun. There seemed to be lots of buildings started, and lots of them stopped, projects empty of workers, or with just one or two puttering around. Most were simply ignored. Krishen noted that this is due to cash flow, or the lack of it at any given time. The place was as Asif said, "in a state of becoming." Everywhere horns blare, as impatient drivers voice their need to keep moving. We pulled up on one of the main streets and were led up a back alley to a typical apartment. It turned out to be the Artisana Center of

Crafts and Textiles, a place that hires and trains poor artists, producing some exciting craft items. Most of us found treasures in that store—paintings, textiles, bronze and brass items, jewelry.

Our morning ended at the prestigious old Bengal Club, founded in 1827, one of the bastions of the Raj era. A sign advised "dogs and Indians not allowed," a condition that existed until 1970. Of course we were met by an Indian member, Atmaran Sarogi, an old friend of Mac's and Krishen's, who told us that the club is now only about a quarter of its original size. He showed us old photographs of the place in its glory time, and from the second floor, pointed out the area that had once comprised the club. Most members today are corporate executives. "If anyone wants to know the history of the club, there is the book over there on the table. I have never read it."

We enjoyed a fine lunch at the club. After the meal, one of Krishen's friends, Ifti, who runs a company called Calcutta Walks, talked about life in the city from the viewpoint of a recent outsider. (Ifti is from Rajasthan.) He mentioned North Kolkata, Black Town, where "all of the houses were picked up and thrown into the air, landing wherever they could." He said that much of the modern city is neither Black Town nor White Town, but more like gray, filled with Chinese, Jews, Muslims, etc. He mentioned that Kolkata is still not viewed as a tourist destination, and struggles to attract people, but says that it is a fine 2-night stay. "10 years ago, Calcutta was deemed a 'dead city'," a Communist city. Today it is 40% Bengali and 60% mixed.

Following lunch we drove a short distance to the Indian Museum, the very one that Mark Twain so raved about. Interesting signs at the entrance: "Ticket Counter is closed before half an hour daily," and "Eatables not allowed inside." The entrance fee is 10 rupees for Indians, 150 r. for foreigners. I was frankly shocked by the place, which didn't seem to have been cleaned since Twain wandered through its halls. The museum is filled with the old religious sculptures of early India, many resembling those we saw *in situ* at Angkor Wat in Cambodia. They are very poorly signed, often with the signs missing or damaged, with nothing posing by way of general explanation. The building labors under stifling heat, with no apparent worry about damaging the collections. Most of us endured the ground floor and gave up on seeing the rest, lasting just a few moments before returning to the hotel. Mary and I walked down to Park St. and the Oxford Book Store to pick up some books on Calcutta.

This evening we again met Atmaran Sarogi, this time at another private club, the Tollygunde Club (est. 1895), the "Tolly," as it is known in Kolkata, one of the prestigious athletic clubs of the city, boasting an 18-hole golf course, tennis, polo, cricket, snooker facilities. The place is overrun with bars. Mr. Sarogi led us into the Wells Lifestyle Lounge, and then on a somewhat rambling tour that took us past the Tipu Sultan Room, the Cruickshank Bar (Where "Smoking here is an offense."), the White Mischief Swimming Pool, the Black Dog Tavern ("Proudly old fashioned"), the Glen Drummond Indigo Lounge, and finally into the Antiquity Lounge, where a sort of dinner was served. Unfortunately Mr. Sarogi had just gone through some serious surgery and seemed to be rather disconnected this evening, and much of what he had to say was difficult if not impossible to follow, not at all as he had been this afternoon. Krishen was very taken back by his performance, but I think that most of us understood the situation.

> "I believe that in India "cold weather" is merely a conventional phrase and has come into use through the necessity of having some way to distinguish between weather which will melt a brass door-knob and weather which will only make it mushy... But this cold weather was too warm for us; so we started to Darjeeling, in the Himalayas—a twenty-four hour journey."
>
> *Following the Equator,* p. 523

We will make most of this journey in a little over an hour, thanks to Jet Airlines' flight to Bagdogra. In Twain's day, the trek was done by train, which he describes with great glee in his journal, filling his mind and the reader's brain with long accounts of the many "man-eating" creatures about which India can boast. His description of riding a handcart down from the mountains is a classic, a route we will be taking part of the way by train, the same train he laughs about during his descent. Twain also lectured in Darjeeling, before retiring to one of the British clubs he so liked. We will leave him in Darjeeling, because he wanders off in the opposite direction from us, on his way to the Afghanistan border area, while musing at length about the glories and tragedies of the Great Mutiny of 1857.

We boarded our Jet Air flight 617 in mid-morning, opting from the outset to skip the lunch that was offered on arrival in Bagdogra, because it was quite evident that the road to Darjeeling was going to take considerably longer than the three hours listed on our itinerary. Just last week, Jim and Ruth drove the exact route we will take today, and they reported that the "shortcut" road to Darjeeling was under construction and we would have to take the longer route. A kind of warm snack was served on the plane, which was enough to get us through the morning. Even that was a remarkable bit of service because the flight lasted only 49 minutes.

On arrival in Bagdogra, we were met by Randeep Khati, the owner of Mystic Tours, who will be our guide for the next couple of days. We opted early on to have two mini buses to split the group, in order to give everyone some extra leg room on these long drives, both to Darjeeling as well as from there to Phuentsholing two days from now. Krishen became the guide in one bus and Randeep in the other. We noted that there was no AC on either minibus but were assured that the high altitudes of Darjeeling made such a thing unnecessary. It was 2:00 when we left the airport, bound for the first of Britain's Hill Stations, a mere 105 kilometers away. The road, named in honor of the first native guide to conquer Everest, follows the route of the old Himalayan Railroad. We weren't very far along when the traffic came to a complete stop, blocked on the narrow road by a motorcycle accident that involved injuries. It probably held us up for a quarter hour, once the police arrived and took their report. Of course this mountain traffic made matters worse as vehicles of all shapes and sizes jammed the shoulders trying to get through, arriving at a fine condition of complete gridlock. The solution as could be expected from our Kolkata experience was obvious—hit the horns!

Again underway, we made our first pit stop at Sikuna, the first train stop on the way to Darjeeling. There we noticed our first posters for the Free Ghurkaland campaign which is very active in the mountains, shutting down Darjeeling a couple of months ago. "We want a separate state of Ghurkaland," read the banner. They don't want complete independence from India, just from West Bengal.

The road began to rise as soon as we left Bagdogra, beginning the ascent which would raise us 6000' to Darjeeling. At another spot, a tree had fallen over the road, although we were able to slip through. "That tree was here a week ago," Jim commented, his head shake an editorial on the road maintenance system in the region. All along the route, we smiled at some of the road signs:

"Donate blood at the blood bank, not on this road."
"Have a slow and joyous ride."
"Do not be rash and end in crash."

"It's your life. Save it!"

"Drive, don't fly!"

The road conditions almost require such signs—a narrow, single lane path that is often filled with potholes, littered with fallen rocks, obstructed by cattle, a few macaque monkeys, goat herds, slow lorries and people. At least seven of us, the deWalls, Petersons, Dolds and Kate were quite prepared for Hill Station Roads, having endured the six-hour road to Shimla two years ago, one of the most exciting rides of our lives. No matter what the conditions here, they couldn't possibly match the thrill of that experience. I even wrote an essay, called "The Road to Shimla."

THE ROAD TO SHIMLA!

I have driven the Road to Hana, and once rode down Highway 1 in California in a lumber truck. I had a mad Italian bus driver skidding down the Amalfi Coast about 10 years ago. We have taken folks on the Cabot Trail in Cape Breton and down the side of the mountain to Flam in Norway. But the Road to Shimla (I'm going to capitalize it for sure) is the wildest ride I have ever been on. For five hours Sonor Singh, our Sikh driver, snaked our bus up an impossible road, big enough for a single bus, but always able to expand and squeeze to two if needed, sometimes even managing to sandwich a darting car between them. Once we left Karka and started rising into the "foothills" of the Himalayas, the demands on his concentration were unbelievable. It is difficult enough to drive a bus up a winding mountain road, where turns always demand you to consider the length of the vehicle. But on this road, you have certain additional considerations that range from obstacles to hazards to moving projectiles to lethargic critters. Imagine a road filled with convolutions, about 65 kilometers of them ranging from hairpins to tortured S-turns. Build that road just about wide enough to hold a pair of cars in most places, and for good measure, make that road rise from 2000' to 8000' in 40 miles.

Give your two lanes a continuous 1000' drop-off for excitement, with a dozen spots where a landslide or crack has sent part of road into the canyon. Now, park cars on the side, quite often both sides. Place random broken-down trucks using a circle of rocks as their warning flares. Take all the random animals available—donkeys, horses, cows (some bulls), pigs, goats, monkeys and give them license to wander as they will. Have people walking, preferably in the middle of the street. Every five or ten kilometers, insert a village, with an open vegetable market, random construction, piles of sand or rock, maybe a festival for fun. Drop some trees here and there, and maybe a landslide or two. How about a bunch of tractors, and even a steamroller looking for something to flatten? OK, that's the road to Shimla. 15% grades, continuous curves, wonderful scenery on the drop-off side. Now, here's the best part—fill that road with insane drivers, mostly in trucks that have been tricked out to look like Guatemalan Chicken Buses. Outlaw the "Do not pass" sign on all hills and curves; set people free. Before you leave make a note of some important signs:

> On the back of the trucks, you will read:
> "Please Honk"
> "At night use your dipper."
> On the road signs, you will find:
> "Always keep to left and be safe."
> And my favorite:
> "Accident is always fatal in the hills."

OK, Ready, Action, Go!

On this road, everyone passes everywhere. Going up a hill with a blind turn at the top, cars will honk (as requested) and breeze past you on the right. Oh, did I tell you, they drive on the wrong side of the road over here in India? That car will get alongside the bus just as a Tata dump truck clears the curve ahead of him. He honks a bit louder; Mr. Singh honks shrilly; the on-coming truck barely slows and the car slides like an eel between the converging vehicles. Up ahead we come to a slow local bus. Mr. Singh hits his louder horn, one that sounds like a trumpet beginning the Kentucky Derby, slides out to the right on a turn and just as he is about to execute a wonderful head-on collision, jumps back to his side of the road, that slow bus having gotten slightly slower to let him in. And so this goes for more than three hours, through villages that permit a single truck at a time but somehow allow several, around stolid cattle and fallen rocks, between rock ledges and broken-down lorries. Mr. Singh's timing is incredible. He slides his bus perfectly into a turn exactly gauging the distance he needs to pass the oncoming truck. And that driver maneuvers just as expertly. In two passes of the Road to Shimla, we never once saw an accident, just one car, broken and finished, hanging over one of the rock walls, somehow avoiding a fall into the valley far below. But that was not a new accident. Patina was already growing on the bumper. I saw a policeman on a motorcycle waiting to nab someone for something. If there is a more useless job in the world, I don't know it. There is nothing to ticket a driver for because there are no rules that anyone follows, except the most important rule of survival.

Other roads have their moments, a few miles or kilometers of heart-stopping exhilaration, but none of them go on for hours and hours. And when we finally reached Shimla, we took the "Bypass" because as Ajay told us, "it is faster than going through the city." That bypass added gravel roads, a major dumpsite, some true hairpin turns and an even crazier brand of drivers who were all on this road because "it is faster."

Mr. Singh may be the best coach driver I have seen from the standpoint of pure driving skill on the road. He leaned his whole body into his turns, in a constant sway from side to side, accelerating always on his turns. Much of time his right hand was waving cars and trucks behind him to go ahead and pass, carefully gauging the distances and angles if another vehicle came around the turn ahead. He seldom braked but used the incline or transmission to slow him down if needed. It is fun to watch, even if your heart is in your throat. Returning from Shimla a couple of days later, I saw a sign at the end of the road: "Accident prone area."

"Time is money, but life is precious!"

"Enjoy your ride; don't commit suicide."

Darjeeling's signs are better than Shimla's.

At Kurseong, almost three hours into our drive, we made our second pit stop at the Kurseong Travel Lodge. Jim has a Swiss Army knife that tells the altitude and he reported 4864' in this bustling crossroads town. Originally, we were scheduled to stop at the tea garden of one of Mac's friends, Ambootia Tea Co., but the day was far too advanced for such a stop, and we decided that we would visit a tea garden tomorrow that was closer to Darjeeling. Here I collected my favorite among the travel admonition signs:

"Hurry Burry spoils the Curry!" Heaven forbid!

We reached Darjeeling around 6:30, relieved at the increasing collection of lights that loomed ahead. It is a city of around 110,000 people, built, like Shimla, on the precipitous cliffs of the foothills of the Himalayas, houses appearing to be propped up by others below. In the 19th century, it was ruled by Sikkim, but the Brits as the East India Co., arrived in the 1820s and 1830s, establishing the tea industry that is still the mainstay of the region. Today Darjeeling is one of the most important regions for West Bengal, a source of considerable revenue from the tea industry, from its long-standing British-founded school systems, and from tourism in general. In recent years it has endured considerable political turmoil from the Gurkhas, Maoists and multiple racial and ethnic groups colliding.

At 6:45 we finally reached the Windemere Lodge, a delightful hotel sitting high in the hills near the old British installations. We were met by Elizabeth Clarke, the manager who simply exudes charm and optimism, qualities that I think were much valued by us weary travelers, but we were quickly led to our rooms, and before long, lodged in the attractive dining room for a gin and tonic and a fine meal.

IV

For our travels today, we are using four Land Rovers, the usual means of transport in this precipitous city. Last night we heard of the political problems the area is experiencing. This morning a few more things were added to the list: a serious drought that is crippling agriculture, especially the tea farms; a crumbling infrastructure; and inadequate roads for transporting materials and especially the tea to market. As a result, the famous Darjeeling tea is declining as a revenue producer. There is a feeling here that the government of West Bengal has deliberately ignored these issues, simply milking the area for its revenue without modernizing the infrastructure. Hence the demand for independence.

Just outside the hotel, down a steep street or two, our drivers executed a rather unusual maneuver—backing down a narrow alley a couple of blocks, so that they would be pointed in the correct direction once they arrived at the bottom. I never did quite figure out the reason for this because the road they began this scheme on seemed to go straight to the road we ended up on. Maybe they just wanted some practice in reverse.

It took us about forty-five minutes to reach the Jay Shree Tea Factory, in the village of Puttabong, filling a hillside with their plantation and factory buildings. It was founded in 1852, advertising "None before us" on their company sign. The plantings are spread over 892 hectares, almost 2000 acres, spread over altitudes ranging from 1500' to 6300'. There are a total of 1636 workers during the most active picking times. Randeep led us through the factory, which didn't seem to have much activity at the moment even though this is one of the harvest times. We were required to remove our shoes and don slippers of sorts, although I have never yet encountered a factory slipper that had grown as large as size 13 and made do with my socks. We were led first up to the second-floor drying area, where 75% of the moisture is removed from the leaves on long drying tables. The leaves are then dropped to rolling machines which break down the leaves but don't remove the juice. From there the tea goes to oxidation tables.

Our tour completed, we were introduced to the plant supervisor, who had a variety of teas available for sniffing and sampling, offering rather attractive boxes for sale. This is not a tourist plant, and it was nice to be able to buy a supply of the famous Darjeeling for folks back home. From the factory, the supervisor led us out to the plantation, where he explained the picking process. Unfortunately there were no pickers working at the moment.

We returned to the city in late morning, making a brief photo stop at St. Joseph's School at North Point, one of the prestigious boarding schools of Darjeeling, a school that we would later discover was the alma mater of several of the Bhutanese speakers we would meet. Darjeeling with its many private schools founded by the British has remained one of the learning centers of the mountain regions. It is one of the major gifts the British left on their departure.

Our next stop is at the Padmaja Naidu Himalayan Zoological Park, which also happens to house the Himalayan Mountaineering Institute. Krishen announced that none of us would be interested in the zoo, and that we would head straight for the Mountaineering museum. Unfortunately we were required to park well down the hill, requiring a long, long walk up the steep grade just to reach the entrance of the zoo. From there it was another serious hill to get to the Mountaineering Institute, by which time we were certified Everest climbers. None of us required pitons however to make the ascent. Along the way, it seemed necessary to stop several times to rest a bit and observe the many unusual mammals the zoo has to offer, including "wild" yaks, and a variety of mountain deer that none of us had ever seen before. We also poked our heads into the Mountaineering Institute as well.

It was getting late by the time we returned to the Windemere, but they had kept lunch ready for us. In the afternoon, Krishen suggested another change in our schedule, opting to have our "Toy Train" experience today instead of tomorrow morning, when we have a long ride to Phuentsholing, Bhutan. Randeep was able to get us tickets on the 3 P.M. train, tickets which included a seat to sit on. He explained that during the week, the train is so crowded that virtually everyone must stand going all the way down the mountain. This being a weekend, the train is not very full, so off we went, backing down that same narrow street, and arriving at the Darjeeling Train Station is just a few minutes. We were soon ensconced in a couple of the cars, which as small as they are, seem way too big for the very narrow-gauge tracks on which the train operates. In a few minutes the engine arrived, a smoke-belching old coal burner that pointed its stack into the lead car, proposing to back its way down the mountain. It seems that everyone in Darjeeling enjoys the sensation of going backwards, perhaps not wanting to see what lies ahead of them. Randeep came through the cars, advising us that we probably should keep our windows closed because with the wind and the slope, there is a tendency for the cars to fill with ashes from the engine.

The Darjeeling narrow-gauge train is a wonderful experience. It has all the noise, the smells, the heat, the stale air, the commotion and the lack of even a semblance of speed to make it truly romantic. The engine is a thing of beauty that only a mother could love, commencing its "run" with a labored chug, then another, a turn of a wheel, then two, until it was positively moving—slowly, slowly, loudly. It was inevitable that someone in our car could not resist: "I think I can; I think I can...." Mark Twain's description of the Darjeeling train is entitled "Sliding down the Himalayas," an entertaining essay that Mac suggested I distribute to everyone yesterday. Of course, Twain was not actually in the train, but rather in a handcart that more or less free-fell along the route, at times stopping to let the much slower train catch up and even pass him.

> "The road fell sharply down in front of us and went cork-screwing in and out around the crags and precipices, down, down, forever down, suggesting nothing so exactly or as uncomfortably as a crooked toboggan slide with no end to it. Mr. Pugh waved his flag and started, like an arrow from a bow, and before I could get out of the car we were gone too. I had previously had but one sensation like the shock of that departure, and that was the gaspy shock that took my breath away the first time I was discharged from the summit of a toboggan slide. But in both instances, the sensation was pleasurable—intensely so; it was a sudden and immense exaltation, a mixed ecstasy of deadly fright and unimaginable joy. I believe that this combination makes the perfection of human delight.
>
> "The pilot car's flight down the mountain suggested the swoop of a swallow that is skimming the ground, so swiftly and smoothly and gracefully it swept down the long reaches and soared in and out of the bends and around the corners. We raced after it, and seemed to flash by the capes and crags with the speed of light; and now and then we almost overtook it—and had hopes...We played with the train the same way. We often got out to gather flowers or sit on a precipice and look at the scenery, then presently we would hear a dull and growing roar, and the long coils of the train would come into sight behind and above us..."
>
> *Following the Equator*, p. 538

I never had the chance to ride the famous Newfie Bullet in Newfoundland, a similar smoke-belching masterpiece of inaction, but I imagine that this "Toy Train" would be a close cousin. I told the story of the Bullet that once a woman gave birth on the train, arousing the indignation of the conductor, who scolded her: "Madame, you should never have boarded in such a condition." Her reply was succinct: "I didn't."

That is a slow train!

Actually, we are not on the Toy Train today, but a modern improvement, so to speak. The engine and cars of that first train are on display at the Ghoom Station where we will disembark today. Meanwhile, within a quarter mile of the Darjeeling station we had worked up a good head of steam and were flying along at about 3 miles an hour, literally filling the immense canyon below Darjeeling and the hills above with dense black smoke, smoke that almost erased at times, the buildings just across the street. Folks walking along the highway, pulled a scarf or sleeve over their faces as they passed us. But in every doorway, in many windows, other natives poked their heads out to watch this apparition rumble by, as though it didn't happen several times a day, and was a totally new experience for them. I think it would be impossible not to look upon the train with interest, no matter how many times you have seen it lumber past.

The rail bed continually crosses the highway, taking the shortest possible route down the curvy hillside, not requiring anything by way of crossing warnings. The fact is, so loud, and smoking and scary is it, that anyone driving a car will be warned a mile away. We never saw anything that looked like a looming disaster by way of a wreck. The train is its own crossing warning.

Before boarding we decided that we would only go to the second stop on the route, the old Ghoom Station, built in 1881, the second highest train station in the world. Our first stop was at a very impressive Soldiers' Memorial, featuring a tall obelisk with a single saluting soldier standing before it. We all got off to walk around the park that surrounds the memorial. Mary was thrilled to find an entire garden filled with California poppies in full bloom, her favorite flower in the whole world.

We returned to the hotel around 5:00. Krishen took the adventurous souls off on a walk of the British part of the city, while the rest of us crashed or, in my case, went for a bird walk. Before dinner this evening, Mrs. Clarke offered to show us a film that she had made about Darjeeling, its people and history, which she did with great aplomb. She positively gushes her love of Darjeeling, in a thick British accent.

Tomorrow we head for Bhutan! Mark Twain never got to Bhutan, but he may have mentioned it, in his own way. Looking out at the mountains to see the immense bulk of Mount Kinchinjunga, he went to the Club after his lecture.

> "...from it you can see where the boundaries of three countries come together, some thirty miles away; Thibet is one of them, Nepaul another, and I think Herzegovia was the other."
>
> *Following the Equator*, p.532

BOOK FIVE

Mark Twain In Hawaii

> "After a three months' absence, I found myself in San Francisco again, without a cent. When my credit was about exhausted, (for I had become too mean and lazy, now, to work on a morning paper, and there were no vacancies on the evening journals,) I was created San Francisco correspondent for the *Enterprise*, and at the end of five months I was out of debt, but my interest in my work was gone; for my correspondence being a daily one, without rest or respite, I got unspeakably tired of it. I wanted another change. The vagabond instinct was strong upon me. Fortune favored and I got a new berth and a delightful one. It was to go down to the Sandwich Islands and write some letters for the Sacramento *Union*, an excellent journal and liberal with employees."
>
> Mark Twain Library, *Roughing It*, p. 421.

That is the whole reason for the trip we are about to take—Sam Clemens/ Mark Twain got a job in Hawaii. Here we go again, following that wonderful writer on one of his adventures.

This will be the fifth tour we have done with our old friend, Mark Twain. It was inspired last year by a random comment on the bus as we were returning from "Mark Twain in the West," an adventure to the gold country and Virginia City. "Didn't Mark Twain go to Hawaii?" someone had inquired out loud, and the idea was immediately born. I have laughed ever since, because when people ask where we are going and we answer, "Mark Twain in Hawaii," we always get a blank stare in response. Nobody ever conceives of those two in the same phrase. But here we are, reliving the twenty-five letters the author penned to the *Sacramento Union* newspaper in 1866, still one of the best descriptions of Hawaii ever written. Mark Twain was as captivated by the islands as has been every person who ever ventured here, and he saw them in a time when at least a bit of the old culture was still around. The old religion based on a draconian web of *kapus* was gone forty years before his arrival, replaced largely by the Calvinist strictures of New England ministers and the worldview of Mormonism. The monarchy founded by Kamehameha I, the Great, was still puttering along, though weakly. Spreckels had not yet cornered the sugar market, but the crop was important in Twain's day and in fact, inspired the commission that sent him to the islands. He spoke at length of its possibilities. Many of the sites and customs that he described can still be experienced. It will be fun to follow him around.

It is not easy to remember that we are still in the U.S, probably because the whole flight is over an ocean, and this shouldn't really be part of our country. It wouldn't be if we hadn't gotten excited back in 1898 and started grabbing up parcels of land from Manila to San Juan. We still have a few of those bits and pieces, like Samoa, Guam, the Marianas, Puerto Rico, the Virgin Islands. Most of them have remained territories, stuck in a sort of no-man's land, but Hawaii got elevated to statehood, having been pretty much an American outpost long before the Spanish-American War. After all, those trouble-making missionaries were Yanks, from New England, and most of the whalers were Americans during the 1830s-1850s. The sugar industry boomed after Spreckels bought up half the crop and Hawaii got a free trade agreement with the U.S. It was the Americans who stood up to the French in several confrontations and who ultimately nudged out the Brits. And of course, it was America who was the target that kicked off the War in the Pacific in 1941. Hawaii has always had better than territorial status. But walking down Kalakaua Avenue is still not the same as strolling along Michigan Avenue or Market Street. It just feels foreign.

We checked in to the Princess Ka'iulani around 2:00, and then walked across the street to kick off our Hawaiian month in style, with a mai tai at the Royal Hawaiian, that magnificent old pink palace that used to be the symbol of Waikiki. It still is, I guess, if you can find it. It used to sit regally in the midst of a lush garden, fronting the surf, one of those special hotels that graced the world in the late nineteenth and early twentieth centuries. Today, having received a complete facelift, it is still elegant, but buried behind the concrete and glass curtain of modern high-rise. Some of the aesthetic damage is self-inflicted because the whole street front along Kalakaua Avenue is now called the Royal Hawaiian Center, a bunker strip of high-end boutiques that hides the hotel from the unwashed public. We finally found the bar, deciding to augment our rum concoctions with a bit of lunch, fashioning a comfortable $75 snack into our stay. It balanced out however, because I asked our vivacious young waitress where she and her boyfriend would go in town for good seafood.

Her immediate response was an exclamation: "Oh, you must go to Uncle Bo's! It is soooo good, and really cheap. All the locals go there."

So we found Uncle Bo's, just a few miles north of Waikiki, and found that she was right. It's a funky little place, nothing fancy, but filled with folks who didn't look at all like tourists. Good recommendation.

9:40 P.M.—I'm sitting alone on the balcony on the 29th floor of the Princess Ki'alauni Hotel, Waikiki. I've made my way to "paradise," that fabled island of O'ahu in the center of the vast Pacific Ocean, a palm-studded piece of utopia that smells of plumeria leis and sounds of beating surf and hula drums. My soul has been craving this catharsis for some time now, the hectic beat of my "laid back" California life taking an unseen toll on my senses. My *manna* is wearing thin; my karma has evaporated. I need the replenishing of the islands.

"Where are you going next?"

"Hawai'i!"

"Oh, that's tough. I feel sorry for you."

"Well, someone has to do it!"

And here I am, ensconced high above Waikiki Beach, where a couple centuries ago, Kamehameha the Great camped in the Royal Coconut Grove as he mustered his troops to conquer O'ahu and the rest of the islands. Not 200 yards away is the ancient temple where the last human sacrifices were made to the impossible gods of the people. Across the street is the statue of Duke Kahanamoku, the fabled Olympian swimmer that brought Hawai'i, swimming and surfing, to the attention of the world; here Don Ho sang "Tiny Bubbles" every night for three decades until they finally named a street after him. Ah! Paradise! For Omar Khayyam it might have been, "a loaf of bread, a jug of wine, a book of verse, and thou!" For me it is a "swaying hula, a strong mai tai, a giddy ukulele, and now! Sitting in the wilderness, ah, waving palm trees are paradise enou'!"

But what's this? All I see are lights, lights edging a bay that has disappeared in the jungle of high rise; lights blocking any view of the crystal clear Pacific Ocean; lights, embedded in concrete blocks filling the land, obviating any thought of a swaying palm or a throwing net; lights blotting out paradise, covering the land, roiling like inverse lava flows up the side of the Waikiki hills, suffocating the land with misuse and overuse. Once I remember the Royal Hawaiian, the pink palace of Waikiki, "the finest resort in the world," standing like a princess on the white sands of the Pacific. I recall the fabled banyan where poets stopped to sing, and lovers hid away, where the air was cooler, and life was sweeter. The Royal Hawaiian is still there, but I can't see it from my balcony, and it is only a couple of football fields away. I see nothing! I hear, not the beat of the drum and ukulele, but a steady drone of cars, and Harley roars, and squealing AC units, an incessant blare of humanity gone crazy. A half dozen planes have cruised through the dark skies as I have been recording this, spewing even more humanity onto this modern wasteland; taxis hit their horns at some wayward driver; a disco beat penetrates the tourist hum; an ambulance screams its urgent message down Ala Moana Road—the twenty-first century symbol of the new paradise. Oh how I yearn once again for the good old days, sitting, sipping a pineapple-infused libation, listening to a besotted Don Ho mumble an inane song that made my foot tap. Coming from a Berkeley background, I fear I can relate: "They took paradise and put up a parking lot."

Tomorrow we begin our study of Mark Twain in Hawaii. I just finished rereading his twenty-five letters to the *Sacramento Union*. I can't imagine what he would have written from my perch here on the 29th floor of paradise, but he would have concluded with, "Brown, let's leave!"

I

At 6:00 this morning, armed with a local map and a description of the thirteen stops of the Waikiki Walking Tour, I decided to visit the city's past. Mark Twain did it a century and a half ago, mentioning the Royal Coconut Grove, the several streams that turned Waikiki into a marshland, an ancient temple where they cut and cooked a great many unfortunates to appease one or another god, and of course, Diamondhead. My tour begins quite a distance from the hotel, in a fishing basin that once belonged to the family of Duke Kahanamoku, but now has been filled, drained and exploited to become several hotels, and the U.S. Military base of Fort DeRussy. I decided to skip that part, since there is nothing there of the ancient times. Stops 3, 4, and 5 are all related to this landfill and military action, so I decided to start with #6, the back lawn of the Royal Hawaiian Hotel. That spot also had the good sense to be directly across the street from my hotel, which meant that my walk wouldn't have to be too long. This was the site of the royal coconut grove, known as Helumoa. Mark Twain described it:

> "A mile and a half from town, I came to a grove of tall cocoanut trees, with clean, branchless stems reaching straight up sixty or seventy feet and topped with a spray of green foliage sheltering clusters of cocoanuts—not more picturesque than a forest of colossal ragged parasols, with bunches of magnified grapes under them, would be.... The king's flag was flying from the roof of one of the cottages, and His Majesty was probably within. He owns the whole concern thereabouts, and passes his time there frequently, on sultry days, "laying off." The spot is called "The King's Grove."
>
> *Letters from Hawaii*, Letter 6

The king is gone. The flag is changed. The thatched houses are gone, and so are just about all the trees. The grove is gone, now become the Royal Hawaiian Hotel. Once there were 10,000 trees serving Kamehameha the Great, who camped on this beach in the summer of 1795 to begin his conquest of O'ahu. Here he also built a stone house often used by his favorite wife Ka'ahumanu, probably for one of her frequent assignations which seemed to cause quite a few of the king's subjects to lose their heads. The land is still owned by the descendants of Kamehameha, The Bishop Trust, funding the Kamehameha Schools, which educate thousands of Hawaiian children across the state. In 1927, the Royal Hawaiian Hotel was built, the "Pink Palace."

Next door is an even older hotel, the Moana Hotel (Now the Sheraton Moana Surfrider), built in 1901, called "The First Lady of Waikiki." And just east of that is a circle of cast iron fencing that encloses a stone altar and four mammoth boulders. They are called "the healing stones of Kapaemahu". The plaque says they were placed to honor four Tahitian healers—Kapaemahu, Kahaloa, Kapuni, and Kinohi, who worked their magic in Waikiki before transferring their skills to these four stones and disappearing. Legend says that the stones were brought here, by the fabled *menahune*, in one night from Kaimuki, two miles away. The largest weighs 7.5 tons.

The shore road leads to Kapi'olani Park, a much-used area that sits in the shadow of Diamondhead, containing a variety of fields and venues for public use, including the Honolulu Zoo and the University of Hawaii Aquarium.

I enjoyed watching two old men, sitting in lounge chairs, well-bundled against the morning coolness. On a blanket in front of them they placed a small pile of bird feed, which soon attracted a pair of lovely Red-crested cardinals, a species related to our Northern cardinal, introduced from South America around 1930. Many, if not most, of the birds found in the islands today were brought here by settlers, often as pets, and released to propagate and thrive. Our Northern cardinal was brought in 1929. Hawaii has at least forty endemic species of birds, those found only here, having somehow managed to migrate more than 2,500 miles and survive and reproduce. Fossil discoveries indicate at least another thirty-five species that lived here but disappeared before the advent of mankind. Another twenty-seven species have become extinct since the first Europeans arrived. Of the present forty endemic species, twenty-four are considered endangered, and two of those may well be extinct now. In addition to the endemics there are at least twenty species that are considered "indigenous," birds that migrate to breed in the islands, but are found elsewhere as well. There are more than 110 species of imported birds in Hawaii, which pose a serious threat to the native birds, because of increased competition for food and introduced disease. Particularly troubling are parrots. More than ten species have been introduced in recent years; two are now reproducing in the wild. The real culprit, however, in the demise of the endemic birds of Hawai'i is the mosquito. That little critter attacks the eyes of the birds. Most of the endemic birds that remain are found at high altitudes, above the mosquito belt in the rain forest.

I found two new birds for my list this morning. The first is the beautiful White tern, or Fairy tern, a species indigenous to the islands; and the tiny Common waxbill, an alien species from Africa. We should have a good chance to see many of the birds of the islands, especially on the "Big Island" of Hawaii, with its many ecosystems.

This afternoon, all our travelers arrive. Mary and I drove back to the airport to greet the people. Twelve came in on a United flight and the other nine arrive on five different Hawaiian Air flights. Mary will meet the UAL group and I will try to gather those on HA. By 2:00 we had found everyone but Michael, who hadn't checked any large luggage and didn't ever make it to the baggage area where we met everyone. By 3:00 we were all in the hotel and heading for lunch or a nap. I didn't schedule anything for this evening because on the first night, everyone is usually worn out, regardless of the length of the flight or the number of time zones involved. Just getting on an airplane seems to take all the energy out of most travelers. I did invite everyone to the bar for an introductory mai tai, but that isn't an event; it's a requirement. Tomorrow our tour will officially begin. It will be interesting to hear in the morning where everyone went for dinner tonight. I am sure that some will go to the famous restaurants, and a few may just stay at the hotel for the totally underpriced $29.50 buffet. Mary and I went almost completely native with Bob, Frank and Alice, walking a couple hundred yards to the California Pizza Kitchen. Hang loose, brudder!

II

Naomi back in our office, said that we had to have James Oda for our driver-guide on O'ahu because he is so good. Yesterday morning, Mary and I met with Sandy, the highly frenetic sales manager for Roberts Tours, who assured us that he would be our guide during our stay here. I am not sure why it didn't come as any sort of surprise that Nick Oducado was waiting at the bus this morning and James Oda was nowhere in sight. Somehow, I knew that would be the case, but I'm not sure why. Anyway, Nick seems a very nice man, with a soft, comfortable voice and the prototypical Hawaiian calm. I went over our itinerary, which he didn't seem to have with him, and he assured me that he fully understood our needs. He had not the slightest problem with Mac or me or Bob jumping on the mike if something occurred to us that the group couldn't survive without. The circle island tour is one of the "standards" for the Roberts drivers, and Nick is one of their most experienced. We know from Mark Twain's letters to the *Union* that he didn't much get out of the general area of Honolulu-Waikiki, probably because his options for travel were walking, riding a horse or sailing. But Bob agreed with my theory that *if* he had a bus at his disposal, he most certainly *would* have circled the Island, so today's tour is in the spirit of Mark Twain and it is up to us to experience it as he would have. So off we go on our circuit of O'ahu.

Leaving the hotel we drove through Kapi'olani Park, created in 1877 by King David Kalakaua to honor his queen. The park later would be the bivouac area for the U.S. army in 1898, when Hawai'i lost its independence. The park skirts several famous beaches, including Queen's Beach and San Souci, where an ailing Robert Louis Stevenson convalesced for five weeks in 1893. Our route took us toward Diamond Head or Mt. Le'ahi (Ring of Fire), which is one of the most upscale districts of the metropolitan area. This area, known as Kohala, was once the site of pig and chicken farms, a waste land on the edge of the city. Nick pointed out the elaborate residence of Doris Duke, an estate she named "Shangri La." I wonder if she would still use such a name as she looks down on the urban sprawl that now fills her paradise. That sprawl continues pretty much around the east end of the island, right around to Hanauma Bay. Most of this land, in fact most of Waikiki as well, is part of the Bishop Estate, former royal lands that now make up the endowment foundation for the Bishop Trust, mainly dedicated to the education and medical care of native Hawaiian children. I suppose that a good amount of revenue in that land comes from the fifty-three golf courses that fill the shores of Hanauma Bay alone. A major development inside the Bishop Estate is Hawai'i Kai, the incredible town of Henry J. Kaiser, a major city, elaborate and expensive that was designed to be a world unto itself, with shopping, schools, huge boat marina, hospitals, etc.

Nick explained that Hawaiians don't use the same directional terms as we do, i.e.. "east, west, etc.," that because they are island dwellers, they give directions as *mauka* (mountain) and *makai* (sea). When your world is a relatively small circle surrounded by water, those directions make more sense. We made a potty stop on the *makai* side of the Kalaneanaoke Highway. I love those words!

"What did Sam Clemens like best about Hawaii, Bob?" Mac inquired over the mike, the first of the Mark Twain in Hawaii questions he would pose over the next ten days.

"I think he liked the peace and quiet."

"Is that a play on words?"

"I didn't mean that piece!"

There is no question that Sam liked the Hawaiian women, many of whom he encountered swimming au natural or riding a surfboard, or dancing one of their enchanting hulas. There is some rumor that he may have left some progeny behind; after all, he was thirty years old in 1866, unmarried and known to enjoy life. Ever since Captain Cook found it impossible to keep the Hawaiian maidens away from his crew, European and American seamen have found the islands to be a very fertile ground, so to speak.

"When the missionaries first took up their residence in Honolulu, the native women would pay their families frequent friendly visits, day by day, not even clothed with a blush. It was found a hard matter to convince them that this was rather indelicate. Finally the missionaries provided them with long, loose calico robes, and that ended the difficulty—for the women would troop through the town, stark naked, with their robes folded under their arms, march to the missionary houses and then proceed to dress!"
Roughing It, p. 460-461

"At noon I observed a bevy of nude native young ladies bathing in the sea, and went and sat down on their clothes to keep them from being stolen. I begged them to come out, for the sea was rising and I was satisfied that they were running some risk. But they were not afraid, and presently went on with their sport. They were finished swimmers and divers, and enjoyed themselves to the last degree. They swam races, splashed and ducked and tumbled each other about, and filled the air with their laughter."
Roughing It, p. 494-495

We made a required stop at the famous "Blow Hole" to watch the Pacific force its better waves through an aperture in the lava into a brief fountain of spray. Nearby is a more impressive site—the famous "From Here to Eternity" beach where Burt Lancaster and Debra Kerr frolicked in the surf, certainly one of the most famous love scenes in movie history. It is a tiny beach really, one that is accessed by a difficult climb down the rock hill.

We suggested to Mac that he and Sita put on their swimsuits and reenact that scene.

"If you can walk down there, Sita," Mac bluffed, "I will too." He was subjected to considerable derision from his audience. I offered $100 bounty to sweeten the deal, but that wouldn't have begun to pay for the resulting hospital bills.

Nick took a bit of time to point out one of the neighboring beaches, saying that it is important in Hawai'i to recognize whether a beach is a "safe" one or "dangerous." He said you had to determine where the waves were breaking, on a reef offshore, or directly on to the beach. Then you needed to see how steep the angle of the beach was entering the water. A steep beach is far more dangerous than one that is relatively level. He showed us Makepu'u Beach, a very steep beach, which he called "the second most dangerous in Hawai'i."

A Waimanalo, we looked across the water at Bellows Air Force Base, still a very active place. Nick said that it and another coastal base were both attacked by the Japanese planes in 1941, before they crossed the Pali and hit Pearl Harbor.

As we progressed around the island, we found ourselves on the windward side of O'ahu. Here as on all the islands, the mountains are a precipitous barrier to the ocean storms, steep cliffs, covered by rampant vegetation, the rainy, unprotected side of the land. Deep valleys are carved between the peaks, running down to the shore. On a sunny day, as it mostly is today, it is a lovely sight. We made a stop at the Byodo-in Temple, an impressive Japanese structure that was a major studio site in the "Hawai'i 5-0" series. It is surrounded by a rambling cemetery, parts of which are filled with dark Japanese headstones. The place, as Nick said, offers "ocean-view condos."

Our lunch stop is at the Kualoa Ranch, a working ranch, cum tourist attraction, founded by Dr. Charles Judd in the mid-nineteenth century. In 1863 he also opened the first sugar refinery on the island, an ill-fated operation, because eight years later, Dr. Judd's grandson was killed, falling into one of the boiling vats. The factory was immediately closed and never reopened.

"Do they have poi here?" Mac asked Nick, the initial inquiry that would carry forth throughout the trip. Mac has a deep interest in any local food, the more bizarre, the better. Over the years I have never known him to pass up something that was either rare or odd in the gastronomic arena, and here he is on the hunt for poi, and would quickly add pulled pork, boiled taro and spam to his list.

We were back on the road for only a minute when Nick pulled over and asked for three of our women to volunteer for a roadside search. They disappeared for a few minutes and returned clutching a rather curious flower, the Naopaka. It is a sort of Hawaiian edelweiss, picked by a young man for his lovely lady. Nick explained the legend that saw the flower split in half, with one side of it growing on the shore, *makai*, and the other *mauka*, in the mountains. You have to get one of each to come up with a complete flower. Mac carried forth on an explanation of zygomorphism, which he assured us is quite common in the botanical world.

"Mac, how do you explain half flowers?" Arville, one of Nick's volunteers, inquired.

"Half-assed bees pollinate them."

This area of O'ahu is the most traditional on the island, small fishing villages clinging to the shore, almost pushed into the sea by the mountain crags. We quickly passed through Kahalu'u, Punalu'u, Hau'ulu, a wonderful collection of glottal-stopped "u"s, but they all had to take a back seat to Ka'a'awa for sheer vowel pollution. I can only recall one other instance, but I know there are probably many, of three of the same letters in a row. I once found *Grosstadt* floating around in German and can now add Kaaawa to form a true collection. Hawaiian is a wonderful language, a fluid, rather melodic stream of grunts and clicks and clacks, something that wasn't even written down until the missionaries arrived in the early nineteenth century. They had to discard most of what they knew because somehow the Hawaiians had managed to get by without most of the verbal riches of the Latin alphabet. The Hawaiian language, as transliterated by westerners, only has twelve letters: a, e, i, o, u, h, k, l, m, n, p, and w. They can get the most imaginative flavor out of those five vowels, by gluing them together, and sticking an upside-down apostrophe in between, forcing you into a full glottal stop to make that sound twice, or three times if you are a fishing village in O'ahu. They also weld their vowels into diphthongs, ae, ai, ao, au, ei, eu, oi, and ou. If you feel like it, you can string a couple of these critters together too, as in *heiau* or temple. If you do, you must put a little screech in the middle to prove to folks that you are capable of flexing four vowels in a row. It comes out as "hay-ee-ow." With so much dexterity in their vowelings, no wonder they don't require so many consonants. They make up for the paucity of their letters by using them all a lot, coming up with words that are long enough to cast a shadow. And then, to make it a bit easier to swallow, they double up on phrases, as in "Kamehameha" or "*humuhumunukunukuapuaa*".

We spent twenty minutes watching a turtle not do anything. It is one of the most interesting things I have ever done. Nick had spied out the place first and informed us that there were turtles to be seen. We all walked down to the beach at Lanea Kea where a gaggle of oglers was already assembled around a bunch of rocks, black rocks, all of which looked like turtles. It took a while for our eyes to adjust to the non-movement of the stones, and to be honest, I felt a little uncomfortable watching them because except for the lack of movement, those rocks really didn't much resemble turtles. But people in flip-flops and tank tops were excitedly snapping pictures. The Japanese among us were busy kneeling in the sand to get their picture taken with the immobility, and they were certainly happy, so I figured I would just have to set aside my feelings and start enjoying the turtles too. Then I noticed a red rope in the sand, a sort of half circle with a sign telling moving people not to move there. Frank was already inside that semicircle trying to get out of the way of the Japanese Minoltas and he almost tripped over one of the rocks stuck in the sand.

An eye opened. The rock had an eye! Frank, not even aware that he was treading on forbidden ground, took a step back and whipped out his camera. Apparently, he has never seen a rock with an eye before. Look! There is a second eye! A young Japanese honeymooner next to me immediately produced a video camera to record the astonishing movement. Bob Hirst walked up looking a little confused, asking why all the turtles looked like rocks, and wondering which one he ought to photograph for the archives back home. I pointed to Frank, who was the most active creature on the strand, and suggested that he might be the best action shot.

"Frank, what are you doing behind the rope?" It was Alice, shocked at her husband's blatant lack of respect for law and order. "You're going to step on that turtle!"

It was then that I really got embarrassed. I took off my glasses, cleaned them on my shirt and tried again. By God! That rock *is* a turtle! That's what we are all doing down here—looking at turtles. We were all wrong, because we have been taking pictures of black rocks that don't move at all. I immediately erased all of the shots I had taken of the non-turtles and turned my fullest attention to the new arrival, who had hit the beach last month on October 10, 1850, and hadn't moved since, according to the Japanese bride next to me who was starting to kneel in the sand next to the eyes for her new husband to snap a shot to send back to Kyoto. It hadn't moved, that is, until Frank kicked sand in his eyes, causing them to open. It was then that I began to appreciate the scene properly. Here, in full view of a busload of folks with a hundred degrees in esoterica, Mr. Slowsky the Turtle, was putting on a command performance. Once we got Frank safely out of the red restraining rope, old Slowsky settled in and really did his thing to the thrill and approbation of the entire audience. He never moved again. And that is certainly worth recording

At the far end of the island we came to the town of Laie. The Mormons had arrived in Hawai'i in 1850, settling on the island of Lanai. In 1914, they moved to O'ahu buying the village of Laie and erecting an elaborate temple which we viewed briefly. In the rear of their property they constructed, between 1961-63, the famed Polynesian Cultural Center, which ever since has been a major tourist attraction, and is probably most responsible for requiring every visitor to the islands to attend a lu'au sometime during their stay. The Mormons have been immensely successful as missionaries in Polynesia, and have built a university on O'ahu, now called Brigham Young University, Hawaii Campus.

The best surfing beaches in O'ahu are on the eastern end of the island: Sunset, Kawela and Waimea. Here waves are commonly recorded at 25' or bigger, attracting the best of the world's surfers. Surfing is an ancient Hawaiian tradition, once reserved only for the *ali'i*, or nobility. There are even temples erected specifically to the gods of the surfers. The closest we can come to that these days is that statue of Duke Kahanamoku on the beach in Waikiki.

Mac has been campaigning for a stop to get a "shave ice," something we have seen on several signs along the highway. For some reason they never put a "d" on the end of the word. Nick turned off the highway into the small village of Hale'iwa to the Matsumoto Grocery, one of those old institutions that seem to crop up in all parts of the islands, often with Japanese names. According to Nick, Matsumoto's is the best place in O'ahu to get a shave ice cone, and the crowd around the old place seemed to back him up. There was even a film crew outside, taking shots of satisfied customers exiting the grocery with their cones. I objected that this is nothing but an old-fashioned snow cone but was hooted down by Mac and Nick who say that the ice is shaved, whatever that is supposed to mean. I later found out, at Jo Jo's in Kaua'i that a snow cone is constructed of crushed ice with some flavoring poured over it. Shave ice is literally shaved by a very sharp knife off a block of ice. They put a scoop of ice cream at the bottom and cover it with the shave ice, add tropical juices on top. I got a large one, called a "rainbow," served with a straw and a spoon. It's a snow cone. I must admit that I couldn't say that about the one Mac got, because at the bottom of his cone was a thick slurry of ice cream and beans, that ungodly concoction topped by fruit-flavored ice. Had it been available I have no doubt that he would have topped the whole thing off with a thick slab of Spam and made it a perfect island meal. We have been laughing about all the Spam (Specially Prepared Army Meat) we have seen on menus and store signs, yet another delicacy that has caused Mac's mouth to water. Most of us remember Spam from our Boy Scout days, but here in Hawaii it is still routinely on the menu. Nick kidded us saying that on the mainland, the most eaten dish is the hotdog, and "hotdogs are made of things that don't qualify for Spam." There are two cookbooks sold in the islands filled solely with Spam dishes.

Our last stop was quite forgettable, at the Dole Plantation store, which quite possibly is the biggest tourist trap of them all in the Hawaiian Islands. Never have so many paper, plastic, and rubber pineapples been gathered together in the same place. Here you can eat pineapple, get your picture taken with a giant Maui Gold, ride in the Pineapple Express, wander through a pineapple garden or get lost in a pineapple maze. Sadly, there are almost no actual pineapples left in Hawai'i, the industry having been moved to South America, Africa or Southeast Asia where labor is not as expensive. Maui Gold just announced their imminent closure and Dole is about gone, moved off to Kenya, and South East Asia. The same has happened to the sugar industry.

This was a nice day, filled with a variety of scenes and experiences. Tonight we topped it off with dinner at the Top of Waikiki Restaurant, the only revolving restaurant in Honolulu or Waikiki. The food was fine, and thanks to a very energetic waiter with a bottomless pitcher, it was washed down with gallons of water.

III

James Oda is our driver today. He is that good friend of Naomi in our office who was supposed to be our driver yesterday too. I have just about given up on the way Hawaiians do business these days, at least the travel business. Naomi had assured us that James is one of the best drivers that Roberts Tours has, and she had put in a special request for him. Two days ago, Mary and I met with Sandy, the group sales manager for Roberts, and she agreed that James would be our O'ahu driver-guide. Nick showed up yesterday. I admit I was a bit disappointed and dismayed at the apparent lack of communication, but happily Nick proved to be a very good guide. I phoned Sandy yesterday, as she had suggested, requesting that we have Nick again today. I received a guarantee to that effect, and Nick assured me that he would be back in the morning. James is here today; Nick is nowhere in sight.

James couldn't be more of a contrast to Nick. Where the latter is soft-spoken, quiet and thoughtful, James is loud, laughing and brash. After two days, I like them both. Nick gives more and better information; James is not so accurate with his facts, but his good nature puts you at ease. Our day today is to take in the part of Honolulu and environs that Mark Twain describes in his letters: the Pali, Kalihi Valley, the Mission Churches, the Foster Botanical Gardens, Iolani Palace, the State Capitol. We are adding the Punchbowl Military Cemetery and downtown Honolulu to the itinerary.

We left Waikiki, driving along the Ala Wai Canal that runs along the back of the city, built originally to deflect the waters of the many streams that flowed from the mountains to the sea, that once made a marshland of what is now Waikiki.

Crossing the canal, we headed into the Ko'olau Mountains, entering the Nu'uanu Valley. The valley on the leeward, dry side of the island, leads up to the famous Pali, which Mark Twain described as a "divide," the bridge between Honolulu and Hanauma Bay, where we were yesterday.

On reaching the Pali, Bob gave us a brief history leading up to Mark Twain's journey to the islands. He was thirty years old, with no job, no money, and probably drinking too much. He began writing daily 2,000-word articles for the *Enterprise*, which he did for five months, and was probably worn out by the exercise. He agreed to write similar reports for the *Sacramento Daily Union* on the sugar industry in Hawaii, giving him an opportunity to leave San Francisco and earn a little money. He boarded the *Ajax* in March, 1866 bound for Honolulu, arriving on March 18. In all he would write twenty-five letters to the *Sacramento Union*, which are still regarded as one of the best nineteenth century descriptions of the Hawaiian Islands. Once he arrived, his letters describe a great many things besides sugar, as he freely wandered around, recording whatever drew his attention or piqued his curiosity. Of course he visited the Pali.

Today the Pali is one of the most visited places on O'ahu, possessed of a fine road that takes the visitor from Honolulu, right over the pass to Hanauma Bay. Yesterday Nick told us that the Pali Highway is one of the most expensive road constructions in U.S. history, because the problems posed by the weather and terrain were matched by those inflicted by the environmentalists. For us this morning, it was an easy ride up the spectacular Nu'uanu Valley. In 1895, Kamehameha the Great won his major victory here, pushing the army of the O'ahu king up the valley to the pass, where they were trapped with the sheer cliff to their backs, and ultimately driven over the precipice to their deaths. It was the last island the king conquered in war, and the islands were finally united in 1810 when the King of Kaua'i agreed to vassalage through a treaty. Mark Twain relates that aboard his rented steed, Oahu, he rode into a plain filled with bones.

It evoked three different explanations out of him, two different versions of the Battle of Nu'uanu and a third discussing an epidemic that hit the city later. A plaque at the Pali tells the story of the famous battle, called Kalelea'anae, ("the Leaping of the Fish"), where 400 warriors lost their lives. The Pali is the easiest way to get through the Ko'olau Mountains from Honolulu to Hanauma, but until the modern highway, that "easy" way was no treat. It was "almost too fearful to be enjoyed," stated the Rev.

Rueben Tinker in 1831. Over the decades there was a narrow path, a steam train, a wagon road, mule and horse trails, and finally a narrow car lane.

> "I have ridden up the handsome Nuuanu Valley; noted the mausoleum of the departed Kings of Hawaii by the wayside; admired the neat residences, surrounded by beautiful gardens that border the turnpike; stood, at last, after six miles of travel, on the famous Pari—the "divide," we would call it—and looked down the precipice of six or eight hundred feet, over which old Kamehameha I drove the army of the King of Oahu three-quarters of a century ago; and gazed upward at the sharp peak close at my left, springing several hundred feet above my head like a colossal church spire—stood there and saw the sun go down and the little plain below and the sea that bordered it become shrouded in thick darkness; and then saw the full moon rise up and touch the tops of the billows, skip over the gloomy valley and paint the upper third of the high peak as white as silver; and heard the ladies say: "Oh, beautiful!—and such a strong contrast!" and heard the gentlemen remark: "By George! Talk about scenery! how's that?"
>
> "It was all very well, but the same place in daylight does not make so fine a picture as the Kalihi Valley... All citizens talk about the Pari; all strangers visit it the first thing; all scribblers write about it—but nobody talks or writes about or visits the Pari's charming neighbor, the Kalihi Valley. I think it was a fortunate accident that led me to stumble into this enchanted ground."
>
> *Letters from Hawaii*, Letter 11

We descended from the Pali back toward the city, stopping at the Punchbowl, the National Cemetery of the Pacific. Like all our national cemeteries, it is a haunting place, this one a bit different because there are no headstones or crosses. In Hawaiian, it is called *Puowaina*, "Place of Sacrifice," where 44,000 souls gave the ultimate sacrifice for their country. There are 33,700 graves in the Punchbowl, which is now completely filled. Today only cremations are done here, with the ashes interred in a new area. MIA are buried around a central memorial which is topped by a sculpture of Lady Columbia.

I had asked James this morning if it was possible to drive into the Kalihi Valley and he agreed, although, nobody ever asked him to do it, and he had never taken a bus into Kalihi. But we did in fact have time, so as we drove past new housing developments, Bob read Sam's description:

> "For a mile of two we followed a trail that branched off from the terminus of the turnpike that leads past the Government prison, and bending close around the rocky point of a foothill we found ourselves fairly in the valley, and the panorama began to move. After a while the trail took the course of a brook that came down the center of the narrowing canyon, and followed it faithfully throughout its eccentric windings. On either side the ground rose gradually for a short distance, and then came the mountain barriers—densely wooded precipices on the right and left, that towered hundreds of feet above us, and up which one might climb about as easily as he could climb up the side of a house.
>
> It was a novel sort of scenery, those mountain walls. Face around and look straight across at one of them, and sometimes it presented a bold, square front, with small inclination out of the perpendicular; move on a little and look back, and it was full of sharp ridges, bright with sunlight, and with deep, shady clefts between and what had before seemed a smooth bowlder, set in among the thick shrubbery on the face of the wall, was now a bare rampart of stone that projected far out from the mass of green foliage, and was as sharply defined against the sky as if it had been built of solid masonry by the hand of man..."

Sam carries on in this vein through a couple of very long paragraphs, concluding,

> "Verily, with its rank luxuriance of vines and blossoms, its groves of forest trees, its shady nooks and grassy lawns, its crystal brook and its wild and beautiful mountain scenery, with that charming far-off glimpse of the sea, Kalihi is the Valley of Enchantment come again!"
> *Letters from Hawaii*, Letter 11

We weren't able to drive to the top of the valley, but could see off in the distance, the spectacular mountain scenery that Mark Twain was describing. Bob commented that this is a great example of the author writing serious prose, something he does often in these letters. "One of the ways that you can legitimize humor," Bob said, "is to show that you can write serious." I have always felt that Mark Twain is one of the best travel writers I have read. His descriptions of the West in *Roughing It,* are both extensive and very accurate. I have read in several places that Hawaiians consider his to be the best description of the islands in his day.

Lunch found us down at the Aloha Tower in Honolulu. Like so many of the old city sites, they have turned the tower area into an eating and shopping venue, much like Ghirardelli Square in San Francisco or Quincy Market in Boston.

Our tour continued after lunch, with the first stop at the Mission Houses Museum in the old section of Honolulu. There we were met by our guides, Mike and Tawny, who took us through the several buildings on the site. In 1820, seven missionary couples arrived in Honolulu from Boston, Congregationalists from the ABCFM, American Board of Commissioners of Foreign Missions, led by the Rev. Hiram Bingham. Their mission was specific: "You are to aim at nothing short of covering those islands with fruitful fields and pleasant dwellings and schools and churches; of raising up the whole people to an elevated state of Christian civilization." Their arrival would prove to be fateful. Only the year before, Kamehameha I had died, and his son, Kamehameha II, at the considerable urging of Ka'ahumanu, the "favorite wife" of the dead king, had effectively eliminated the old *kapu* system of the traditional Hawaiian religion. With the singular act of dining with the queen, he destroyed that religion.

Enter the New Englanders on a mission to "civilize" the islands, arriving to find a virtual religious vacuum. They were allowed to stay for a year, quickly building four thatched houses and a similar church, and they never left. A year later a more substantial frame house was erected. After four thatched church buildings, the present Kawaiaha'o Church was built, constructed out of 14,000 coral blocks. We visited several of the buildings on the property, including the 1821 frame house, the 1831 Chamberlain House, which today houses a collection of "flag quilts," and the coral Kawaiaha'o Church. I collected a fine Hawaiian name from that church, a tablet memorializing the improbably named Laura Kakuakapuokalani Coney, d. 1929.

In his *Sacramento Union* letters, Mark Twain had some very pointed words about the missionaries:

> "They are "pious, hard-working, hard-praying, self-sacrificing; hospitable; devoted to the well-being of this people and the interests of Protestantism; bigoted; puritanical; slow; ignorant of all white human nature and natural ways of men, except the remnants of these things that are left in their own class or profession; old fogy—fifty years behind the age..."
>
> *Letters from Hawaii,* Letter 14

Our last stop today is at the State Capitol, which occupies the very central position in Honolulu, across from the old royal palace and the equally imposing statue of Kamehameha I. The capital is unique among our fifty capital buildings. There is no dome, no neo-classical capitals, no rotunda. Instead there are eight "Hawaiian" capitals, idealized palm trees. A pair of volcanoes grace the sides of the building, which, apropos of the only state that is surrounded by water, is encircled by a water moat. A statue of the recently canonized Fr. Damian stands in front. Across the street is the famous statue of Kamehameha the Great, one of four such statues that are found on the islands and in the rotunda of the Capitol in Washington D.C.

IV

Kakahiaka! Good morning!

It was sewn into our Good Morning quilt in the elevators of the hotel. They are switched for Good Afternoon and Good Evening, but I forgot to write those Hawai'ian phrases down. We leave the Princess Ki'aolani and Waikiki this morning, bound for Kona on the Big Island. Georgiatina was standing there smiling at the Hawaiian Air desk, with not a soul in line and nothing else to do but check us in. She was holding a stack of boarding passes, ours, and handed them over to me almost before I identified myself.

"California Alumni?"

"Yes, how did you know?"

"You look like it."

She told me to bring the bags in and line them up near her desk while she printed the claim checks. Done!

"Do you need to see our driver's licenses?"

"Do you know all of them? That's enough for me."

And that was it! We are on our way to Kona. In 40 years of mushing groups through airports, this may have been the easiest passage of all, and I told that to Georgiatina.

"Oh, I'm so sorry," she moaned with fine irony. "I thought it was always this way."

What a refreshing experience to have at an airport, just as I had become convinced that there is no such thing anymore. And she didn't even charge us the $10 a bag that the airline just imposed last month. I should have collected it anyway and provided a fund for mai tais the rest of the trip.

Today we begin our Big Island adventure, one in which we can follow Mark Twain pretty much around Hawai'i, because he described many sites that are still extant, places that are important in the history of the formation of the Hawaiian kingdom. Here Kamehameha was born, came to power and launched himself into the unification of all the islands. Hawai'i today is probably the main repository of historical sites, with places of refuge, temples and holy sites preserved in a string of national parks. Of course it is also the home of the most active volcano in the nation, perhaps in the world depending on the definition of "active." Mark Twain reveled in the natural world of Hawai'i, describing the volcanic places in great detail.

It was as easy to arrive in Kona as it was to leave O'ahu. An agent from Roberts Tours met us in the baggage area, escorted us to our waiting bus and in a short time we were driving through the arid lava fields of Kona to our hotel in Kailua, the King Kamehameha. It sits right on the water at Kailua-Kona, the very place where the great king lived in his old age and passed away. Today the hotel is half under reconstruction; the west tower is completely closed. We were all assigned ocean-view rooms overlooking the harbor and small beach. This afternoon we will cruise to Kealakekua Bay to relive the experiences of the unfortunate Captain James Cook.

At 3:30 we boarded the Body Glove catamaran, a very nice vessel with comfortable benches and seats, a big central bar and a good PA system. We are off on a three-hour cruise from Kailua to Kealakekua Bay and back. The cruise offered a rather curious "historian" named Mike, who exhibited all the style and vocabulary of a surfer dude but managed to cover most of the details with some semblance of order. When Mike wasn't talking, a singer was belting out loud music that would eventually drive Mac to the stern of the boat and Russ to turn off his hearing aids. But it is a nice evening, the ocean is placid, the scenery attractive. A pod of playful dolphins entertained us with a series of acrobatic, twisting jumps. And at the end of the outbound leg is the monument to Captain James Cook, who arrived in Hawaii as the god Lono and departed in a bag of bones.

The monument is a tall obelisk, erected in 1874 "by some of his countrymen." It is placed on British soil on the far end of the bay. In Mark Twain's day, there was no such obelisk, but rather several brass plaques on a rotting palm trunk.

"Tramping about in the rear of the warehouse, we suddenly came upon another object of interest. It was a coconut stump, four or five feet high, and about a foot in diameter at the butt. It had lava boulders piled around its base to hold it up and keep it in place, and it was entirely sheathed over, from top to bottom, with rough, discolored sheets of copper, such as ships' bottoms are coppered with. Each sheet had a rude inscription scratched upon it—with a nail, apparently—and in every case the execution was wretched. It was almost dark by this time and the inscriptions would have been difficult to read even at noonday, but with patience and industry I finally got them all in my notebook. They read as follows:

Near this spot fell
CAPTAIN JAMES COOK,
The distinguished Circumnavigator,
who Discovered these islands A.D. 1778
His Majesty's Ship Imogene,
October 17, 1837

...After Cook's murder, his second in command, on board the ship, opened fire upon the swarms of natives on the beach, and one of his cannon balls cut this coconut tree short off and left this monumental stump standing.... up on the mountain side we had passed by a large inclosure like an ample hogpen, built of lava blocks, which marks the spot where Cook's flesh was stripped from his bones and burned; but this is not properly a monument, since it was erected by the natives themselves, and less to do honor to the circumnavigator than for the sake of convenience in roasting him."
Letters from Hawaii, Letter 19

Nearby the land ends in a sheer cliff, highly important in Hawaiian history. On this cliff, which is filled with holes and crevices, were interred the bones of the Hawaiian chiefs. A commoner was dangled down the wall with those bones, placing and concealing them in various holes. Since the Hawaiians believed that the bones possessed the *manna* of soul of the chief, they were anxious to keep their whereabouts secret to prevent desecration. When the dangling subject was finished with his task of interring the bones, he announced it to the *ali'i* standing on top of the cliff, who then cut the line, sending the undertaker to his own death. It was a curious honor to bury a chief.

Bob had his first talk this evening, since we got back from our dinner cruise fairly early. The King Kam Hotel was kind enough to give us a room in the middle of their great hall-museum. The hotel is being renovated and this curious hall, filled only with a couple of massive marlin trophies, will be redone as a Hawaiian museum, filled with displays of ancient artifacts. Presently they have a good collection, but it is spread all over the old hotel.

Bob's topic was one of the major stories contained in Mark Twain's *Sacramento Union* letters—the burning of the Clipper Ship *Hornet*, and the survival of part of the crew. The Hornet burned to the water just north of the equator, the crew embarking in three longboats, one of which was led by Captain Mitchell. Fifteen men, including the captain, survived for forty-three days, finally landing, in critical condition, at Laupahoehoe, on the Island of Hawaii. Mark Twain was captivated by the story, which he followed with great interest, sending the details to the *Sacramento Union*. Letter 15, the longest of the *Sacramento Union* reports, is the complete story of Captain Mitchell and the *Hornet*. Mark Twain writes it virtually without humor, a straightforward journalist's submission, which was a major scoop for the *Sacramento Union*. He meets with the crew in the hospital in Honolulu and tells the story pretty much through the report of the Captain himself. Bob emphasized the journalistic nature of the letter, showing that Mark Twain could report a story as a serious writer, rather than a writer of humor.

It is clear, Bob states, that Twain considered the Captain a very strong man, and he is captivated by such personalities, even comparing the captain to one of his good friends whom he greatly admired, President Grant. His writings are filled with the characters of strong men. He returned to San Francisco on the same boat with Captain Mitchell and two shipmates. In addition, he knew immediately that this was a major story, and he made the most of it, as a journalist. The story was printed in the *Sacramento Union* and again in *Harper's*, a major achievement in Mark Twain's mind. Bob says he looks on it as the beginning of his literary career. However, in the *Harper's* index, the story is listed, "BOAT, IN OPEN, 43 DAYS IN..... *Mark Swain*"

Despite the misspelling, the *Hornet* article was important in Mark Twain's career, a fine example of pure journalism, an article he kept throughout his life. To Bob it is a "very good example of his ability to write straight prose."

V

We have a walking tour of Kailua this morning, or more precisely, Kailua-Kona, to distinguish it from Kailua, O'ahu and probably a couple of other towns on the other islands. There are only so many "K"s to go around. Two guides from the Kona Historical Society were waiting under the banyan tree outside the hotel, Fred and Pumahana. I told them that we had about an hour and a half at most and needed to be back at the hotel by 10:00 because we have a 10:30 bus to catch. I could immediately tell from the look on their faces that they couldn't make that deadline and I mentally girded my loins for a battle in about an hour. I have seldom met a local guide who didn't think in three-hour tour increments, and I have never met a local guide who wasn't convinced that his/her information was essential to a decent life. No way are Fred's and Pumahana's messages capable of being condensed into a mere ninety minutes. At least not without a well-placed salvo or four being fired by me around 8:30, 9:15, 9:25 and 9:30. They will get angry, will tell everyone that we didn't get a very good tour because we didn't give them enough time, and they will waste twenty of their precious minutes voicing that disclaimer. Most of the local guides I have met are pretty much incapable of prioritizing their information—factoid #2 always follows from nugget A, and informational gems #8, 9 and 10 must stay in sequence to be properly comprehended. Take any element away and the whole house of cards comes falling down.

We divided into turtles and hares, depending on the relative speed of our walking gaits. Fred started us "turtles" off with a twenty-minute intro under the banyan tree while Pumahana led the "hares" over to the Ahu'ena Heiau over on the shore, where she initiated her own twenty-minute intro. Kailua is a very historic town, the place where Kamehameha I, the Great, solidified his conquest of the island, where he settled down in his last years and died in 1819, where the first missionaries landed from New England

271

in 1820, where the famous cattle herds from Parker Ranch were floated out to waiting ships to be sent to the market. Near here Captain James Cook made his triumphal arrival as the God Lono, and where he made his disastrous departure as butcher meat not much later.

> "We landed at Kailua (pronounced Ki-loo-ah), a little collection of native grass houses reposing under tall coconut trees—the sleepiest, quietest, Sundayest looking place you can imagine. Ye weary ones that are sick of the labor and care, and the bewildering turmoil of the great world, and sigh for a land where ye may fold your tired hands and slumber your lives peacefully away, pack up your carpet sacks and go to Kailua! A week there ought to cure the saddest of you all."
> *Letters from Hawaii,* Letter 18

Today is indeed Sunday, but there are no grass houses in sight.

Just a few yards from the banyan tree is a little cove and beach, tiny really, where the Parker Ranch *paniolo,* Hawaiian cowboys (their name is derived from "Espaniolo"), cornered their rambunctious steers in preparation for shipping them off to slaughter. They funneled them into the beach pen, literally dragged them into the water, roped them to the sides of whaleboats and floated them out to the waiting cargo ship, where they were winched onto the vessel on a stomach strap. 120 at a time made the voyage to market, a process that continued right up to 1956, when a 747 was substituted for the transportation.

But that is modern history. The real story for Kailua begins in the late eighteenth century when a strapping young prince who had participated in the "welcome" given to Captain Cook, conquered the island of Hawai'i. Kamehameha the Great was born about sixty miles north of Kailua and probably because of his stature and charisma quickly rose to power, consolidating his rule across the island. Eventually he would unify all the islands, creating the Hawaiian Kingdom. Kailua was his first capital, until he moved it to O'ahu. As an old man, he returned to Kailua in 1812, making Ahu'ene Heiau his personal place of worship as well as home for him and his twenty-two wives. Eventually we were led over to that restored temple, which today displays all the elements necessary in a *heiau.* Kamehameha dedicated his *heiau* to Lono, god of peace and prosperity, the same god that Cook was thought to be on his first arrival in Hawai'i. The traditional *heiau* is built on a stone platform (*paepae*), on top of which are placed several structures: the *hale mana*, a thatched hall used for meetings and community events; the *hale pahu*, or house of drums, the *'anu'u*, a white oracle tower where the chief priest announced the will of Lono, and a bunch of *ki'I akua*, temple images that resemble tikis or totems. All these elements can be found at this Kona spot. Kamehameha didn't have long to enjoy his new home, dying seven years after his retirement arrival, in 1819.

By this time it was closing in on 9:30, and Pumehana was proposing to stop and discuss every king's portrait in the hotel hall, and every artifact in their considerable collection of Hawaiiana. I feel bad that I was compelled to stop her show in mid-sentence and push her out to the street to show our folks that "Sundayest" place that Mark Twain had extolled. She didn't take my prodding well and hurried off in a huff with her rabbits in tow. But even in a tizzy, the tour guide came to the surface, as she couldn't ethically get past the display with the feather cape, the case with the feather headdress, the pictures of Kam II, Kam III and Huumanuhu, and yet another case featuring a discussion of a *hulua* slide and a *papamu*, a stone checker board for playing *konane*. And then, finally, she led us off to that village!

There are two main historic sites extant in Kailua. The first is Mokuaikaua Church, the first Christian church in Hawaii. Kamehameha I was barely cold in his grave when on April 20, 1820 Bingham Whitney arrived with his small band of New England missionaries, with definite instructions: "You are to aim at nothing short of covering those islands with fruitful fields and pleasant dwellings and schools and churches; of raising up the whole people to an elevated state of Christian civilization." He immediately established Mokuaikaua Church, and baptized Henry Opukahaia, the first Hawaiian Christian. The present church, impressively constructed out of stone, was built in 1836. Unfortunately, or from the standpoint of our schedule, fortunately, this is Sunday and services are going on in the church, rather loud Congregational services I might add, preventing us from entering and extending our stay at least another twenty minutes. Instead we walked across the street to the village's second historic building, also not open—Hulihe'e Palace. The palace was built in 1838 by Governor Kuakini. The governess, Princess Ruth Ke'elikolani, she of the tremendous girth, moved to a grass house (*hale pili*) on the grounds, and in 1884, King Kalakaua and Queen Kapi'olani modernized the original palace in Victorian fashion.

We did in fact get back to the hotel by 10:00, with time to spare to freshen up for our bus ride to the south end of the island. A smiling Jeff, the driver-guide from Roberts, met us in the lobby of the King Kamehameha when we got back from our walk of the town. The first thing he told me was that he would be our driver for the next three days. I introduced him to some of our folks sitting there, relaying that information.

"Do you think I'm going to believe you?" Frank asked with only half a smile. "We have heard that about all the drivers we have had." Jeff held his own though, insisting that he would be here tomorrow and all the way up to the transfer to Hilo Airport on Wednesday morning. We'll see. I couldn't have expressed Frank any better.

Our itinerary both today and tomorrow is quite full, with too many sights to take in and too many miles in between. But Jeff suggested that we drive straight to Punalu'u Black Sand Beach, the furthest south we will go, and then work our way back, "playing it by ear," judging the time. Jeff is another of those very outgoing, Hawaiian-happy drivers that Roberts has collected, and I look forward to having him as our driver the next three days, if in fact that happens.

Right off the bat, the banter started as we passed a Bougainvillea tree in full view.

"That was named by a French botanist, after himself," Mac announced. "Botanists have a habit of naming things after themselves."

"Oh, I suppose I can say that the Macadamia nut was named after you then, Mac," Jeff responded.

"Only the 'nut' part!" That came from the audience. I think it was Les.

Kailua-Kona is a town of about 33,000 people, which usually doubles in size with the tourists that descend on it throughout the year. It sits on the dry side of the island, virtually surrounded by lava flows that fill the land with black rock, and line the shore with black beaches. There is even a green beach, formed by the sands of a green silicate named olivine. The lava is of two types, *a'a*, jagged and shattered, and *pahoihoi*, that flows out and down in a viscous pudding, and cools in smooth slabs.

Jeff, who lives in Hilo, is a very fluent speaker with a good grasp of the natural history of his island. He has an attractive, outgoing personality, which quickly melded with our style of travel, engaging Mac in word games almost from the start.

"Jeff, what is that flat area down on the water's edge?" Mac inquired as we moved down the coast road. Jeff had to reconnect his mike to provide an answer.

"Mac, that land down on the water's edge is a flat area."

He went on to surmise that it is probably an outflow from Moana Loa, which has filled this section of Hawai'i with enormous expanses of lava. We passed through the tiny village of Ki'alakeku'a, famous for that "little grass shack" in the song. Then came the strange sounding town of Captain Cook, a slight diversion into English before resuming reasonable names like Nonaunau and Kealia, just past Kealakekua Bay, to which we will return later this afternoon. Before long we were on the narrow Mamalahoa Highway, which cuts across a dozen lava flows from Mauna Loa. It took a bit over an hour to reach our destination, the village of Na'alehu, and the Punalu'u Black Sand Beach. This is as far south as we will go today.

This is the route that Sam Clemens took on his way to the volcano. From Kealakekua Bay he took a boat south to the windy tip of the island. There in the village of Wai'ohinu, he rented a horse and rode the rest of the way to Kilauea and the Volcano Lodge. Tomorrow we will reach that same destination from the opposite direction.

The black sand is not at all like the normal beach sand. Rather it is shredded lava that shatters into tiny pieces when it comes in contact with the relatively cold water. It is like a beach filled with miniscule stones, rather than the water-worn grains we are used to. Punalu'u Beach is a major tourist attraction because of that distinctive sand. It seems also to be an attraction for the giant Green turtles like the one we saw yesterday on O'ahu. Today it multiplied the excitement factor by five, a heart-stopping experience since all five turtles today were not working just as hard as the one yesterday. To be fair, however, four-fifths of today's inertia was plopped in the surf, showing only a round shell back to us viewers, and those backs were positively bobbing at times as waves rolled in. The excitement at such times is palpable.

From the turtles doing nothing on black sand, we retreated up the highway back to Na'alehu where we stopped for a lunch break at the Punalu'u Sweetbread Shop. They are advertised as the "southernmost bakery in the United States," a title that Jeff says is often disputed by Floridians, who can't conceive of anything that is south of Key West. The bakery was bustling with customers, most eager to indulge themselves in generous chocolate éclairs, and a variety of *malasada*, a sort of sugared Portuguese jelly donut that is filled with apple, mango, pineapple or other types of fruit.

Near the bakery is the famous "Mark Twain Monkeypod Tree," which apparently has no real basis in fact. Bob was consulted about its authenticity, but he was forced to report that he has never read anything that could corroborate the truth of Mark Twain planting anything during his stay in the islands. I am not sure all our folks believed Bob because they were looking at an official state sign that announced the tree to the general public, and such signs being permanent, must be believed. Whoever planted the tree, it was blown down in a hurricane in 1957, the present tree being the result of shoots rising out of the wreckage.

The main object of our day is approaching, the massive site of Pu'uhonua'a Honaonao, the famous "City of Refuge." This impressive site on Kealakekua Bay, the same bay where Captain Cook was killed, was one of several areas of asylum during the brutal days of kapu. In the old days, commoners' lives were regulated by the kapu system, taboos to cover hundreds of acts, most of which resulted in death. Men and women were not allowed to eat together, or to consume the same foods. There were many kapus that regulated the commoner in the presence of the chiefs, including the prohibition of allowing his shadow to cross that of the chief. Fishing and hunting areas were often declared kapu to replenish the stock. Death was almost inevitable, by strangulation, club, fire or spear. At times entire families were executed for a particularly egregious offense. The only way out was the pu'uhonua, or place of refuge, an asylum where the wrongdoer could perform some rituals and escape his fate. Warriors defeated in battle could also find a new life in the sanctuary, as could women and children during warfare. Built in the 1500s, Pu'uhonua Honaonao is the best of the Places of Refuge in the islands, declared a National Park in 1961. It features a massive wall, 1000' long, 12' high and 17' thick. There are a few reconstructed dwellings on the grounds, including a thatched A-frame structure, called Hale-o-Keawe, which once contained the bones of twenty-three chiefs. The main platform for the heiau is quite impressive, a large stone rectangle that has been fully restored, sitting behind the long wall of the refuge. Nearby is the Keoua Stone:

> "Outside of these ancient walls lies a sort of coffin-shaped stone eleven feet four inches long and three feet square at the small end (It would weigh a few thousand pounds), which the high chief who held sway over this district many centuries ago brought hither on his shoulder one day to use as a lounge! This circumstance is established by the most reliable traditions. He used to lie down on it in his indolent way, and keep an eye on his subjects at work for him… He was fourteen or fifteen feet high. When he stretched himself at full length on his lounge, his legs hung down over the end, and when he snored he woke the dead. These facts are all attested by irrefragable tradition."
>
> Letters from Hawaii, Letter 22

Frank, hearing this story, had no patience with old King Keoua. "If he was that strong, why wouldn't he carry a stone long enough to fit his legs?"

There is an even bigger stone in the *heiau,* called Ka'ahumanu's Stone, which legend has it, was a refuge for Kamehameha's wife. It is said she hid under it to get away from her angry husband, a fact that Mark Twain hotly disputes:

> "…Kaaumanu was six feet high—she was bulky—she was built like an ox—and she could no more have squeezed under that rock than she could have passed through the cylinders of a sugar mill. What could she gain by it even if she succeeded? To be chased and abused by her savage husband could not be otherwise than humiliating to her high spirit, yet it could never make her feel so flat as an hour's repose under that rock would."
>
> Letters from Hawaii, Letter 22

Jeff laughed when I read him this passage about the buxom Ka'ahumanu, saying that she must be the model for all Hawaiian women. "Hawaiian woman don't eat 'til they're full; they eat 'til they're tired."

❧ ❧

Arville had suggested that we make a stop at "the Painted Church," which sits just a couple of streets away from the City of Refuge. In the old days, it was much closer, sitting on the water in Honaunau, known then as St. Francis Regis Chapel. In 1899, Father John Berchmans Velghe arrived from Belgium and helped the parishioners move the chapel up the hill, in the process becoming St. Benedict's Church. In an effort to bring his Christian message more clearly to his parishioners, Father John, an amateur painter, painted the entire interior of his church with biblical scenes, using ordinary oil-based house paints. Many of the panels have been erased by time and the elements and others appear to be under repair, but the church is still impressive as an admirable piece of folk art.

Mac, who has become an expert at devising unusual talking topics was in fine form heading back to the hotel. He lamented the lack of writing paper at the hotel in Waikiki, surmising that people were so used in our modern era to emails and computers that the art of letter writing has disappeared, causing hotels to discontinue the tradition of supplying post cards, stationery and free pens for their clients. At the same time, that hotel had fine, thick and wide toilet paper, as opposed to the puny, poorly absorbent panels of the King Kam. This led naturally to India, where people use the much more efficient and efficacious water and left-hand system instead of relying on perforated paper. It is irrelevant that the water itself may be polluted, or the paper non-existent. And that of course opened the subject of computerized Japanese toilet seats, which soothe, amuse, warm and cleanse almost anything on your body and mind. I am sure that Mac could have extended his subject much further, but we had arrived back at the hotel and everyone was inspired to run for the loo.

VI

THE KINGS

1795 – 1819	Kamehameha I
1819 – 1824	Kamehameha II (Liholiho)
1825 – 1854	Kamehameha III (Kauikeaouili)
1855 – 1863	Kamehameha IV (Alexander L. Liholiho)
1863 – 1872	Kamehameha V (Lot Kapuaiwa)
1873 – 1874	William Lunalilo ("Whiskey Bill")
1874 – 1891	David Kalakau
1891 – 1893	Lili'oukalani (Kamaka'eha Paki)

You can't be a king in Hawaii if your name doesn't begin with a "K". Everyone has heard of King Kamehameha—there were a bunch of them. But just try to negotiate the sea of "K"s on Kamehameha the Great's drive to his throne. Twice he had been defeated by the great king of Maui, Kahekili, but in 1790, with Kahekili away on Oahu, Kamehameha invaded Maui and whipped Kahekili's son Kalanikupule, much to the joy of the war god Kukailimoku. After Kamehameha's defeat of Kalanikuipule, Kahekili immediately made an alliance with his half-brother Kaeokulani, king of Kauai. Kamehameha had to hurry back to the Big Island because Keoua, who had just defeated Keawemauhili, was attacking Kamehameha's lands. Keoua went home to his lands in Kao, but was invited by Kamehameha to a feast to celebrate the completion of his new temple at Kawaihae. Keoua accepted. His retinue was met by Kamehameha's lieutenant, Keeaumoku, who earlier had slain Kiwalao. Keeaumoku immediately put a spear in Keoua's chest, and his retainers were all slain as well. It seems that Kamehameha needed a sacrifice to christen his new temple. Hearing this awful tale, Kahekili and his half-brother Kaeokulani sailed for Hawaii.

The armies met in the indecisive battle of Kepuwahaulaula. But Kahekili died in Waikiki in 1794, turning his kingdom over to Kalanikupule, with Kaeokulani in control of Kawai, Maui, Lanai and Molokai. They immediately started fighting among themselves, with Kalanikupule defeating Kaeokulani, as well as an American named Kendrick, who somehow managed to have a K-name in a Hawaiian battle, and died defending it. Kalanikupule decided to attack Kamehameha in Hawaii and make himself king of all the islands. He was joined by Kamehameha's ally, Kaiana, who had been having an affair with Kamehameha's favorite wife, Ka'ahumanu. Finally all the "K"s met in the great battle of Nuuanu, where Kaiana, his back to the cliff at the Pala, died. Kamehameha then turned his sights on Kau'ai, but more problems at home, this time led by Kaiana's brother Namakeha (All of the good "K" names had apparently been taken). Six years later, Kamehameha was finally ready to deal with Kau'ai. Kalanikupule was dead by now, succeeded by Kaumualii, who was building a ship to escape if he lost the battle. The Hawaiian army was not defeated in battle, but by a terrible epidemic, probably cholera, and Kamehameha again failed to add Kau'ai to his lands. In 1805, Kaumualii agreed to become Kamehameha's vassal, retaining his title of King of Kau'ai, but unifying the islands under the great king. Kamehameha never fought another battle, issuing a decree: "Let the old men, the old women and the children sleep in safety by the road side."

Kamehameha died in 1819 and was succeeded by his son, Liholiho. "Aha!" you say. "There's a king without a 'K'!" But not so fast, as soon as Liholiho became king, he changed his name—to Kamehameha II. As a sidelight, by the way, that favorite wife of Kamehameha I, Ka'ahumanu, who had been sleeping all around the islands much of her life, went looking for a husband after the great king died, and settled on Kaumualii, King of Kauai, whom she forced into wedlock. She then added Kaumualii's 7' son, Kealiiahonui as a second husband. If she hadn't then converted to Christianity, she could have gone on collecting "K"s for the rest of her life.

We are heading south this morning and our first stop is at Pu'ukohola Heiau. This impressive temple was built by Kamehameha in 1790-91, called a *lu'a kini heiau*, a sacrifice temple. The construction was aided throughout by the sacrifice of workers to keep the god happy. On completion, the king invited his enemy, Keoua, to the dedication. The visitor was executed on arrival and became the cornerstone sacrifice for the new temple. According to the ranger who hustled us into the visitor center for his canned speech, the temple was the second of three prophecies that foreshadowed the career of the young Kamehameha. The first was that he would be born under a shooting star. Could that have been the same Haley's Comet that ushered in Sam Clemens? Second he would have to move the *naha* stone, a 3,000 pound behemoth that is still sitting in the middle of Hilo, a feat he is said to have accomplished as a young man. And third, he had to build this *lu'a kini* to satisfy his war god, Kuka'ilimoku. The temple built, Kamehameha then proceeded to subdue the rest of Hawaii.

I think that Pu'ukohola is the most impressive of the "ancient" sites in Hawai'i. It is being completely restored by the National Park Service, sitting impressively on a steep hill overlooking the ocean. A pair of crossed sticks topped by white balls, the traditional symbol that the place is *kapu*, blocks the visitor's way up the hill. The *heiau* was constructed of smooth lava rocks collected from the Pu'o'olu Valley, twenty miles away, transported to the site by a chain gang of the king's soldiers. Kamehameha himself took an active part in carrying the stones. It must have been most intimidating when viewed by the subjects of the king, especially after his treatment of King Keoua, who had only recently defeated Kamehameha in battle. I asked the rangers why Keoua would so meekly have gone to his death, but none had any explanation other than a misplaced sense of fate. He certainly knew that he was going to die because our guide told us that he intentionally castrated himself on the way to the *heiau* to make his sacrifice less acceptable to the gods.

Had we the time, we would have continued out the Kohala Peninsula to other historical sites, including the birthplace of the ferocious Kamehameha, but we will run out of time before we reach our destination tonight at the Volcano House. So we turned inland to Waimea, the center of the famous Parker Ranch. Originally, I wanted to visit the ranch house museum, which is somewhat like the old ranch houses of South Fork or Ponderosa from TV lore. But the Parker Ranch, once the largest privately held cattle ranch in the world, has been going through some tough times lately. Just this morning in the local papers it was announced that they were selling off their real estate division to concentrate solely on their cattle enterprises. Even the cows lost money last year in these hard times. In 1793, George Vancouver brought a gift to King Kamehameha—a bunch of long-horned cows. The king issued a *kapu* from harming them for ten years to build up the herd, during which time they grew wild, roaming the hills of the Big Island, a threat to all who ventured into their realm. In 1815, the king hired a Massachusetts man, John Palmer Parker, to hunt down the wild beasts, salt them and sell the meat to whaling captains in search of provisions. Parker began assembling his own herd as payment for his services. In 1816, he married Kamehameha's granddaughter, and he was allowed to purchase two acres of land. His new wife later was granted a princess's 640 acres. Parker added another 1000 acres to the ranch, which would eventually grow to nine percent of the entire island, 225,000 acres, the largest privately-owned ranch in the world. Much of the ranch, 139,000 acres, was deeded in the 1990s to a non-profit trust, which today operates several disconnected segments with 39,000 head of cattle. They are tended by a small force of twelve *paniolo*, Hawaiian cowboys. The cows are grazed here for five to six months and then flown to Canada or the mainland for fattening and slaughter. Back in Kailua we had seen the ramp from earlier days when those cattle were tied to whaleboats and rowed out to waiting ships in the harbor.

It was on Parker Ranch that the Scottish botanist, David Douglas, met his fate, while walking along Mana Road. He fell into a bull pit, and though he survived the fall, he was gored to death by a wild bull who had found the same pit. The botanical world decided to name the Douglas Fir after the fallen Scot, even though he was not the man who first described the tree. Douglas was impressive nevertheless, having walked across Canada, east to west and back, down to San Diego and back up to the Columbia River. Finally he came to the islands and met his tragic death.

Waimea is a beautiful green pastureland, sitting in the saddle between two of Hawaii's five volcanos, the old worn out Kohala and the majestic Moana Kea, at 13,796 the highest on the island. It is only slightly higher than its sister Moana Loa (13,679). Mt. Hualalai, visible from the hotel this morning, is a meager 8,271, while the active volcano, Kilauea, is barely a mountain at all, but rather a big pit of smoke and rubble. The Big Island, the youngest of the Hawaiian Islands, is constantly growing as Kilauea continues to dump its excess into the ocean, adding to the shoreline.

From Parker Ranch our route took us along the Hamakua Coast, through small towns with tongue-twisting names: Honoka'a, Pa'auilo, Laupahoehoe, Papa'aloa. Our first stop was at Akaka Falls, one of the "musts" of this coast. A circular path takes you to the falls, a very tall ribbon that descends to a quiet pool at its base, and then winds to a second less impressive waterfall, Kahuna. In the process you get to climb 134 steps.

We were greeted back on the bus by Mac, who was wielding a pair of sugar cane sticks, each with about three nodes, ready for his next planting. He launched into a brief lecture on cane that included such terms as chloroplasts, photosynthesis, carbon fixing and lateral buds. I saw Jeff's head snap up on that last one and knew that it would immediately be inputted to his next Circle Hawai'i tour. Mac has a wonderful way of throwing in botanical and scientific terms in such a way that you never quite get them right, unless you have your Botany I or Biology II text handy and can study them by candlelight. Jeff is right to just pick one such term and add it to his working vocabulary, somewhat like going into the Smithsonian and collecting one artifact in your memory. Try to absorb more and you lose everything. (Note: later in the trip, Jeff publicly thanked Mac for teaching him about lateral buds.)

Presently we arrived in Hilo, a tropical town that seems to sleep beneath the cover of its considerable rain, once again on the windward side of the island, with the great volcanic barrier behind it. There could not be a greater contrast between Hilo and Kona, the contrast between green and wet and black-brown and dry. Hilo is a place of luxuriant growth and beautiful flowers; Kona is one of arid lava flows, graffitied by white coral messages from teenagers, lovers and migrant tourists. Ironically, it is Hilo that is now experiencing the constructive flow of volcanic effluents, as Kilauea disgorges its lava into the ocean nearby.

We stopped in the old part of town at the second of those four statues of King Kamehameha. The third is along the Kona coast, near Kamehameha's birthplace, which we missed in our haste this morning. The fourth is one of the two statues that each of the states selected to represent it in the basement of the capitol rotunda in Washington D.C. Jeff explained that this area of Hilo, which is now an expansive park, was once densely settled, mostly by his Portuguese nationals. In 1946 a tsunami hit Hilo wiping out this part of town, which was called New Town (Shinmachi to the Japanese residents), including his own home. He was saved, he said, only because his father was sitting on the john that morning and realized that the cadence of incoming waves had stopped. He grabbed him and his mother and they ran for high ground just as the wave hit.

From Kamehameha's statue we drove down the most impressive Banyan Drive, through Lili'aukalani Park, a magnificent park that pretty much fills the area of Hilo that is most vulnerable to the periodic tsunamis. The dozens of banyans are named for prominent visitors to Hilo, I suppose planted in their honor, such luminaries as FDR, Neville Chamberlain, and other politicians and statesmen. Babe Ruth has a tree there as well.

Our last stop this afternoon is at the Nani Mao Botanical Gardens. There we boarded a tram for a half-hour tour of those gardens, which are mainly an arboretum of the trees of the tropics. A young guide narrated the tour and did pretty well until he stated that the mongoose, introduced to combat the rats of the island, didn't maintain the same life cycle as those rats, but did succeed in eliminating the snakes from Hawaii. That got an immediate and loud reaction from Mac, and several more of us, since there are fewer snakes in Hawaii than there were in Ireland when St. Patrick arrived. There is a worry now however, that an Asian brown snake, brought in on tankers, may be establishing itself on the islands, and authorities are keeping a close watch. There are already so many noxious imports in both flora and fauna that Hawai'i can ill afford to add a reptile to that list.

The very last paragraph in Mark Twain's letters describes the Volcano House where we are staying.

"It is only at very long intervals that I mention in a letter matters which properly pertain to the advertising columns, but in this case it seems to me that to leave out the fact that there is a neat, roomy, well-furnished and well-kept hotel at the volcano would be to remain silent upon the very highest importance to anyone who may decide to visit the place. The surprise at finding a good hotel in such an outlandish spot startled me considerably more than the volcano did. The house is new—built three or four months ago—and the table is good. One could not easily starve here even if the meats and groceries were to give out, for large tracts of land in the vicinity are well paved with excellent strawberries. One can have as abundant a supply as he chooses to call for. There has never heretofore been anything in this locality for the accommodation of travelers but a crazy old native grass hut, scanty fare, hard beds of matting and a Chinese cook."

Letters from Hawaii, Letter 25

As he said, the place only opened in March, 1866, just before he arrived. It was basically a thatched building with a fluted gable end, replaced in 1877 by a frame building with a wooden roof. That 1877 version was expanded and saved from destruction in a later fire. It was moved away from the rim of the crater to occupy the spot where it now rests, serving as the art gallery, a very expensive art gallery for the new Volcano House Hotel. In talking with the folks at the front desk, the "new" hotel is now scheduled for a complete remodeling, much needed, and may be out of commission for up to a year. Since it is presently the only restaurant in the park, this will cause a considerable problem for tourists, especially those arriving from Hilo and from the cruise ships, who now fill it virtually every day at lunch time. We had a very nice dinner this evening, of prime rib, a meal that would have gotten fine praise from Mark Twain.

VII

We have the morning to relax. I think that means that we don't have to get onto a bus until the afternoon. Jeff is scheduled to pick us up at 12:30 for a ride around Kilauea, to view all the vents, flows, eruptions, flumes, plumes, tubes, cones and craters. By the end of the day we should be able to put one of those tongue-twisting Hawaiian names at the back of each of those. I have been listening to Jeff spew out such names for two days now, and I always wonder if he is making them up. I have heard so many: Huluhulu, Kulanaokuaiki, Kealakomo, Kipukapuaula, Namakanipalo. For the uninitiated, does any of it actually matter? Will my life be enriched if I take the time to memorize these verbal processions? I think I am going to consign Hawaiian place names to my "Castle on the Rhine" storage. I never was able to come up with the actual names of those rock piles, so I decided to just collect the rocks themselves. I gathered *stein*, and *feld*, and *herr, nieder* and *ober, berg* and *burg, alt* and *neu, gau, volk, hoch, mehr,* and maybe a *wunder.* Whenever one of our travelers asked for identification, I just glued three or four of these rocks together and shot it into the conflict:

"That castle? Oh, it's called Altfeldstein, built in 1472."

"Niederoberneuburg!"

"I think they call that one Neuscheissweinwunder."

"Hochwaldobersteinherrschaftenberg." That was my favorite.

That's what I am going to do with my Hawaiian names. Here it is so much easier because you only need a couple of letters, maybe an "A" or ten, some "L"s, "N"s, "P"s, certainly a gross of "K"s and "U"s. Heck, there's only twelve grains in the whole shotgun shell. I figure I can just set a wide spray and come up with something that should satisfy anyone. You also need an apostrophe every so often so you can double or triple your vowel of choice. I saw a town called Ka'a'a'pa. How can you account for such a dearth of alphabetic imagination?

287

"What's the name of that crater, Jack"

"Kanukanupailo'o."

"That's Nukaika'nao'i. It erupted in 1492, same year that Kamehameha discovered the islands."

It helps to double everything, because everyone here has a double-barreled shotgun. "Humuhumunukunukuapua'a go swimming by."

I am certain that Jeff has been launching these verbal mortars at us ever since Mac told him we were all college graduates. How else could he have come up with Huluhulu, Kulanaokuaiki, Kealakomo, Kipukapuaula, Namakanipalo, all of which were included in our tour today?

&⚬&

Bob gives his second formal talk this morning after breakfast, on a subject I have been greatly anticipating, "The Sandwich Island Lectures." Or as Mark Twain formally called it, "Our fellow savages of the Sandwich Islands." It was a lecture that he would give more than 100 times, carrying it throughout the West and into his East Coast circuit.

Twain found himself back in San Francisco after returning from the islands, without a job and without any foreseeable means of income. The idea of a lecture occurred to him, and he began scribbling notes, on the first page of the first draft: "85 pages, 1 hour." He agonizes over the thing, asking his friends for their opinion. They told him he would ruin his literary career with such a thing. It was a great risk, financially and professionally, but he rented the Opera House in San Francisco, with a seating capacity of 1500, selling the tickets at $1 each. He sold about 200 tickets to friends, wishing to have an appreciative audience, and he arranged for them to clap and applaud. "Doors open at 7 ½. Trouble begins at 8!" This was a great gamble. Even though he was well known in San Francisco, he worried that he would not get a good crowd, that the reviews would be horrible. And to his great shock, when he looked out, the theater was filled.

"Little by little, my fright melted away, and I began to talk."

His lecture was a huge success. Though there were some critics, his comment showed his mental state afterwards, "They have their opinions and I have their dollars, and I am satisfied."

In October, 1866, he took his lecture on the road, beginning in San Francisco and San Jose and back again in San Francisco. Then he headed for the gold country, speaking in a variety of gold mining towns and camps in California and Nevada: Red Dog and You Bet (near Nevada City), Grass Valley, Nevada City, Gold Hill, Silver City, Dayton and Virginia City. Then he moved his lecture to the East Coast. Bob said that Mark Twain loved manipulating his audiences, changing his lecture to meet the needs of the night. He added that he hated the idea of being driven to lecture, but they were "a big part of Mark Twain's career and a fundamental part of his talent."

Bob said that the Mark Twain Papers don't have the whole manuscript of the "Sandwich Island Lecture." Many of the manuscript sheets he gave away, when admirers requested something of his work, and the talk was constantly changing as well. There was no standard lecture. It was arranged "like beads on a string," you could take one off or add one on and it made no difference at all. This is what he called "his natural gait," something that he used on his novels as well as on his lectures. For instance, he didn't plot out *Huckleberry Finn* from beginning to end; he just created it as he went along. Bob mentioned several problems he had with that novel as he moved with it, particularly with the ending. Evidence that he changed the "Sandwich Island Lecture" comes from some notes he made, but mostly from reports of the talks in newspaper accounts and letters. He always disliked the formal introductions that were made introducing him to his audiences.

His lecture mixed humor with description. On cannibalism: "If anyone will lend me an infant, I will demonstrate the matter." His descriptions of Hawaii are accurate; he called Kilueia "the chief attraction of the Hawaiian Islands." Even though his lectures were closely timed, eventually he had to add stories to fill the time. In one version he described a man blowing himself out of a hole and disappearing into the sky. "Would you believe it, that poor fellow was only gone for fifteen minutes, his company docked him for loss of time."

Much of Mark Twain's writings are really travel narratives: *Innocents Abroad* and *A Tramp Abroad, Following the Equator, Roughing It, Life on the Mississippi.*

Mary asked if Mark Twain only lectured about travel. Did he ever lecture on politics? Bob's answer is that he didn't give political speeches and didn't really speak out on politics until the Spanish-American War, which he greatly opposed. While he didn't give political lectures, there are plenty of comments on politics in his writings and letters. Religion was always a favorite subject, but he generally steered clear of politics because of its possible harmful effects on his livelihood. He did give speeches other than the "Sandwich Island Lecture" however, including "Famous People I Have Met," "Vandals Abroad," based on *Innocents Abroad*, and another based on *Roughing It*.

As good as he was as a lecturer, Mark Twain is "still thought of as a novelist." He is the "first one to write an entire novel in the voice of a fourteen-year old boy."

Bob was asked if Mark Twain ever put the Sandwich Island Lecture into a book. He did, but it was never published. Then the notes were incorporated into *Roughing It,* because he needed more pages to finish that book. The Hawaii notes were simply tacked on to the end, along with some other stories.

Asked if Mark Twain had a formula for writing, Bob answered that he generally wrote from about 10 A.M. to 5 P.M. At Elmira, he would read his day's work to his family in the evening. In his life he penned more than 50,000 letters, of which the Mark Twain Papers have about 11,000. Bob said that they find an average of two new letters a week. The Mark Twain Papers Project has thus far has published six volumes of letters to 1885. "It is hard for him to write a dull letter," Bob added.

What is so remarkable is that this literary and verbal master left school at age eleven. But he was thoroughly versed in the literature of the world, especially the Bible, Shakespeare and Dickens. His was a skill learned by doing.

⁂ ∞

The ship is in Hilo today, the *Pride of America* which docks in Hilo every Tuesday. We are scheduled to have our lunch at the Volcano House, but by 11:00, there was a line of hungry tourists lined up outside the front door of the hotel, and they just kept arriving. A few of our more famished folk, went to the desk and were told that as hotel guests they didn't have to wait in line, so they were properly fed. Most of us however took one look at the line and made other arrangements, such as skipping lunch. Mac opted for a "cultural fusion lunch,"—taro chips and a Milky Way, along with a satisfying cigar on the veranda.

The cigar sparked a brief discussion of the noxious gases being puffed out by Kilauea, hydrogen sulfide and sulfur dioxide. He groused that visitors gave him evil glances as he sat there smoking his cigar, while at the same time they were inhaling sulfuric acid without a hint of anxiety or concern. Those gases do cause concern for the National Park Service however. Whenever the winds shift and blow the vapors toward inhabited areas, that section is evacuated. About half of the volcano rim road is closed at this time because of the danger of the volcanic emissions.

Lunch or not, Jeff was at the hotel at 1:00 and we were off on a half circle of Kilauea, our first stop being at the Jagger Museum, on the very rim of the large caldera, and the closest to Halema'uma'u Crater, which is presently spewing out the chemicals that are filling the skies, not only of this region but all of the Kona coast, and even into Maui. Down on the flat lands, they call this mixture "vog," volcanic fog, a condition we saw very clearly when we took our cruise over to Kealakekua Bay a couple of days ago. Halema'uma'u Crater is said to be the home of Pele, that ferocious god who casts a spell on any who would steal part of her hoard of rocks. From 1823 to 1924 it was filled with an enormous lake of molton lava, something Mark Twain describes vividly:

> "By the path it is half a mile from the Volcano House to the lookout house. After a hearty supper we waited until it was thoroughly dark and then started to the crater. The first glance in that direction revealed a scene of wild beauty. There was a heavy fog over the crater and it was splendidly illuminated by the glare of the fires below. The illumination was two miles wide and a mile high, perhaps.... Arrived at the little thatched look out house, we rested our elbows on the railing in front and looked abroad over the wide crater and down over the sheer precipice at the seething fires beneath us. The view was a startling improvement on my daylight experience..."
> *Letters from Hawaii*, Letter 25

I turned my eyes upon the volcano again. The "cellar" was tolerably well lighted up. For a mile and a half in front of us and half a mile on either side, the floor of the abyss was magnificently illuminated, beyond these limits the mists hung down their gauzy curtains and cast a deceptive gloom over all that made the twinkling fires in the remote corners of the crater seem countless leagues removed....

"The greater part of the vast floor of the desert under us was as black as ink, and apparently smooth and level, but over a mile square of it was tinged and streaked and striped with a thousand branching streams of liquid and gorgeously brilliant fire! It looked like a colossal railroad map of the State of Massachusetts done in chain lightning on a midnight sky. Imagine it—imagine a coal-black sky shivered into a tangled network of angry fire!

"...the little fountains scattered about looked very beautiful. They boiled, and coughed, and spluttered, and discharged sprays of stringy red fire—of about the consistency of mush, for instance— from ten to fifteen feet in the air, along with a shower of brilliant white sparks—a quaint and unnatural mingling of gouts of blood and snow flakes!"

Letters from Hawaii, Letter 25

Mark Twain used up a month of exclamation points on his description of Kilauea. Last night a few of us walked out on the veranda of the Volcano House and got very excited because we could see a faint glow in the darkness across the black expanse of the crater floor. That glow comes from Halema'uma'u, which is pumping gases out at a considerable rate. On the other end of Kiluaea, she is continuing to pump mass into the ocean, adding to the land, building the island.

In 1924, the crater erupted, expanding in size from a quarter to a half mile. It still contains a reservoir of molten lava two miles deep. The Jagger Museum is named for MIT geologist, Thomas Jagger. It contains fine displays explaining Kilauea and Halema'uma'u, as well as a variety of seismographs and other instruments for measuring volcanic activity, earth tremors, etc. Unfortunately, the museum sits at the end of the rim road, which encircles Kilauea, the activity of the crater causing the national park people to close almost half of that highway. So Jeff reversed course, driving us back past the Volcano House to the Chain of Craters Road that leads down to the ocean. We also passed the Kilauea Military Camp, a large R&R facility for active and retired military personnel.

The Chain of Craters Road leads all the way from the summit to the ocean. In past years, Kilauea has wiped out large sections of the road that circles the island. The Chain of Craters Road runs through that cooled flow, a wasted land of black rock, with scattered 'o'hia trees holding on to a bare existence on the slope, their dark green skeletons peeking a bright red blossom out at the wasteland around them. The first vegetation to appear after a lava flow, the 'o'hia is the subject of many Hawaiian legends, and also the sustenance for many of the endemic honeycreepers when they were able to survive at lower altitudes.

Jeff made a stop at the Ke'alakomo overlook where you get a great panoramic view of the devastation inflicted on the land by Kilauea, from the mountain, right down to the ocean, and indeed, beneath the ocean. Thirteen miles of road have been covered in the most recent flows, in 1969 from the nearby vent of Mauna Ulu. Jeff pointed out several little oases of green, called *kibuka* in Hawaiian, bits of land and forest that are left untouched, completely surrounded by the lava. We stopped at a pullout to inspect the lava more closely. This is *pahoehoe* lava, flat, generally smooth, often with curious circles and designs that seem almost intentional. Mauna Ulu spewed forth its magma for five years leaving the land covered with all sorts of interesting shapes and configurations.

There are several craters hidden in the forest along the Chain of Craters road. Jeff pulled us off at Echo Crater and we all trudged in the rain just to hear ourselves talk. "Go Bears!" echoed through the land, to the delight of everyone. Jeff said this was the only one of the craters where you can achieve an echo, asserting that he tried them all. We next stopped at Pujmao Crater, to see Pu'u Pua'i, "gushing hell," the tallest lava fountain in recorded history, shooting some 1900 feet in the air in 1959. Near here is a trail, called Devastation Trail, which is dense forest on one side and lava field on the other.

Finally we arrived at the Thurston Lava Tube, a massive tunnel that once was the pipeline through which the lava flowed. It was pouring rain by now, but most of us braved the weather to stroll through the cave, which has rain forest on both ends.

We settled back in to the Volcano House for an evening at leisure. Tomorrow we get up very early to catch our flight to Maui and the last leg of our Mark Twain adventure.

VIII

We are up early today! I put in a wakeup call for 4:45 and a bag pull for 5:30. We have to leave for Hilo at 6:00 in order to catch an 8:10 flight to Maui. Originally, we had planned a late afternoon flight, but that was before I discovered that Frank and Alice's son is getting married in Maui this afternoon, at 5 P.M. to be exact. Alice thought it would be fun if they could make the wedding, so rather than get just her and Frank on that morning flight, I moved the whole group. It will give us a free afternoon in Lahaina, which will be welcome for a variety of reasons. Our driver this morning is a Hawaiian named Spencer, a rough-hewn man with a style of speaking that is right off the beach. Mac immediately plied him with questions because he likes to "talk to the locals."

"I'm not a very good thoughter," Spencer replied to one of Mac's queries, and that only spurred our professor on.

Hawaiian Air was almost as efficient in Hilo as they were getting us to Hana. They had all the boarding passes ready when I got to the desk, and they processed the luggage just as quickly. They don't seem to worry much about looking at driver's licenses or things like that, figuring that the folks at the security check point will handle those sorts of details. It is purely refreshing to see how easily these agents handle their tasks, and they seem to do it with a perpetual smile.

We landed in Maui's Kahului Airport, met there by a new driver-guide from Roberts, Richard, an experienced driver with a very wide knowledge of Maui natural history. He has an interesting cadence when he speaks, moving along nicely, easily understood, and then for no apparent reason, his words stack up on each other and come out in a blur for a few phrases. Once the logjam is cleared, he settles back again as understandable. I later checked my notes and found a whole bunch of phrases that I couldn't read.

Immediately on leaving Kahului Airport we stopped at the Sugar Museum, part of the last existing sugar mill on Maui, the Alexander and Baldwin Sugar Company. It was part of H.C. & S., Hawaiian Commercial and Sugar Co., a mega company that once included Matson Lines, pineapple plantations, hotels, trucking and storage, macadamia nuts, power companies and the Kahului Railroad. Today the plant operates with 35,000 acres of sugar cane, running eleven months a year, twenty-four hours a day. The mill is visible from the museum. Sugar is experiencing the same decline as pineapples, suffering from labor costs that can't compete with the world. Domestic sugar costs 21¢ to produce; the world's cost is 7¢. C&H Sugar in Crockett, which we all know from driving across the Carquinas Bridge, gets only 4 percent of its sugar from this mill.

Sugar occupies a very important role in Hawaii's modern history, not only as an important economic factor in its development but because of the many changes it wrought in the culture. In 1850, the government decreed that foreigners could buy land in fee simple, causing a land boom with an eye to supplying the gold fields in California. Many bought lands planning to expand the wild sugar that was common throughout the islands. By 1851, the gold rush was gone, and depression hit the islands. But the possibilities of sugar as a cash crop remained. By 1860 there were twelve plantations operating and the populations of Oregon and California were rising. The same Civil War that ruined the whaling industry here made the Hawaiian sugar industry. The sugar plantations of the south were closed to the Union and Hawaiian prices exploded. In 1860 less than 1.5 million pounds were exported; in 1867, it had risen to 17.75 million pounds. Walker, Allen & Co. was the biggest producer with twelve plantations. The sugar industry struggled along after Walker, Allen and Co. went bankrupt in 1867, when the Civil War ended and the demand slipped. Between 1852- 76, several thousand Chinese coolies were imported as workers on five-year contracts, beginning a major shift in cultural developments in the islands. Chinese, Japanese and Portuguese were all imported to work the sugar cane.

The real change in Hawaiian sugar came in 1876 with the signing of the Reciprocity Treaty of Trade with U.S. It eliminated U.S. tariffs and allowed for the free importation of sugar, rice and other products between the two countries. The following year, Claus Spreckels landed in Hawaii and bought half of the islands' 1877 sugar crop. The treaty lasted for eight years, called the "fattest years in Hawaiian history." Spreckels would become almost the ruler of the islands as he dominated the industry as well as the government.

We were greeted warmly at the museum, met by our guides Warren and Tamiko. They began with the myth of Maui, who captured the Sun God one day at dawn, forcing her to slow down and allow more time for the crops to grow. The crop, of course, was sugar cane. The museum has an interesting collection of tools and artifacts from the historic company, which was largely worked by Portuguese laborers. Particularly interesting are the pictures from the late nineteenth century and early twentieth. A couple of different films show the harvesting and milling process. Today of course, the harvest is done with huge tractors and trucks, not with hand cutting, horse-drawn wagons and coal-fired mills. Much of the power today is fueled by bagasse, the dried debris of the cane, supplemented by low sulfur coal from Australia.

At least part of Mark Twain's commission from the Sacramento Union was to report on the sugar industry. Most of Letter 23 is devoted to that subject. Throughout his stay in Hawaii he kept a keen eye out for all elements of the economy, discussing both the sugar and whaling industries, and even providing sharp insights into developing trade between California and Hawaii. He proposed that America should build a fleet of fast steamers to reduce the travel time to the islands, thus reducing the influence of both England and France who were competing with the United States over control of the islands.

> "It is a matter of the utmost importance to the United States that her trade with these islands should be carefully fostered and augmented. Because—it pays. There is no better reason than that. …the Sandwich Islands, which cost the United States but little, have paid her, in customs, as high as $400,000 in gold coin in a single year!"
> *Letters from Hawaii,* Letter 3

Leaving the Sugar Museum, we drove across the isthmus, called "the Pali," that separates the two round landmasses of Maui. Off the coast is the small sickle-shaped island of Molokini, with Lanai in the background. As we turned west we could see Molokai in the distance.

I am trying something different for the next three nights, using condos instead of the normal big hotel. Naomi in our office suggested the Aina Nalu Condos in Lahaina, because they are just a block from the center of town with nice facilities. Still I have been nervous about it. I shouldn't have been. The Aina Nalu has very nice units, most of the ones we were assigned, very large with two bedrooms. Mary and I were ensconced with two bedrooms, two baths and three TV sets. No chance for arguments here.

We arrived around noon, and fortunately our rooms were already clear, so we settled in and headed for town to find lunch and supplies for three days of breakfasts at the markets. Mac, Sita, Bob and I found a nice table at the Pioneer Inn at the harbor. We were just finishing when Arville and Clair strolled past.

"Are you ladies looking for a good time?" Mac inquired with a waterfront tone in his voice.

"Exactly what are you looking for, big boy?" Arville retorted to Mac's confusion.

Arville watched me pull my notebook out of my shirt pocket.

"Don't you dare write that down in your journal, Jack!" Arville commanded.

"I won't. Don't worry."

Lahaina was the main whaling port of the islands beginning around 1820, at a time when the sandalwood trade with China was winding down. Whaling took the ships all over the Pacific moving from the South Seas to the eastern areas and finally to the Arctic. The Hawaiian Islands were placed right in the middle of the trade as ship captains followed the supply of whales. The native population moved to the cities and then it began to decline. Both were mainly due to whaling, which prospered after 1820, using Lahaina and Honolulu as the main ports, but also Hilo, Waimea and Koloa (Kauai). The sailors brought money into the ports, and diseases that the Hawaiians couldn't combat. Since Captain Cook's day, VD was rampant throughout the islands, spreading from the sailors in the cities and to the rural communities on the islands when the women went home after the whaling season. Whaling boomed in the 1840s and 1850s when hundreds of vessels made Hawaii their port. Eight times before 1860 more than 500 ships made Hawaii their base. 1846 was the record year of almost 600 ships. Ships moved the trade from equatorial waters to the Japan Sea to the Arctic, with Hawaii in the center of the trade. Whaling's decline came with the American Civil War, when many of the ships were commandeered in the Union cause. That same war provided the replacement in the islands' economy—sugar.

ʗ ʘ

We all walked to the edge of town this evening to I'o Restaurant, a modern fusion place in a new mall area. We probably had our best meal of the trip, beautifully presented and served, and delicious. The dessert was something they called "chocolate paté," a devilish concoction of chocolate so concentrated it almost withstood the knife. Everyone exclaimed and protested the richness, but those were weak protests. Mary even set a record by asking for a "doggie bag" for a desert and assembled a fine collection from fellow diners. "We have a refrigerator you know. These will make a great midnight snack."

During dinner, Mac and Mary decided that they ought to get a tattoo. Everyone at the table offered to pay for them, figuring it would be less expensive and more fun than a Broadway play. They talked and talked about the design and style, and if we only had had a bottle or two of fine scotch, they probably would have pulled the trigger, so to speak. I fear we will have to wait a bit to see the idea brought to fruition.

IX

We have seen Kilauea, skirted Moana Loa and Moana Kea, looked at the crater that became Diamondhead. Today we get to the top of Haleakala, the House of the Sun God. It was here that Maui, using a fishing net, snared the sun and forced him to slow down to give the people enough light to grow their crops. The volcano has been dormant for a couple of centuries except for the flow of tourists clambering to the top and coasting on bicycles down from the summit. It is a torturous road, weaving madly through the scrub and rock to the top, where on a clear day you can see the crater, worn away to the south and west as the lava escaped through the Kaupa Gap to the ocean, building the island with its flow.

Richard is our driver again today, but we didn't even let him have the mike until we were halfway up the mountain. Bob read a brief description of Haleakala from *Roughing It,*

"But the chief pride of Maui is her dead volcano of Haleakala—which means, translated, "the house of the sun." We climbed a thousand feet up the side of this isolated colossus one afternoon; then camped, and the next day climbed the remaining nine thousand feet, and anchored on the summit, where we built a fire and froze and roasted by turns, all night. With the first pallor of dawn we got up and saw things which were new to us. Mounted on a commanding pinnacle, we watched Nature work her silent wonders. The sea was spread abroad on every hand, its tumbled surface seeming only wrinkled and dimpled in the distance. A broad valley below appeared like an ample checker-board, its velvety green sugar plantations alternating with dun squares of barrenness and groves of trees diminished to mossy tufts. Beyond the valley were mountains picturesquely grouped together; but bear in mind, we fancied that we were looking *up* at these things, not down. We seemed to sit in the bottom of a symmetrical bowl ten thousand feet deep, with the valley and the skirting sea lifted way into the sky above us! It was curious, and not only curious, but aggravating; for it was having our trouble all for nothing, to climb ten thousand feet toward heaven and then have to look *up* at our scenery....

I have spoken of the outside view—but there was an inside view, too. That was the yawning dead crater, into which we now and then tumbled rocks, half as large as a barrel, from our perch and saw them go careening down the almost perpendicular sides, bounding three hundred feet at a jump...The crater of Vesuvius, as I have before remarked, is a modest pit about a thousand feet deep and three thousand in circumference; that of Kilauea is somewhat deeper, and ten miles in circumference. But what are either of them compared to the vacant stomach of Haleakala! I will not offer any figures of my own, but give official ones—those of Commander Wilkes, U.S.N., who surveyed it and testifies that it is twenty-seven miles in circumference! If it had a level bottom it would make a fine site for a city like London..."

Roughing It, p, 522-24

The author says in his *Sacramento Union* letters that he was going to Maui, and in fact spent five weeks there, but his Maui notebook hasn't been found, and he stated that he would be writing about the island after he returned. He thought Maui a beautiful place and didn't want to spend his time there writing. Besides the section in *Roughing It*, Bob mentioned that he also had written to his mother and sister about Maui. He wrote from the Wailuku Sugar Plantation where he was staying, mentioning a young woman who had particularly attracted him. This brought up the whole subject of Mark Twain and woman, and Bob was armed and ready for any and all questions. He said that the author admitted that he had a very difficult time picturing women in his writings.

"Mark Twain had definite ideas about how wealthy a wife should be."

The most interesting of Mark Twain's women, other than Livy and his daughters, is Laura Wright. He wrote to her many times, and often he pictured her in his dreams, in a variety of settings—Rome, New York, Hawaii, mentioned in what Bob called his dream essays. It is a sign of just how thorough and elaborately informed Bob is, that he took the name Laura Wright and discussed her for nearly half an hour, her marriage (to a man named Dake), her general life history, her protective mother, her death. The letters she received from Mark Twain were given to her student Wadi Bowser and were burned after her death. Bob said that there were five or six other women who were of interest to Mark Twain as well. Bob was asked if he ever had affairs with some of the women friends. His answer was a definite "No." There is not a hint of any sort of dalliance in his letters, Bob said. "We have been reading his mail for forty years!"

By now we had crossed over to West Maui and were beginning the climb up the mountain, so Richard took over. Somehow the subject of Maui Gold came up, the distinctive pineapple that is still being grown on the island, although the company just announced its impending close. Someone asked if that was marijuana, and Richard laughed. "No, marijuana is Maui Wowie. You're thinking of Kona Gold. The Hawaiians call it 'polalolo,' stupid tobacco, whacky tobacky." Richard said that we were driving into "up country Maui" as we climbed the flanks of Haleakala. In 1881 the first cattle ranch was established here with 33,000 acres of grazing land up to 6,500'. There are about 4,000 head of cattle and 350 sheep grazing here today. Richard said that there are thirty-five miles of fences that have been placed encircling the National Park, to keep the wild pigs and goats out. There is a year-round season on wild pig hunting with no bag limits, so destructive are the animals to the natural environment of the islands. Axis deer were also imported from Japan years ago and have proliferated, with an estimated 15,000 now on Maui. We passed a well-organized lavender farm as we got higher, and several nurseries and gardens that were growing the impressive protea. Richard promised that we would stop at one on the way back down.

By the time we reached the Haleakala Visitor Center at the crater's rim, the place was completely fogged in. The actual summit of the mountain (10,008') bears the remarkably Hawaiian name of Pu'u'ula'ula, another word for my collection with three "u"s in a row. It was both fogged in and very cold. At one time, Haleakala was one of five active volcanoes building a single large island. Two of the five remain today at the centers of East and West Maui. Flooding and erosion separated the other three; by 150,000 years ago they had become the separate islands of Moloka'i, Lana'i, and Kaho'olawe. Haleakala rose to the greatest heights, at one time considerably higher than today, at 10,023'.

The mountain has a remarkable diversity of ecosystems ranging from Alpine-Aeolian at the top, to coastal lowland at the ocean level. In between are Sub-alpine scrublands, dry forest, pastureland and dense rain forest, with rainfalls ranging from 20" to 400". The alpine region is almost devoid of living things, because as the brochure says, its "bare surface becomes summer every day and winter every night." One of the plants that can survive in such an environment is the Silversword (*'ahinahina*), a plant that Mark Twain describes. Richard pointed out several at the Park Headquarters Visitor Center, and one in full bloom at our stop on top of the mountain. They may say it is summer every day, but by the time we reached the summit, it was extremely cold with a high wind. Our folks had been warned to bring a coat because years ago, Mary and I and our daughters arrived there wearing T-shirts and driving a Jeep. There were several such tourists here today, their arms and legs quickly becoming a fine shade of blue as they hustled from their jeeps to the Visitor Center. One buxom woman, clad in a swimsuit, hurried along with a lovely flower in her hair, frozen.

Sadly there was not much to be seen on top in the thick fog that had enveloped Haleakala, so we retreated to warmer climes. Richard was true to his word, stopping at a protea nursery on the way back down. We enjoyed a lunch break at the Kula Lodge, a most attractive restaurant with a spectacular garden that cascaded down the mountainside.

Originally, we had scheduled another of Bob's talks for this evening, but he had arranged a dinner meeting with friends near Lahaina, so we put the lecture off until tomorrow morning. I have been working on Bob the whole trip to get him into a semblance of Hawaiian garb, and on our return to the Aina Naula, he agreed to accompany me to Hilo Hattie's emporium, a block or two from our condos. He emerged as the very picture of a tropical savant, with fine flower shirt and stylish woven hat, even sporting the bead necklace that the store imposes on everyone who walks through the front door. I can't express how proud I was to help him become a Hawaiian!

X

Yesterday I got a call from Maui Nei Nature Expeditions, confirming our walking tour this morning of old Lahaina. I had completely forgotten that we had a guide and had scheduled Bob to give his talk at 9:00. But we quickly moved Bob back to 11:00 and hurried down to the Old Court House at 8:30 to meet our guide, a young man named Kalapana. What followed was a very fine, and well thought out tour of the old Hawaiian village, before and at the time of the monarchy, delivered in a casual, yet serious manner.

Lahaina, he said, means "cruel sun," in Hawaiian, although that is precisely what has drawn folks to the town since it began. It sits in the rain shadow of the West Mountains, receiving less than 20" of rain a year, while on the other side of those mountains, 300" is common. In the old days it was known as *Lele*, meaning to jump, a central jumping off place for controlling the islands. The Polynesians called it *Keala te Kahiki*, "Path to Tahiti," part of what Kalapana called "The Polynesian Triangle." The place was settled probably around the time of Christ.

We met Kalapana by the Old Court House, under the marvelous Lahaina banyan tree. He walked us down to the water where a woman awaited us, Hanao Okomoku, who chanted a prayer for our wellbeing. She stood near the *Hauolo* Stone, which sits exposed in the water, a curiously shaped stone, resembling a large chair. It was used by the *ali'i*, the nobility, as a birthing stone, where royal children would be born and confirmed in their family.

We walked from there to the Missionary House across the main street of the town, the home of Dwight Baldwin who arrived in Lahaina in 1834. As we have heard many times before, the missionaries would be fundamental in the nineteenth century history of Hawaii, both for good and for bad. In 1819, when the great king Kamehameha died, there had been a decade of peace on the islands. The following year his son, Liholiho, Kamehameha II, overthrew the *kapu* system by dining with Ka'ahumanu, the Queen Regent. In the process, the door was opened for the Missionaries who first arrived on the *Thaddeus,* in 1820. Many of the taboos that had stabilized the society were now overturned. Many foods had been *kapu* for women. The *hula* had been reserved only for the men of nobility. Hundreds of things that affected the daily life of the people were now overturned. The missionaries came into a vacuum, and formulated their own order for the people, often with good intentions, but just as often misguided in their zeal. Liholiho followed up his destruction of *kapu* with a more physical destruction, tearing down all the temples, the *heiau* that were spread throughout the islands.

The work of the missionaries was not all bad. The Rev. Ephraim Spaulding, who built the present Missionary House in 1854-57, saved thousands of lives on Maui when he vaccinated most of the populace against smallpox. While 11,000 died throughout the islands, only 350 perished on Maui.

We walked from the Missionary House, down one of the back streets to Waiola Congregational Church, built in 1823. There we were directed to look at the West Maui Mountains, the Kahalwai Mountains. On Mt. Pa'upa'u, a large "L" sits above the Lahaina School, the oldest public school in the western U.S. David Malo, the first local Hawaiian to learn to read the "words that stay" is buried on top of that mountain, a tribute to one of the great Hawaiian historians who preserved much of the history and legend in the new writing. Kalapana pointed out a large valley next to Mt. Pa'upa'u, the Kao'aula Valley, from whence, about every fifty years or so, a great wind erupts, of hurricane force, called the Kao'aula Wind. The last time it occurred, it blew the great bell right out of the church where we were standing. Next to the valley is Mauna Ka Wahine, the women's mountain, so named because of its shape, that of a woman's vagina, so placed to complement the Ia'o Needle on the other side of the mountain, the great phallus column that we will see this afternoon.

Our tour finished in front of a large vacant lot, which was the site of Okomulu, the fortress of King Kamehameha III. We were met again by our chanter who chanted a song she called "Returning the Glory to Okomulu." The plans are to rebuild that fortress, the groundbreaking for which will commence shortly. Kalapana finished with a slogan: *I ka wa mamua ka wa mahope*—the future is in the past.

❧ ❧

We all met Bob back at the hotel for another Mark Twain presentation. This morning his talk is a report, on the progress and the future of his present project, a most significant one in the literary world, the autobiography of Mark Twain.

The author first thought about writing his autobiography at the age of forty, stating that it must be published posthumously. He later stipulated that it couldn't be published until 100 years after his death, exactly as it is being done. Elsewhere he raised that to 500 years, but that is expecting too much. The work is haphazard to say the least, exactly as his overall writing was, starting and stopping with no identifiable pattern. "If he's writing at age forty and thinks of something at age four, he just adds it in right there." He started writing the work in 1885, spurred by his friendship with President Grant, and decided to work with a stenographer. He talked about his relationship with Grant pouring out 80 pages, which he calls "a botch." From 1885 to 1910 there are a dozen different false starts.

In 1904, in Florence, just before Livy died, he started dictating to Isabelle Lyon. It worked just fine because she didn't know shorthand, writing everything in long hand, and he spoke very slowly. There is an eighteen- month layoff after Livy's death. Prompted by Albert Bigelow Paine, he began a biography. From 1906-1909 he dictated daily, producing a manuscript of 5,500 typescript pages. Paine took his notes and produced an autobiography in 1924, rearranging everything into chronological order, a two- volume edition.

Mark Twain wanted his autobiography published in the order it was dictated. When the project began, Bob says he didn't know how to proceed, but finally it was agreed that it should not be a chronological work but the way the author's mind and dictation set it. Their work began officially in 2000, with the goal set for the 100th anniversary of Mark Twain's death, 2010. Bob says it was a daunting task of editing. Many pages are marked up by as many as twelve different handwritings: Mark Twain's, Paine's, stenographers, etc. In June, 1906, Mark Twain went back through all the pages to put them in order. His reasoning in not publishing the work for

100 years was that in this way he could be honest, and not harm anyone about whom he spoke ill. Bob said that he was never able to reveal the depth of himself, was never able to speak the truth about himself, but was much more honest about others, his friends and acquaintances.

The work will be published by U.C. Press in three volumes, the first volume coming out next year, right on time. Bob just laughs when asked what the final publishing date will be for the entire work. It is wonderful to hear the inside workings of a major project like this. Bob is so easy to listen to, we could easily have spent eight hours a day listening to him talk with sincere love and reverence, and honesty, about the great author. And Bob could easily have filled all those hours, so conversant is he with his subject. What a prize we have had to have him with us.

❧ ❧

Our last touring is this afternoon, when Dwayne picked us up to take us to the Ia'o Valley. Dwayne is not at all one of Robert's driver guides, but rather a refreshingly simple, life-loving Hawaiian who is far more comfortable talking about his family and life in the islands that he is about history, formal culture, etc. He made a half-hearted attempt at that history, but we are pretty good at that ourselves by this time. You only want to hear about Kam II and the dissolution of the *kapu* system and the arrival of the missionaries so many times.

"What do you want to talk about?" Dwayne asked as we were driving through the isthmus around West Maui.

"How about the way you live," I suggested and that is all it took. He began talking about the importance of family in the island culture, the simplicity of their life, really, of taking time with his sons for fishing and hunting.

"What do you hunt?" Mac asked.

"Deer, but mostly boar. There's no limit on wild boar."

It seems he hunts them with his dogs, using knives instead of rifles. He said they couldn't use rifles in Hawaii, but I wasn't able to check if that is a universal law or just for boar hunting. I later saw some bow hunters with their dogs, but nobody with rifles.

We drove through Waikapu, once a pineapple village. "They only grow houses here now," Dwayne observed. At Wailuku, where Mark Twain

310

stayed and wrote several letters, we turned into the Ia'o Valley, the cloudy, rainy side of the West Maui Mountains, getting as much as 400" a year. It was in this valley in 1790 that Kamehameha I won the great week-long battle that would result in his conquest of Maui, the Battle of Kepaniwai. Once again, as later in Nuuanu in O'ahu, he would drive his opponents into a wall where they all perished. Mark Twain describes the Ia'o Valley,

> I still remember, with a sense of indolent luxury, a picknicking excursion up a romantic gorge there called the Iao Velley. The trail lay along the edge of a brawling stream in the bottom of the gorge—a shady route for it was well roofed with the verdant domes of forest trees. Through openings in the foliage we glimpsed picturesque scenery that revealed ceaseless changes and new charms with every step of our progress. Perpendicular walls from one to three thousand feet high guarded the way, and were sumptuously plumed with varied foliage in places, and in places swathed with waving ferns. Passing shreds of cloud trailed their shadows across these shining fronts mottling them with blots; billowy masses of white vapor hid the turreted summits, and far above the vapor swelled a background of gleaming green crags and cones that came and went, through the veiling mists, like islands drifting in a fog; sometimes the cloudy curtain descended till half the canyon wall was hidden, then shredded gradually away till only airy glimpses of the ferny front appeared through it—then swept aloft and left it glorified in the sun again.... Presently a verdure-clad needle of stone, a thousand feet high, stepped out from behind a corner and mounted guard over the mysteries of the valley. It seemed to me that if Captain Cook needed a monument—here was one ready made, therefore why not put up his sign here, and sell out the venerable coconut stump?"
>
> *Roughing It*, p. 522

We reached the parking lot of the Ia'o Needle, the male counterpart to the female mountain, Moana Ka Wahini that Kalapana had pointed out this morning. "We'll hang out in this place for a while," Dwayne announced. The Ia'o Needle, Kuka'emoku, is also called "the Phallic Stone of Kanalona". A stairway (of 135 steps) leads up to a good vantage point for the Needle. Otherwise, this valley is protected by the state, devoid of hiking trails, off limits to campers. There is a botanical garden of sorts in mid valley, and a camping area around some models of historic cultural dwellings, but the upper valley is left pristine.

෨෪ ෫෬

We complete our Hawaiian experience tonight with the Old Lahaina Luau, considered by many to be the best of the luaus the islands have to offer. Dwayne was back to transfer us to the edge of the town, where we were met by Neil, a bare-chested, loin-clothed hunk of a man who really ought to have a name with a couple of "u"s in it and maybe a "k" or two. We were all properly lei-ed and escorted into very nice seats at stage level, right in front. The luau is set in what is meant to be an old Hawaiian village on the edge of the ocean. The seating is surrounded by palm-studded sand areas where craftsman display and explain their art. On one side is the cook pit, where the pig is buried on top of hot river rocks, and buried in banana leaves, canvas and earth. In many ways the process resembles one of our old-fashioned clambakes back in New England. The opening of the pit was announced, attracting many of the guests with their cameras, to photograph something that is not very photogenic—an overcooked porker that gives the very definition to the meaning of "pulled pork." I took a picture though.

This is a very well-organized venue. All drinks are included in the hefty price of the ticket, but that saves all sorts of lines and frustration, since every table has an overseer like our Neil who quickly procures tropical drinks whenever you want one. The buffet is divided into about six lines, so the whole crowd was fed in less than half an hour, with no long lines at all. Then the show started, that traditional sequence of chanting, drums, a few legends thrown in, and of course, the hula in a bunch of different varieties. Whatever the costumes, whatever the grass type, you can't get away from those hips!

> "At night they feasted and the girls danced their lascivious hula-hula—a dance that is said to exhibit the very perfection of educated motion of limb and arm, hand, head, and body, and the exactest uniformity of movement and accuracy of "time." It was performed by a circle of girls with no raiment on them to speak of, who went through with an infinite variety of motions and figures without prompting, and yet so true was the "time," and in such perfect concert did they move that when they were placed in a straight line, hands, arms, bodies, limbs and heads waved, swayed, gesticulated, bowed, stooped, whirled, squirmed, twisted, and undulated as if they were part and parcel of a single individual; and it was difficult to believe they were not moved in a body by some exquisite piece of mechanism."
>
> *Letters from Hawaii,* Letter 8

The ladies are amazing in their maneuvers, and so are the men. Most of us didn't realize that the hula was originally a dance only for the men, a sort of warming up exercise for war, where the men revved their bodies up for the considerable bloodshed that was a fundamental part of the Hawaiian culture. In the early days, hula was *kapu* for women, but thank God such a thought has been abandoned. Actually, the hula was banned by the missionaries during most of the era of the kingdom but was reinstituted by King David Kalakaua on the evening of his coronation. Our ladies tonight, in their smiling faces, long hair, coconut shell bras and grass skirts were impressive. Neil disappeared right after the buffet was served, reappearing on stage as a very significant *ali'i* dancer. No wonder there are so many Hawaiians and other Polynesians playing in the National Football League.

This was a nice ending to our Hawaiian experience. Sam Clemens described much of what we saw tonight—the hula, the native culture, the food, especially the poi. I must admit that I dobbed a few globs of that viscous taro blend somewhere in the middle of my plate, but it was too dark to discern exactly when I was consuming it. Perfectly camouflaged between the sashimi salmon and the pulled pork, the poi was as delicious as it is possible to become, overwhelmed by its neighbors.

Poi is a perfect way to bring Mark Twain's view of Hawai'i to a conclusion:

"The poi looks like common flour paste, and is kept in large bowls formed of a species of gourd, and capable of holding from one to three or four gallons. Poi is the chief article of food among the natives, and is prepared from the kalo or taro plant (*k* and *t* are the same in the Kanaka alphabet, and so are *l* and *r*). The taro root looks like a thick, or, if you please, a corpulent sweet potato, in shape, but is of a light purple color when boiled. When boiled it answers as a passable substitute for bread. The buck Kanakas bake it under ground, then mash it up well with a heavy lava pestle, mix water with it until it becomes a paste, set it aside and let it ferment, and then it is poi—and a villainous mixture it is, almost tasteless before it ferments and too sour for a luxury afterward. But nothing in the world is more nutritious. When solely used, however, it produces acrid humors, a fact which sufficiently accounts for the blithe and humorous character of the Kanakas. I think there must be as much of a knack in handling poi as there is in eating with chopsticks. The forefinger is thrust into the mess and stirred quickly round several times and drawn as quickly out, thickly coated, just as if it were poultice; the head is thrown back, the finger inserted in the mouth and the poultice stripped off and swallowed—the eye closing gently, meanwhile, in a languid sort of ecstasy. Many a different finger goes into the same bowl and many a different kind of dirt and shade and quality of flavor is added to the virtues of its contents. One tall gentleman, with nothing in the world on but a soiled and greasy shirt, thrust in his finger and tested the poi, shook his head, scratched it with the useful finger, made another test, prospected among his hair, caught something and ate it; tested the poi again, wiped the grimy perspiration from his brow with the universal hand, tested again, blew his nose—"Let's move on, Brown," said I, and we moved."
Letters from Hawaii, Letter 8

XI

Our first group left this morning at 9:00—Claire and Michael, Ed, Carol and Barbara. I have been battling with Roberts Tours about these transfers, because they had scheduled our entire group to leave for the airport at 9:00, but most of us have a 2:00 flight, which will mean four hours at a rather small Kahului Airport. I asked them to send us a van at 9:00 and a minibus at 11:00 instead of a big 53-passenger motorcoach at 9:00. Roberts readily agreed, but parenthetically announced that there would be an additional $195 cost for this new maneuver. Yesterday I had talked to a taxi driver named Trung who said he could take the five people to the airport at 9:00 for $60. So I cancelled the 9:00 pickup from Roberts and went with Trung. This morning at 9:00 a Roberts minibus pulled up to pick up our five people, just as we were loading the taxi. Ken, the driver didn't have a clue about when he was supposed to be there, so I called Roberts once more. It seems that they didn't tell Ken the move had been cancelled so they said he could just wait for the 11:00 pickup. I told the manager in Kahului that I would only accept the minibus if there was a refund of our transfer money because we had paid for a full motorcoach. Otherwise Ken would have to go and someone else would have to come with a big bus. I just got a call from Lori at Roberts, saying there would be a $195 refund for the smaller bus. So after all the arguing, and all the yelling, and all the considerable lack of common sense, I saved $130 in the matter, which should keep Mary and me in mai tais for at least a week.

My last official act as a Golden Gate Tours tour director was to assist Frank and Alice in repacking their suitcases at Kahului Airport in Mau'i. There was a sign at the check-in counter at United Airlines that demanded a fee of $125 for any suitcase over fifty pounds, a ridiculous amount, but the airlines these days are frantic in their efforts at financial survival. Thank goodness they had a scale there and Alice's suitcase weighed in at a hefty 63.5 pounds, Frank's only at 35 pounds. I figured we could redistribute and save them the money, a simple thing really, but much more complicated because it entered the embarrassment area for both of them. But I insisted, and Frank started dragging things out of the outside compartments of Alice's trunk, but wasn't making much headway.

"We have to get to those iron-lined nightgowns, Alice," I suggested, and she blushed like a South Pacific sunset. Opening both suitcases fully, I peeled off several layers of ladies' clothes and plopped them into Frank's. After a couple of re-shifts we arrived at 49 and 48, a perfect division. Next came the computer check-in, another mystery for this wonderful couple. In just a couple of minutes they were checked in, had their seat assignments, luggage tags and boarding passes. And no penalties!

Frank and Alice are precisely why I have so loved my job. It is such a pleasure to travel with them, and all the wonderful couples like them that we have met over the last two decades.

kk

Sam Clemens tried to return to Hawaii in 1895 but was stopped by a cholera epidemic in Honolulu, preventing him from again seeing "the loveliest fleet of islands that lies anchored in any ocean." (Letter to H.P. Wood, Nov. 30, 1908). His earlier "prose poem" about Hawaii is a fitting ending to our own Mark Twain in Hawaii adventure:

> "No alien land in all the world has any deep, strong charm for me but that one, no other land could so longingly and so beseechingly haunt me sleeping and waking, through half a lifetime, as that one has done. Other things leave me, but it abides, other things change but it remains the same. For me its balmy airs are always blowing, its summer seas flashing in the sun, the pulsing of its surf-beat is in my ear; I can see its garlanded crags, its leaping cascades, its plumy palms drowsing by the shore, its remote summits floating like islands above the cloud rack; I can feel the spirit of its woodland solitudes, I can hear the splash of its brooks; in my nostrils still lives the breath of flowers that perished twenty years ago".
>
> April 8, 1889, Delmonicos, New York City. Quoted in www. twainquotes.com

AFTERTHOUGHTS

I suppose we just ran out of time. There is so much more of Mark Twain left out there in the world, whole countries and civilizations to rediscover as he did. High on my list of favorites is *A Tramp Abroad*, that wonderful jaunt through Germany, France and Switzerland. Samuel Clemens could literally have wandered through those countries in the vernacular. Had we the time, we certainly could have followed our author through those lands, adding England and Italy, of course, with perhaps a stop in Spain and Morocco

Because of the world political situation, much of his *Innocents Abroad* experience in the Middle East isn't possible just now. But just try to imagine following the young Clemens into the Holy Land, when there wasn't any Jordan, or Syria, or Iraq—just the "Holy Land," based in the Bible.

If the Holy Land is out of the question, we also have the incredible world tour he took so vividly described in *Following the Equator*. We touched a few days of that tour in India, but he spent eight weeks there. Then there are eight weeks in Australia, six weeks in New Zealand and seven in South Africa.

It would be interesting to read his take on the modern world. I fear that sarcasm would be battling hard to break through the veneer of humor. His take on governing bodies is probably valid in any era, and his eye to detail would have been no different now than in his day. On the other hand, he would have reveled in the new gadgets of Internet, lasers, clones and drones. Essays and stories would have flown out of that incredible mind, that wonderful imagination.

He left a world in awe of his genius. Perhaps the New York Times spoke for all elements of the world of Mark Twain, the life of Sam Clemens.

The New York Times, **April 22, 1910**
[Editorial]

MARK TWAIN.

That SAMUEL L. CLEMENS was the greatest American humorist of his age nobody will deny. Posterity will be left to decide his relative position in letters among the humorists of English literature. It is certain that his contemporary fame abroad was equal to his fame at home. All Europe recognized his genius, the English people appreciated him at his own work, and the University of Oxford honored him with a degree. His writings commanded a higher price in the market than those of any other contemporary whose career was solely devoted to literature. His "public" was of enormous extent. From "The Jumping Frog" to the "Diary of Adam" everything that came from his pen was eagerly read and heartily enjoyed by multitudes.

Much that he wrote has already been forgotten, inevitably, and in spite of definitive editions and the admirably practical management of his business in the later years of his career. But nearly all that JONATHAN SWIFT, FIELDING, STERNE, and SMOLLETT wrote has been forgotten, though their fame, resting on a few books, still lives. ARTEMUS WARD, MARK TWAIN'S greatest predecessor as a National jester, is now little more than a name. NASBY belonged exclusively to the Reconstruction period. For any American humorous writer it would be fit to compare with MARK TWAIN we must go back to WASHINGTON IRVING. But the author of Knickerbocker's ironical history and the Sleepy Hollow legend did not surpass, in those denotements of the humorous genius, the author of "The Adventures of a Cub Pilot on the Mississippi" and "Huckleberry Finn." Indeed, it is hard to say that IRVING ever surpassed CLEMENS. Without belittling the first great American prose writer we are compelled to doubt if posterity will name him in the same breath with the humorist who has just passed away.

The "Innocents Abroad" and "A Tramp Abroad" are likely to be remembered among the great travel books of all time. Full of the audacity, the wild exaggeration and violent contrasts which distinguish the National humor, they are equally remarkable as the veracious record of fresh impressions on a fertile and responsive mind. Mr. CLEMENS'S more serious works, such as "The Prince and the Pauper," an incursion into the field of historical romance; "A Yankee at the Court of King Arthur," and "Joan of Arc," have been read by multitudes with great delight. He has been quoted in common conversation oftener, perhaps, than any of his fellow-countrymen, including BENJAMIN FRANKLIN and LINCOLN. He has been honored by misquotation, too, and the humorous sayings of the ancients have been attributed to him, though he never borrowed. His wit was his own, and so was his extravagance, and his powers of observation never failed him.

We have called him the greatest American humorist. We may leave it an open question whether he was not also the greatest American writer of fiction. The creator of Mulberry Sellers and Pudd'nhead Wilson, the inventor of that Southwestern feud in "Huckleberry Finn," which, with all its wildly imaginative details, is still infused with rare pathos, has certainly an undying vitality. An emotional and quite unconventional sort of man, CLEMENS was, whose early life was a hard struggle for existence. He obtained his education where he could get it. Presumably his faults were as large as his merits. Intellectually he was of Herculean proportions. Hs death will be mourned, everywhere, and smiles will break through the tears as remembrance of the man's rich gift to his era comes to the mourners' minds. However his work may be judged by impartial and unprejudiced generations his fame is imperishable.

Published on-line at www.twainquotes.com

"You had better shove this in the stove—for if we strike a bargain I don't want any absurd 'literary remains' & 'unpublished letters of Mark Twain' published after I am planted." —Letter to Orion and Mollie Clemens, 19 and 20 October 1865

ACKNOWLEDGMENT

It has been my great privilege to travel extensively with Bob Hirst, the General Editor of the Mark Twain Papers & Project. The tours that we experienced with U.C. Berkeley Alumni could not have been possible without his participation as a fellow traveler and as a willing lecturer. During the compilation and editing of this book, he has generously offered his immense expertise, directing me to every area of Mark Twain's voluminous works.

The Mark Twain Papers and Project at the Bancroft Library in Berkeley is a combination archive and publishing program. The library houses, in original and photocopy, virtually every document in Mark Twain's hand known to survive, and the Project has the stated aim to publish every work in the collection. This will result in at least seventy volumes, of which more than thirty are already in print. Recently the Project published the three volumes of Mark Twain's *Autobiography*.

The Mark Twain Papers & Project receives only about a quarter of its funding from the University. It relies on the generous support of individuals and foundations to maintain its vast collection of the papers of Samuel L. Clemens, and to continue the crucial work of the editorial project. Your support is deeply appreciated. All are invited to join the Mark Twain Luncheon Club and the Mark Twain Book Club. For information, contact:

MARK TWAIN PAPERS & PROJECT
The Bancroft Library
University of California
Berkeley, CA 94720-6000

mtp@library.berkeley.edu
(510) 642-6480
(510) 642-6349 FAX

All Mark Twain photographs are used with permission
of the Mark Twain Papers Project at the Bancroft
Library, University of California, Berkeley.

Mark Twain passages are taken from the following:

Twain, Mark, *Roughing It*, The Mark Twain Library, Publication of the Mark Twain Project of the Bancroft Library, University of California Press, (Berkeley: 1996)

Twain, Mark, *Mark Twain's Letters*, 6 volumes, Publication of the Mark Twain Papers Project of the Bancroft Library, University of California Press, (Berkeley: 1988-2002)

Twain, Mark, Newspaper articles, *www.twainquotes.com*.

Twain, Mark, *Life on the Mississippi*, The Oxford Mark Twain, Oxford University Press, (New York, London: 1996).

Twain, Mark & Warner, Charles Dudley, *The Gilded Age*, The Oxford Mark Twain, Oxford University Press, (New York, London: 1996).

Twain, Mark, *Following the Equator*, The Oxford Mark Twain, Oxford University Press, (New York, London: 1996.

Twain, Mark, *Private History of a Campaign That Failed*, Rise of Douai Publishing, 2015

Twain, Mark, *Europe and Elsewhere*, Harper & Brothers, (New York, London: 1923)

Twain, Mark, *Autobiography of Mark Twain*, 3 Volumes, Mark Twain Papers, University of California Press (Berkeley: 2010)

Twain, Mark, *Collected Tales, Sketches, Speeches, & Essays 1852-1890*, The Library of America, 1981.

Twain, Mark, *Sketches New and Old,* The Oxford Mark Twain, Oxford University Press, (New York, London: 1996.

Twain, Mark, *Notebooks,* Mark Twain Papers Project, Bancroft Library, University of California, Berkeley.

Twain, Mark, *Mark Twain's Letters From Hawaii,* ed. A. Grove Day, University of Hawaii Press, (Honolulu: 1966)